RHETORIC IN
GRECO-ROMAN EDUCATION

THE ALLEGORY OF LADY RHETORIC

RHETORIC
IN GRECO-ROMAN
EDUCATION

By DONALD LEMEN CLARK

COLUMBIA UNIVERSITY PRESS

MORNINGSIDE HEIGHTS, NEW YORK

Frontispiece

The allegory of Lady Rhetoric owes its popularity in postclassical times and later to Martianus Capella, whose *Marriage of Philology and Mercury* combines a compend of the Seven Liberal Arts with allegorical descriptions of these Seven Learned Ladies. Lady Rhetoric, as presented in the woodcut from the medieval encyclopaedia *Margarita philosophica* (1504), reflects a remarkably accurate and full statement of Greco-Roman rhetoric. By the sword and the lily which extend from her mouth she represents allegorically the two traditional functions of rhetoric: to attack and defend by verbal arguments and to embellish speech with verbal adornment. The beauty of her gown and the charm of her coiffure represent beauty of style as first taught by Gorgias. The words embroidered on the hem of her robe remind us of the *colores,* or figures of speech, and the enthymemes and exempla, types of deductive and inductive argument.

Aristotle at the top of the picture represents rhetorical and natural philosophy; Justinian, the use of rhetoric in support of law; Seneca, moral philosophy and the educational system of the Roman schools of rhetoric; and Sallust, history. Rhetoric is embraced by the Zone of Justice. The presence of Virgil with laurel crown emphasizes rhetorical influence on the style of poetry. In the foreground Cicero is clearly shown defending Milo in a court of law, and the Senatus Populusque Romanus figures forth the scene of deliberative rhetoric.

A companion allegory in the *Margarita philosophica* shows Lady Grammar as schoolmistress unlocking the narrow gate of the Tower of Knowledge so that the children may enter and meet the grammarians: Donatus on the ground floor and Priscian on the floor above. Above that sits Cicero, teaching both poetry and rhetoric.

To the *Memory* of

NATHANIEL WARING BARNES

1884–1953

condiscipulum atque magistrum
collegamque dehinc

AUSONIUS *Professores* III

PREFACE

THIS BOOK is about teaching. It is written primarily for teachers. To be sure, it tells the story of the literary theories developed by teachers of rhetoric in Greece and Rome, but it is not a history of literary criticism in antiquity. It is an account of the educational methods used by ancient teachers in the grammar schools and schools of rhetoric in their successful efforts to train young men in the artistic control of Greek and Latin as media of communication in speech and writing. The influence of this schooling on the literature of Greece and Rome has never been lost to the sight of teachers of the classics. My book, *John Milton at St. Paul's School* (Columbia University Press, 1948), is only one recent publication pointing how much ancient educational methods in teaching the arts of language influenced Renaissance literary theory and practice. Modern developments in radio have restored the importance of the spoken word as a medium of mass communication. "The art of speaking well," as Quintilian defined rhetoric, is everywhere recognized as of the greatest value by teachers of public speaking. Its value is ready to be rediscovered by all teachers of English composition, creative writing, or the arts of communication in our schools and colleges, devoted as they are to furnishing a general education for a democratic society.

I have undertaken to show how the ancient teacher trained the youth of his day in the art of discovering and evaluating whatever might supply arguments in support of his theme; how he trained the youth to marshal material for presentation to an audience and to clothe it in clear and appropriate and sometimes over-embellished language.

I have chosen to begin with a chapter discussing the question, "Can the art of speaking well be taught?" This question would have seemed absurd to the ancient teacher, because he knew that boys could be taught to speak well. He himself taught them every day. He might quarrel with other teachers as to the relative importance of different methods, and he admitted freely that any boy must have some natural aptitude for an art at which he hoped to succeed. But I have been impelled to present the evidence of the ancients because so many modern romantics, who consider one spark of nature's fire all that is necessary, continue to assert that writing and speaking cannot be taught. Perhaps the classic ancients and the modern romantics discover a different semantic content in the word "teach."

I have next undertaken to answer the question, "What is rhetoric?" The ancients, like the moderns, had different views. Some hated it as a sinful and seductive siren. Most approved of it as a useful instrumental art, susceptible of abuse like all good things save virtue. Some defined rhetoric very narrowly as the art of persuading in a law court; others defined it broadly to include all prose communication in speech or writing. It seemed useful to let the ancients speak freely on this matter of definition before taking up teaching methods.

In teaching the art of speaking well the ancients used three methods in closely related combinations. First they inculcated the accepted precepts of good writing and speaking; next they led the student to imitate the methods of successful writers and speakers; finally they set the student many and varied exercises in the writing and speaking of themes. Hence I devote a chapter to the precepts of rhetoric, many of which can be found adapted in textbooks of public speaking today. Then I devote a chapter to such traditional exercises in imitation as learning good prose and poetry by heart, translating, and paraphrasing. Finally I explain in some detail the ancient exercises in writing and declaiming themes. These were on two levels: the elementary exercises usually taught by the professor of literature in the grammar school, and the advanced exercises in judicial and deliberative public speaking taught in the declamation school by the professor of rhetoric.

Although I present these three teaching devices separately for ease of comprehension, my reader should bear in mind that the teacher used all three methods simultaneously day after day, proceeding year after year from easy lessons for little boys to difficult exercises for youths, until the student was finished with school and took his place as a free man in a civilized society. This was the schooling which gave its characteristic bent to the genius of Cicero, Saint Augustine, and Boethius. Students with lesser literary aptitudes cultivated such aptitudes as they had and at least became more literate citizens than they otherwise would have been.

When Charles Hoole, an enterprising schoolmaster of the seventeenth century, set about explaining his educational innovations, he entitled his book *The Rediscovery of the Old Art of Teaching School*. Had he not made this title so much his own, I would be tempted to borrow it for this book. For the old art of teaching rhetoric, or the art of speaking well, has helped me, at least, to identify and solve many of the problems which I have had to confront in forty years of teaching thinking, speaking, and writing. As I became aware, bit by bit, of ancient teaching wisdom, as I learned the ancient precepts, imitated ancient methods, and practiced on generations of college students, I became increasingly effective as a midwife to others' thoughts. And I have made some progress towards learning to avoid the mistakes of other teachers. So it is my hope that I may make available to younger teachers something of what I have learned.

As I recall now, my first impulse to write this book came in 1917 while I was working on my *Rhetoric and Poetry in the*

Renaissance (Columbia University Press, 1922) and simultaneously teaching Freshmen. Then as now the names of Aristotle, Cicero, and Quintilian were constantly on my lips, and I was delighted to discover that their wit and wisdom quickened and illuminated the Freshman mind.

The great teachers who set my feet on the path which led to the great teachers of antiquity are dead, but they live in my memory and continue to guide and encourage me. Nathaniel Waring Barnes, my teacher of English composition at DePauw, later my colleague when I taught my first classes, and always my friend, was in the tradition of George Rice Carpenter at Columbia University, a tradition to which I have been loyal. Charles Sears Baldwin, who directed the rhetorical studies of my doctoral dissertation, *Rhetoric and Poetry in the Renaissance,* put me in the great tradition of Aristotle, Cicero, and Quintilian. It was Fred Newton Scott who asked me to promise, when I should write on ancient rhetoric, to begin with Plato, not with Aristotle. I learned to realize that he was right, and in my second chapter I have kept my promise. LaRue Van Hook exacted no promise, but over the years, more than any one else, taught me to know and respect that third great rhetorician of Greek antiquity, Isocrates. My faults are my own, but whatever is good in this book owes much to these men.

I am happy to acknowledge my debt to the reference librarians and staffs of the British Museum, the Henry Huntington Library, and the Bodleian for their cheerful help, and especially to Roland Baughman of the Columbia University Libraries; Dorothy Mason, reference librarian of the Folger Shakespeare Library; and H. M. Adams, Librarian of Trinity College, Cambridge. For thirty years the late E. P. Goldschmidt guided me in forming my collection of Renaissance editions of treatises on rhetoric.

Some parts of this book have previously appeared in adaptations for periodical publications. "Some Values of Roman Declamatio," in *The Quarterly Journal of Speech,* XXXV (October,

1949), 280–283, is from the section on Controversiae in Chapter VII. "Imitation: Theory and Practice in Roman Rhetoric," *The Quarterly Journal of Speech*, XXXVII (February, 1951), 11–22, is condensed from Chapter V. "The Rise and Fall of Progymnasmata in Sixteenth and Seventeenth Century Grammar Schools," *Speech Monographs*, XIX (November, 1952), 1259, contains several paragraphs from Chapter VI. My use of this material is with the kind permission of the editors of *The Quarterly Journal of Speech* and *Speech Monographs*.

Certain translated passages are reprinted by permission of Harvard University Press, American publishers of The Loeb Classical Library, from: Diogenes Laertius, *Lives of Eminent Philosophers*, translated by R. D. Hicks; Philostratus, *The Lives of the Sophists*, translated by Wilmer Cave Wright; Dio Chrysostom, *Eighteenth Discourse*, translated by J. W. Cohoon; "Longinus," *On the Sublime*, translated by W. H. Fyfe, and Demetrius, *On Style*, translated by W. Rhys Roberts; Isocrates, *On the Antidosis, Against the Sophists*, and *Panegyricus*, translated by George Norlin, and Gorgias, *Encomium of Helen*, translated by LaRue Van Hook (in Volume III of the translation of Isocrates); Tacitus, *Dialogus*, translated by William Peterson; Suetonius, *On Grammarians* and *On Rhetoricians*, translated by J. C. Rolfe.

Passages are reprinted by permission of Oxford University Press from: Lucian of Samosata, *Works*, translated by H. W. Fowler and F. G. Fowler; Plato, *Dialogues*, translated by B. Jowett; Aristotle, *Rhetoric*, translated by W. Rhys Roberts, and *Poetics*, translated by Ingram Bywater.

Passages from C. S. Baldwin's translation of Hermogenes are reprinted from *Medieval Rhetoric and Poetic* (The Macmillan Company) by permission of Mrs. Frederick J. Woodbridge, Baldwin's daughter and literary executor.

The translations from Cicero, *De oratore*, and Quintilian, *Institutes of Oratory*, are adapted from the translations of John Selby Watson.

All other translations, unless otherwise noted, are my own.

For reading the manuscript and making valued suggestions I am grateful to Bower Aly, William Bridgwater, Philip De Lacy, and Magdalene Kramer. I am indebted to my colleagues John H. Middendorf and Elva D. Hoover, who read the proofs, and to the officers of Columbia University Press. My wife, Mary Read Clark, in the face of difficulties and delays, has continued to admonish and encourage.

Donald Lemen Clark

Columbia University
November, 1955

CONTENTS

RHETORIC IN
GRECO-ROMAN EDUCATION

I. LEARNING TO SPEAK AND TO WRITE

CAN A TEACHER train a student to speak and to write effectively? Is one spark of nature's fire the sole requirement? Was Horace right when he said that "neither training without rich gifts nor genius rude and untrained is sufficient"? And if so, what training? The ancients, like the moderns, voiced divergent views. Although formal instruction in rhetoric was intrenched in the Greco-Roman school system, just as instruction in written composition and oral public address is intrenched in our schools and colleges, formal instruction in rhetoric in the schools was on the defensive. No one denied that some natural aptitude was necessary for success in oratory. No one denied that nurture of some sort was needed to make the most of nature's gifts. But educational philosophers and critics did debate whether nature or nurture contributed more to success, and they did debate whether the traditional system of the schools afforded the best training for making the most of natural aptitudes.

Some preferred a sort of apprenticeship system under which a boy would accompany a successful speaker to the forum, much as in the United States at the turn of the century a boy read law in a lawyer's office instead of going to a law school. Some preferred for the boy to learn by trial and error in the hard school of experience. Some demanded an encyclopedic education in the liberal arts for the boy who was preparing for a career as a public speaker. Others believed that a thorough grounding in the precepts of rhetoric put into practice in school exercises would be sufficient. Moreover, there was never complete agreement as to which were the best exercises or what was the best method of teaching them. I shall now endeavor to expose the modern reader to the conflicting winds of ancient doctrine in the hope that he will be enabled better to understand and to evaluate modern discussions of the same problems in the teaching of rhetoric.

The Greeks were early aware of these questions and made a sound beginning by agreeing on an analysis of the elements which contribute to success in speech and writing—an analysis so sound that it has never seriously nor for long been challenged. By the fourth century B.C. an analysis of those elements into nature, art, and exercise had been accepted.[1] Diogenes Laertius reports, "Aristotle declared three things indispensable for education: natural endowment, study, and constant practice" (v.18). In the *Phaedrus* Plato makes Socrates say, "The perfection which is required of the finished orator is, or rather must be, like the perfection of anything else, partly given by nature, but may also be assisted by art. If you have natural power and add to it knowledge and practice, you will be a distinguished speaker. If you fall short of either of these, you will be to that extent defective" (269).

Before we go farther, we should pause to examine briefly what the ancients meant by these terms. By nature, natural endowment, and natural power, they did not mean such irrational faculties as we sometimes include in the term genius. In Harper's *Latin Dictionary, ingenium* is defined by the words innate or natural quality, nature, natural disposition, temper, mode of thinking, character, bent, inclination, talents, parts, abilities, genius. Nature to writers on rhetorical theory included the innate mental, moral, and physical qualities which might aid a man to attain success in oratory.

[1] D. L. Clark, in "The Requirements of a Poet," *Modern Philology*, XVI (December, 1918), 8. In that article I discuss the influence of the rhetorical analysis on the theory of poetry in antiquity and in the Renaissance.

Mentally it included imagination, intelligence, and memory as well as special aptitudes for language and rhythm. Morally it included courage, prudence, justice, and temperance—the four cardinal virtues, as well as persistence and industry, the infinite capacity for taking pains. Physically it included a pleasing voice of adequate power and range, the kind of good looks to win friends and influence people, bodily poise and grace, physical strength, and good health.

As nature meant what a man was born with, art and knowledge meant what might be acquired by study. Both Plato and Aristotle expected the distinguished speaker to benefit by wide and philosophical knowledge, as did Isocrates and Cicero, but most of the professors of rhetoric who wrote textbooks confined their remarks to knowledge of the art of rhetoric. The Greek word *techne* and the Latin word *ars* meant the systematically arranged rules, principles, or precepts of rhetoric which a boy should learn from a textbook or from the lectures of his teacher. Indeed *ars* often meant quite simply a textbook or technical treatise. In the discussion which follows only context can indicate whether or not the writer includes some study of logic, psychology, political science, or philosophy, as well as precepts of rhetoric, under the general head of art.

The third element, practice or exercise, might be taken in two ways. It might mean learning by trial and error as one gets on and falls off a bicycle until, by practice, one is able to stay on and go somewhere. Usually, however, exercise meant specific classroom assignments; outlined by the teacher, struggled with by the student, and finally criticised by the teacher, who never failed to guide the student. A few teachers made imitation a fourth element, as I do in this book, but logically precepts for imitation are part of "art," and imitative practice is an exercise.

In Greece in the fourth century B.C. there was a three-cornered quarrel among the leading teachers concerning what it takes to make a successful speaker. From this quarrel Isocrates (436–

338 B.C.) came out triumphant. More than any other Greek rhetorician he left his stamp on subsequent Greek and Roman educational theory and practice.

Isocrates was a sophist when the word meant one who professed wisdom and professed the ability to transmit this wisdom to his pupils—in other words, a professor. The sophists were innovators in Greek education who emphasized intellectual, literary, and oratorical training rather than ethical, athletic, and military training. Their activities centered in Athens, though some of the innovators were Greek colonials, such as Gorgias from Sicily and Prodicus from Ceos. Cicero tells us that Isocrates was a pupil of Gorgias (*Orator* 176). The other teacher who influenced him was Socrates.[2] To the traditionalist all sophists were anathema. Aristophanes, in *The Clouds,* attacks all sophists with his coarse and witty satire, lumping them together as corrupters of youth and singling out Socrates as the worst of the lot. Plato, on the other hand, was careful to set Socrates aside as a philosopher (lover of wisdom) not a sophist at all. In his dialog the *Gorgias* he represents Socrates as attacking the views of Gorgias and other sophists. To Plato the sophists were dishonest in their pretensions to wisdom and their claim that they could teach wisdom. Moreover they were ignoble because they were devoted to the practical arts of getting on in the world instead of to the disinterested search for abstract and theoretical truth.

Thus the word sophist had by the time of Isocrates suffered a semantic change for the worse, and when Isocrates was having a literary and philosophical quarrel with Alcidamas, another sophist, he wrote an attack which he titled *Against the Sophists*. Alcidamas, like Isocrates, had studied under Gorgias. Both conducted schools of rhetoric at Athens. Isocrates attacked Alcidamas (among others) because he claimed to be able to teach anyone who paid tuition to become an eloquent speaker and because he

---

[2] An excellent approach to Isocrates is the Loeb Library edition in three volumes and George Norlin's Introduction, in Vol. I.

narrowed his teaching to the immediately practical skills of pleading in the law courts.[3]

As a teacher and head of an important school of rhetoric Isocrates, in *Against the Sophists,* endeavored to defend honest teaching by repudiating such extravagant claims. "If all who are engaged in the profession of education," he writes in his first sentence, "were willing to state the facts instead of making greater promises than they can possibly fulfil, they would not be in such bad repute." And he proceeds to the earliest and best-balanced evaluation of the interrelations of the three requirements for proficiency in an art.

"Ability, whether in speech or in any other activity, is found in those who are well endowed by nature and have been schooled by practical experience. Formal training makes such men more skilful and resourceful in discovering the possibilities of a subject; for it teaches them to take from a readier source the topics which they otherwise hit upon in haphazard fashion. But it cannot fully fashion men who are without natural aptitude into good debaters or writers, although it is capable of leading them on to self-improvement and to a greater degree of intelligence on many subjects" (14–15).

Thirty-five years later Isocrates resumed the discussion in a long passage in *On the Antidosis* (178–214), a self-justification of his long life as a teacher. His discussion of nature, art, and exercise is so full that I can not reproduce it all; I shall only summarize and introduce brief quotations. He begins by comparing the training of the mind by rhetoric or the art of discourse and the training of the body by gymnastic. The teacher or trainer is able to help his pupils to be stronger in their thinking or in the use of their bodies: "However, neither class of teachers is in possession of a science by which they can make capable athletes or

---

[3] Van Hook, "Alcidamas versus Isocrates," *Classical Weekly,* XII (January 20, 1919), 89. Van Hook translates Alcidamas's answer to Isocrates. The quarrel involved much more than I mention.

capable orators out of whomsoever they please. They can contribute in some degree to these results, but these powers are never
found in their perfection save in those who excel by virtue both
of talent and training" (185).

He proceeds to point out that the pupil must have a natural
aptitude, submit to training, and become versed in the use and
practice of the art. "In this process, master and pupil each has his
place; no one but the pupil can furnish the necessary capacity;
no one but the master, the ability to impart knowledge; while
both have a part in the exercises of practical application; for the
master must painstakingly direct his pupil, and the pupil must
rigidly follow the master's instruction" (188).

He then lists as natural aptitudes of greatest importance in the
education of an orator: a mind capable of learning the truth,
industry, memory, a clear and charming voice, and assurance. A
man might, with only superficial training, become an excellent
orator if he had these aptitudes. "Again we know that men who
are less generously endowed by nature but excel in experience
and practice, not only improve upon themselves, but surpass
others who, though more gifted, have been too negligent of their
talents" (191).

So much Isocrates says on the relative value of nature and
exercise. With strong help from either a man may attain success. Both together "might produce a man incomparable among
his fellows." But what of art, the training one gets in school?
This he rates as of less importance than nature or exercise. "For
if one should take lessons in all the principles of oratory and
master them with the greatest thoroughness, he might, perhaps,
become a more pleasing speaker than most, but let him stand up
before the crowd and lack one thing only, namely, assurance,
and he would not be able to utter a word" (192). We may be
reminded that Isocrates here speaks with the voice of experience.
He himself lacked assurance. His great reputation as an Attic
orator was gained by speeches he wrote for others to deliver,

by written speeches which were circulated in manuscript, and by his outstanding success as a teacher of rhetoric.

Thus he refuses to claim too much for the teacher of the arts of discourse in a school, but he is firm also in defending what a school can and does do for the intelligent student who applies himself diligently for long enough under a competent teacher. Only a few will become champions in the contests of oratory, but all will gain some intellectual training, all will become better educated. "For who among you does not know that most of those who have sat under the sophists have not been duped . . . but that some of them have turned out competent champions and others able teachers, while those who have preferred to live in private have become more gracious in social intercourse than before and keener judges and more prudent counsellors than the great majority. How then is it possible to scorn a discipline which is able to make . . . men of that kind?" (203–204.)

A little later Isocrates reverts briefly to the analogy between the physical education of gymnastic, in which all Greeks believed, and the mental education of rhetoric, which many conservatives belittled. And he goes on to enlarge on a related analogy between training animals and training men. It is absurd that some critics, who know very well that some people have the art of training dogs and horses, yet refuse to believe that anyone has the art of training human nature. "And most absurd of all, they behold in the shows which are held year after year lions which are more gentle towards their trainers than some people are towards their benefactors, and bears which can dance about and wrestle and imitate our skill, and yet they are not able to judge even from these instances the power which education and training have, nor can they see that human nature will respond more promptly than the animals to the benefits of education" (213).

Thus Isocrates kept well to the middle of the road, avoiding the extreme positions. Without belittling the importance of nature, he staunchly defended nurture in the arts of discourse offered by the new schools of the sophists. And he pointed out that in this nurture there was a place for the precepts of rhetoric formulated by the theorizers as well as for the exercises practiced by the empiricists.

Jebb justly sums up the relative importance of theory and practice in the effective teaching of rhetoric in his comparison of Aristotle and Isocrates as teachers. "If a philosophical treatment is required Aristotle stands alone. Yet the school of Aristotle—in which rhetoric was both scientifically and assiduously taught—produced not a single orator of note except Demetrius Phalereus; the school of Isocrates produced a host. Why was this so? Clearly because Isocrates, though inferior in his grasp of principles, was greatly superior in the practical department of teaching. It was not by his theory, it was rather by exercises, for which his own writings furnished models, that he formed his pupils." [4]

Doubtless many teachers both before and after Isocrates used the imitation of models as a teaching device to illustrate rhetorical theory and guide the pupil's exercises, but the earliest surviving textbook that makes the imitation of models coordinate with art and exercises is the work of a Roman teacher, whose name we do not know, addressed to C. Herennius. This work (81 B.C.), usually called the *Ad Herennium* and long thought to be an early work by Cicero, is dull, overanalytical, and methodical. In it the author makes scant mention of native talent as essential to oratorical success and gives no discussion of it at all. He says, "As rhetorical theory is nourished by talent, so natural talent is by precepts" (III.xvi.29). He does emphasize imitation. "We may attain success in public speech by the means of art, imitation, and exercise. Art gives precepts which provide a certain method and reason in speech. By imitation we are impelled to emulate others in speaking. Exercise is assiduous and habitual practice in speaking" (I.ii.3). Practitioners of all arts learn a great deal by playing the ape to other artists. Speakers and writers are no exception. I shall

[4] Jebb, *Attic Orators,* II, 433.

devote a separate chapter to the classic doctrine of imitation because of its intrinsic importance and subsequent influence.

Cicero's earliest treatise on rhetoric, the *De inventione,* in many ways resembles the *Ad Herennium,* so much so that it seems probable that as a boy he had read it or had heard the author's lectures. But when he left the Roman schools for the schools of Greece, he found better teachers who introduced him to Isocrates and Aristotle, whose theory and practice furnished the basis for his mature and considered views on rhetoric. These views are best presented in a charming dialog *De oratore* [concerning the orator]—not to be confused with the *Orator,* a treatise on oratorical style. The "orator" whose qualifications and education Cicero had in mind is best exemplified by himself: statesman, publicist, administrator, politician, lawyer, preacher, and general leader of public opinion in the affairs of the state. Such a person, then as now, used rhetoric as a means to mold public opinion.

In the Preface to this dialog, addressed to his brother Quintus, Cicero states his position, "I consider eloquence to be the offspring of the accomplishments of the most learned men, but you think it must be regarded as independent of learning and attributable to a kind of natural talent and exercise" (1.ii). Later in the Preface he speaks of the early Roman orators: "For a time, indeed, being ignorant of all method, and thinking there was no course of exercise for them or any precepts of art, they attained what they could by the single force of natural talent and thought. But afterward, having heard the Greek orators and having gained an acquaintance with Greek literature and procured instructors, our countrymen were so inflamed with a passion for eloquence that to that learning which each had acquired by his individual study, frequent practice, which was superior to the precepts of all masters, was at once added" (1.iv.14–15).

Firmly convinced as he was that education through both precept and practice was essential, Cicero was equally convinced that the kind of training he himself had had in the Roman schools was too narrow. Romans should not "trust that they can reach the height at which they aim by the aid of the precepts, teachers, and exercises which they now follow. They must adopt others of a different character" (i.v). He adds, "In my opinion, indeed, no man can be an orator possessed of every praiseworthy accomplishment unless he has attained the knowledge of all liberal arts" (i.vi).

Cicero is said to be the first to use the term "liberal arts" to designate the cycle of instruction (*encyclios paideia*) which had been the basis of Greek education since Isocrates. By the time of St. Augustine these had been codified as "the seven liberal arts": grammar, rhetoric, logic, arithmetic, geometry, music, and astronomy—the trivium and quadrivium of the medieval schools. Cicero was thus urging a scheme of education which placed rhetoric in a frame of liberal-arts training—where in enlightened colleges it is today, largely as a result of Cicero's influence.

Cicero continues his discussion of the relative importance of nature, art, and exercise in the body of the *De oratore*. He uses the literary device of imagining what several distinguished Roman orators of a generation before his own might have said about oratory and the orator. He uses Lucius Crassus most consistently as the mouthpiece for his own views. Here, then, is what Crassus-Cicero has to say.

First he disposes of the arguments of those who deny that rhetoric is an art at all. "All the disputation about it arises from a difference of opinion about the word. For if art is to be defined . . . as lying in things thoroughly understood and fully known, such as are abstracted from the caprice of opinion and comprehended in the limits of a science, there seems to me to be no art at all in oratory. . . . Yet if those things which have been observed in the practice and method of speaking have been noted and chronicled, have been set forth in words, illustrated in their several kinds, and distributed into parts . . . I do not understand why speaking may not be deemed an art" (i.xxiii).

He thus concedes that rhetoric is not an exact science but what we ourselves would today call an art, and in describing such an art as rhetoric he describes something which sounds very much like the preparation of a textbook or course of lectures on rhetoric.

Crassus goes on: "I am, then, of opinion that nature and talent in the first place contribute most aid to speaking . . . for there ought to be certain active powers of the mind which may be acute to invent, fertile to explain and adorn, and retentive to remember, and if any one imagines that these powers can be acquired, what will he say of those inborn qualities: volubility of tongue, tone of voice, strength of lungs, and a particular conformation and aspect of the whole body? I do not say that art cannot improve these particulars, for I am not ignorant that what is good can be made better by education, and what is not very good may be in some degree polished and amended" (i.xxv).

Later he adds another inborn requisite, "a passionate inclination, an ardor like that of love, without which no man will ever attain anything great in life" (i.xxx). The lack of this inclination is in any age on the part of students undoubtedly the greatest obstacle to teachers. The lack of passion in teachers also has its bad effects on students.

When urged to describe the course of studies which he himself had followed in youth, Crassus proceeds, "I shall say nothing abstruse, nothing previously unheard by you, or new to anyone. In the first place I will not deny that, as becomes a man well born and liberally educated, I learned those true and common precepts of teachers in general; first that it is the business of an orator to speak in a manner adapted to persuade. . . ." (i.xxxi), and he goes on to summarize the whole theory of rhetoric—the "art"—as it was taught for hundreds of years. In concluding his remarks on the art of rhetoric Crassus says, "And if I should say that art is of no assistance, I should say what is not true."

Having discussed native ability and the precepts codified as the art, Crassus turns to the exercises. "Those who are to enter upon a race, and those who are preparing for what is to be done in the forum, as in the field of battle, may alike previously learn and try their powers by practicing in sport" (I.xxxii).

"I like that method," Crassus continues to his young friends, "which you are accustomed to practice, namely, to lay down a case similar to those which are debated in the forum and to speak upon it as nearly as possible as if it were a real case." This exercise, called declamation, later became almost the only one practiced in the schools of rhetoric.

The following exercises he says are especially useful: writing, paraphrase, translation, imitation (II.xx.90–92), reading of poetry and history as well as of oratory, and the study of law and politics. As he has said before, Cicero believed that the orator must be a truly learned man. In this insistence he goes much farther than the Greek and Roman schools ever went. Otherwise he recommends the technical precepts and plan of exercises which the best teachers followed in their schools.

These classic principles enunciated by Cicero continued to hold sway and were echoed and expanded by Quintilian in the first century A.D. Indeed, a fairly adequate knowledge of Greek and Roman rhetorical education could be based on Quintilian alone. He comes at the close of the great period and sums it up. His treatise *De institutione oratoria* [on teaching rhetoric; or, the education of an orator] contains a God's plenty of common sense, erudition, intellectual honesty, practical experience, and professional expertness. The outstanding teacher of his day, he has had a profound influence on education in England and America.

Quintilian's earliest mention of the relative importance of nature, art, and exercise occurs at the conclusion of his Preface: "Neither precepts nor textbooks are of any value without the assistance of nature. Hence the student who lacks native capacity will derive no more benefit from this book than would sterile soil from a book on agriculture. There are also other natural aids such as a good voice, strong lungs, health, endurance, and grace. If these gifts are possessed to a moderate degree, they may be improved by training. But they may be so far wanting as to render abortive the advantages of natural capacity and study. And they are of no profit in themselves without a skillful teacher, persistent study, and continued exercise in writing, reading, and speaking" (Proem 26–27).

In the very first words of the treatise Quintilian voices his considered confidence in the human mind and in the power of education to improve it. "Therefore as soon as his son is born, let a father have the best possible hopes of him. Thus he will care for the boy more carefully from the beginning. The complaint is groundless that very few people are granted the power of comprehending what is imparted to them and that most people through slowness of mind waste their labor and time in study. On the contrary you will find most people ready in reasoning and quick in learning. Reasoning and learning are natural to man. As birds are born to fly, horses to run, and wild beasts to be ferocious, so to us peculiarly belong activity and sagacity of mind, whence it is believed that the soul has its origin in heaven.

"Dull and unteachable persons are no more the law of nature than are deformities and monstrosities, and there are very few of them. A proof of this is that among boys good promise is shown by most; when such promise dies away as they grow older, it is manifest that it was not natural ability that was lacking but the proper care.

"But, it is urged, some exceed others in natural ability. I grant it, but only to the extent that some will accomplish more and some less. There is no one who has not gained something from education" (1.i.1–3).

Quintilian resumes the discussion in his second book. Here, instead of dealing with the nature and nurture of all boys, he takes up specifically the nature and nurture of the orator.

"I know there is a question whether nature or education contributes more to eloquence. But this problem has no concern with

my work, for a perfect orator can be formed only with the aid of
both. For if either be completely separated from the other, nature
will be able to do much without education, but education will be
able to do nothing without nature. But if they be united in equal
parts, I am inclined to think that with the average orator the influence of nature is greater, while the perfect orator owes more to
education than to nature. Thus even the best farmer cannot improve soil of no fertility whatever, while rich land will yield
something useful without cultivation; but with the rich land the
cultivation will produce more than the goodness of the soil itself—
in a word, natural capacity is the raw material for education. The
one forms, the other is formed. Art can do nothing without
material; material even without art has value, the perfection of art
is better than the best material" (ii.xix.i).

That Quintilian analyzes education (*doctrina*) in the conventional way is evidenced by a later statement: "Oratorical skill is
brought to the highest degree of excellence by nature, art, and
exercise, to which some add a fourth, imitation, which I include
under art" (iii.v.i).

As a professional educator Quintilian had great confidence in
school training, both rhetorical and encyclopedic. But not all
writers on rhetoric agreed with him. Philodemus, in his *Rhetorica*,[5] discredits the precepts or art of rhetoric, claiming that
proficiency in speaking comes from much practice and natural
ability, and Tacitus, a younger contemporary of Quintilian, prefers the old Roman system of education to the schools of rhetoric.
Messalla, one of the speakers in the *Dialogus,* says that in the old
days, after a boy had had sound training at home, he studied with
a successful orator in the forum; nowadays a boy is sent to a
professor of rhetoric, who knows less than a practical lawyer, to
debate with boys as ignorant as himself. Hence it is natural to
find Tacitus agreeing with Quintus, Cicero's brother, in attribut-

[5] *Rhetorica* is translated with a commentary by H. M. Hubbell in *Transactions
of the Connecticut Academy of Arts and Sciences,* XXII (1920), 243–382.

ing eloquence to natural talent and practice independent of study in the schools.

So in Tacitus, Maternus says to Messalla, "What I want to know about is this: By what exercises were the young men, about the forum, in the habit of strengthening and developing their natural capacities? For the basis of eloquence is not art or learning, but rather native talent and practice."

Messalla answers: "Since I have given you enough of the beginnings and the seeds from which eloquence sprung—I shall now take up their exercises. Yet art itself involves exercise, and it is impossible for anyone to grasp so many diverse and recondite principles unless his theoretical knowledge is fortified by preparatory exercise, his exercise by natural ability, his ability by practice in speaking" (33).

Postclassical rhetorical treatises kept up this same tradition of the threefold analysis. At the beginning of the sixth century Cassiodorus from his monastery repeats Quintilian's words quoted above and Isidore of Seville in the early seventh century was still saying, "Skillful speech is derived from three things: nature, precept, practice" (*Etymologiae* ii.iii.2). Indeed, the threefold division of nature, art, and exercise, with its insistence that speaking and writing are taught by precept, example, and practice exercises, would seem obvious and indisputable. It would be but a waste of time to recapitulate the ancient story, were it not for the objections of romantic critics who assert that rhetoric cannot be taught by teachers in schools. In Greece and Rome, at least, the leading speakers and writers testified that they themselves had learned from their teachers in schools.

Who Taught the Poets?

Although my topic is rhetoric, not poetry, I hope I will be pardoned if I deviate by dealing briefly with nature, art, and exercise as they involve the requirements of the poet. Perhaps it is not really a digression, for many literary critics of antiquity considered poetry, like rhetoric, a skill pertaining to utterance, although others did indeed consider poetry a divine madness.[6]

Plato, as we have seen, was quick to urge the rule of reason in the training that should be offered in rhetoric. But he is much more famous for having pointed out the irrationality of the poet. His theory of inspiration in poetry has been much more influential on the critical theorizing of the moderns than it was on the theorizing of the ancients. It furnishes a philosophical basis for those of our contemporaries who assert that, "You just can write or you can't, and no teaching can make any difference." But what did Plato really say? What is the Platonic theory of poetical inspiration?

In the *Phaedrus* Socrates analyzes the divine madness into four categories: the prophetic, the initiatory, the poetic, and the erotic. "The third kind," he asserts in a memorable passage, "is the madness of those who are possessed by the Muses; which taking hold of a delicate and virgin soul and there inspiring frenzy, awakens lyrical and all other numbers; with these adorning the myriad actions of ancient heroes, for the instruction of posterity. But he who, having no touch of the Muse's madness in his soul, comes to the door and thinks he will get into the temple by the help of art—he, I say, and his poetry are not admitted; the same man disappears and is nowhere when he enters into rivalry with the madmen" (245).

Another memorable passage is in the *Ion*. Ion the rhapsode tells Socrates that he is not interested in reciting from poets other than Homer, but Homer awakens all his feeling. Socrates tells him why. "The gift which you possess . . . is not an art, but an inspiration; there is a divinity moving you, like that contained in the stone Euripides calls the magnet. . . . In like manner [i.e., like a magnet] the Muse first of all inspires men herself, and from these

[6] D. L. Clark, "The Requirements of a Poet," *Modern Philology*, XVI (December, 1918), 8.

inspired persons a chain of other persons is suspended, who take the inspiration. For all good poets, epic as well as lyric, compose their beautiful poems not by art, but because they are inspired and possessed. . . . So the lyric poets are not in their right mind when they are composing their beautiful strains. . . . For the poet is a light and winged and holy thing, and there is no invention in him until he has been inspired and is out of his senses and the mind is no longer in him."

One poet "will make dithyrambs, another hymns of praise, another choral strains, another epic or iambic verses . . . and he who is good at one is not good at any other kind of verses: for not by art does the poet sing, but by power divine. Had he learned by rules of art, he would have known how to speak not of one theme only, but of all; therefore God takes away the minds of the poets and uses them as his ministers, as he also uses diviners and holy prophets, in order that we who hear them may know them to be speaking not of themselves who utter these priceless words in a state of unconsciousness, but that God himself is the speaker" (533–534).

But when Plato says that the poet is out of his mind and inspired by divine madness, he is not quite so complimentary as some have supposed. His deference is, in part at least, ironic. The popular Greek notion of the poets was that they were wise, clever men, like physicians and engineers. They practiced a craftsmanship. Hence one read the poets in order to learn something solid. The poet was a teacher with knowledge to impart about war, statecraft, morality. He was an adequate guide to truth and right conduct. Hence poems were the body of grammar school education.

Plato has Socrates attack both these notions. Poets produce poetry, not by craftsmanship, but by nonrational inspiration, for they cannot explain what they have written, they write better than they know, and they cannot control their medium (*Apology* 22; *Phaedrus* 245; *Ion* 533–534). Moreover, the poet is not a specialist in any kind of knowledge, hence is not the person to go to if we want to learn. We should go to philosophers for truth and true guidance, not to poets.[7] So we see there is no real contradiction between Plato's statements on the one hand that poets are divinely inspired and on the other that "No poetry should be admitted [in his ideal commonwealth] save hymns to the gods and panegyrics on famous men" (*Republic* 606). One reason for the banishment of most poets from the Republic is that they *are* inspired—nonrational.

Modern psychological studies bear out the nonrational basis of a great deal of creative thinking—including literary creation.[8] Today, however, we do not invoke the Muses or refer to divine inspiration. We are more likely to refer to the subliminal, the subconscious, or the unconscious. But the ancient poets and critics held to their guns and insisted on craftsmanship and rationality. The long-haired madman rolling his eyes in frenzy was not the conventionally approved image of the good poet in antiquity. Although in the *Rhetoric* Aristotle says that poetry, unlike oratory, is inspired (III.7), in the *Poetics* he is more cautious and conventional, saying that the poet must have a strain of madness in him or else must be happily gifted by nature with a quick feeling for metaphor (17).

Horace, however, was much more representative of Greek and Roman notions of the requirements of the poet than was Plato or even Aristotle.[9] He sought in poetry a happy balance of native talent and art, as a famous passage from the *Epistle to the Pisos* declares: "It is asked whether poetry originates from natural capacity or from artistic training. I answer that neither training without rich gifts nor genius rude and untrained is sufficient. Each requires the aid of the other, and they should work together

[7] For a full discussion of Plato's attack on poetry see Atkins, *Literary Criticism in Antiquity,* I, 33–70.

[8] Prescott, *The Poetic Mind,* and Downey, *Creative Imagination,* will start the reader on this investigation.

[9] D'Alton, *Roman Literary Theory and Criticism,* pp. 446–447, 474–475.

as friends." He amplifies his argument by an analogy of the
runner who must train for the race and the flute player who must
practice for hours under a severe master, and makes a memorable
statement of his reconciliation of philosophy and poetry: "Sound
thinking and knowledge is the source of sound poetry." This
knowledge is derived from a study of books and from a study of
life, not from inspiration.

When a boy is just starting to school it is hard to know whether
he is going to be a lawyer, a politician, a soldier, a farmer, or a
poet. It was just as hard two thousand years ago as now. So then
as now little boys got pretty much the same schooling in the liberal
arts. In the grammar school they learned correct spelling, grammar, punctuation, and usage, the use of synonyms and figures of
speech, and the rules of prosody. They studied and memorized
the same school poets of the classical past. They wrote elementary
exercises in verse and prose. When they proceeded to the school
of rhetoric, they studied the same famous orations of the past and
practiced the same rhetorical exercises in declamation. Future
poets got the same training as future orators and future generals,
and it was a rhetorical training. But were they influenced by this
training? Did the professors of rhetoric impress their stamp on
the plastic wax of future men of letters? Did the teachers of speaking and writing teach boys to speak and write?

That the schools of rhetoric did indeed influence poets and
prose writers balefully is recognized by any historian of late Latin
literature.

"The main clue to the literary qualities of Silver Latin," says
Duff, "is to be found in education, and particularly in rhetorical
education. No social or political factor exercised so determining
an influence upon the literature of imperial Rome." And again,
"Manner of expression came to be deeply modified by the systematic instruction in rhetoric and by the declamatory exercises
composed by students practicing the use of figures of speech, ex-
clamations, apostrophes, interrogations, and innumerable other

artifices." [10] Eduard Norden urges the influence of Hellenistic rhetoric on Roman poetry as resulting in a learned content and a laborious style. The poets were burdened by technic. Their native abilities were disciplined and governed by the art of rhetoric.[11] When Henry Osborn Taylor considers the early Christian sermon, he points out that the early Fathers of the church, of whom many had been professors and all had been students of rhetoric, show definitely in their florid styles the rhetorical sophistications they had been taught in the schools.[12] And W. C. Summers testifies, "The conventional censure of Silver literature as rhetorical understates the case against it. . . . For the love of epigram, antithesis, paradox and allusion, all that for want of a better name is called point, the declamations were not of course solely responsible. . . . But the pointed flowers of the declamation are something more than a mere escape from the large garden of contemporary taste: they were the principal objects of its cultivation. . . . We have definite proof of the influence which a school point could exercise upon alumni in their years of maturity. Seneca, for instance, mentions that Ovid borrowed from his master Latro the suggestion that his Ajax makes in regard to the arms of Achilles for which he and Ulysses are candidates, 'Fling them among the foe, and bid us thence retrieve them.' For a careful reader of the declamations, indeed, the literature of our period is full of such echoes." [13]

More recently S. F. Bonner points out good as well as bad effects of the schools of rhetoric on Silver literature: "On the credit side, they gave the style point, neatness and condensation, and also a means of expansion of ideas and literary embroidery; on the debit side, they were undoubtedly responsible for much rant and bombast, false effect, and artificial expression." [14]

[10] Duff, *A Literary History of Rome in the Silver Age*, pp. 23–29 and *passim*.

[11] Norden, *Die antike Kunstprosa*, pp. 182–183, especially note 1.

[12] Taylor, *The Classical Heritage of the Middle Ages*, p. 224.

[13] Summers, *The Silver Age of Latin Literature*, pp. 12–13.

[14] Bonner, *Roman Declamation*, p. 167. He devotes Chapter VIII to declamatory influence on literature.

The consensus then, ancient and modern, is that natural ability is not enough to produce poets and orators. The best of natural talent is improved by training. So is the worst. At least in antiquity teachers taught successfully. The worst a modern historian can say about them is that they were fiendishly successful in inculcating in their students bad taste, empty glibness, and choppy sententiousness. If our fellow teachers were thus successful in cultivating perverse flowers of evil in their rhetorical gardens, we teachers today can be assured that we too can teach young people to speak and write, each according to his capacity. We should be on our guard, of course, to cultivate wholesome and useful plants as well as beautiful blossoms. Our efforts are not fruitless. Let us use the greatest care that the fruits be good.

I have saved for the end of the chapter a sentence from Dionysius of Halicarnassus which expresses wittily and maliciously what I have frequently felt during many years of teaching. "No rules contained in rhetorical manuals can suffice to make experts of those who are determined to dispense with study and practice" (*De compositione verborum* xxvi).

II. WHAT THE ANCIENTS MEANT
BY RHETORIC

THIS CHAPTER will be devoted to definitions of rhetoric. It will study the efforts made by the greatest minds of antiquity to define the nature and aims of rhetoric, to orient rhetoric in an educational system and in a civilized society, and to appraise it as a social good or evil. The ancients were never in any more complete or philosophical agreement on any of these points than we are today. But since we devote so much space in educational journals and so much time in meetings and conventions to discussing the restudy of educational aims for the society of tomorrow and to the reorientation of education in the society of today, we may very well benefit from study of the discussion of the same and similar problems by the great educational philosophers of the Greek and Roman past.

From the beginning there were three characteristic and divergent views on rhetoric. There was the moral philosophical view of Plato, who condemned rhetoric because it seemed to him to deal with appearances, opinion, and pleasure whereas it ought to deal with reality, truth, and the good life. There was the philosophical scientific view of Aristotle, who tried to see the thing as in itself it really was, who endeavored to devise a theory of rhetoric without moral praise or blame for it. There was, finally, the practical educational view of the rhetoricians from

Isocrates to Cicero to Quintilian, who praised rhetoric, practiced it, and taught it as an essential attribute of the free citizen in a civilized society. In this chapter I shall exhibit these three views in some detail.[1]

Rhetoric, like so much else in life, can best be understood if first approached historically. As a formal study it first grew up in Sicily about one hundred and fifty years before Aristotle as an instrument for training speakers to carry on litigation in the law courts. Since Greek law required every free man to speak for himself in court, every free man needed the training—not merely a small class of professional advocates. The first treatise on rhetoric was written by Corax, a Sicilian,[2] and limiting rhetoric narrowly to the conduct of legal dispute was urged by some teachers throughout antiquity. In this narrow view the whole aim of rhetoric was to win cases, to win the verdict by hook or by crook, and if truth was trampled on in the process, so much the worse for truth. Envisaged thus and thus practiced—as it is on occasion to this day—rhetoric becomes the target of all the opprobrium that indignant moralists from Plato down can heap upon it. Yet when practiced by well-matched advocates, umpired by a competent judge and evaluated by a jury of our peers, this rhetoric gives us the nearest thing to justice any of us will see this side the pearly gates. It may be said, however, that ancient Greek judicial procedure offered many more opportunities for abuse than does our own.

In Sicily from the earliest times rhetoric had literary as well as legal aspects. Quoting from works now lost, Diogenes Laertius says, "Aristotle in his *Sophist* calls Empedocles the inventor of rhetoric. . . . In his treatise *On Poets* he says Empedocles was of Homer's school and powerful in diction, being great in metaphors and in the use of all other poetical devices" (viii.57). This sug-

---

[1] McKeon, in "Rhetoric in the Middle Ages," *Speculum*, January, 1942, traces the combinations and permutations of these views from postclassical times to the Renaissance.

[2] Roberts, *Greek Rhetoric and Literary Criticism*, pp. 22, 35.

gestion that the literary artifices of rhetorical prose style had their origin in poetry is borne out by Aristotle in the *Rhetoric:* "Now it was because poets seemed to win fame through their fine language when their thoughts were simple enough, that the language of oratorical prose first took a poetical color, for example, that of Gorgias" (iii.i.9).

Gorgias of Leontini in Sicily was a pupil of Empedocles. When on an embassy to Athens in 427 B.C., he introduced rhetoric to the Athenians, both the rhetoric of the law courts and the rhetoric of literary artifice. Of his pupils, Alcidamas carried on the tradition of legal pleading; Isocrates carried on the literary tradition—each, of course, with developments of his own. The oratory of Gorgias himself was by no means limited in range and interest. Philostratus in his *Lives of the Sophists* mentions three of his orations: the *Pythian* was delivered from the altar of Apollo at Delphi; the *Olympian* was a plea for Greek unity against the barbarians; the *Funeral Oration* (of which a fragment survives) cleverly combined commemoration of the dead with a plea for Greek unity (493).

The Moral Plato

It was this Gorgias of Leontini whom Plato made the protagonist of his Socratic dialog, the *Gorgias.* In this dialog Plato launched an attack on rhetoric and rhetoricians. Plato did not like rhetoric (any more than he did poetry), did not teach it in his Academy, and ruled it out of his utopian republic. But then Plato disapproved of almost everything in human life as he saw it about him in Athens. He disapproved of Athenian democracy, poetry, art, education, and religion as well as of Athenian rhetoric—all fundamentally on the same grounds.

The grounds are inherent in Platonic metaphysics, which postulate as the only truth, the only reality, an idea or form in the mind of God. All else is appearance. The appearances are more or less imperfect imitations of true reality laid up in heaven. In the *Republic* he has Socrates explain by the example of a bed. "Now there are three beds, first the bed which exists in nature, which we should say, I fancy, was made by God. Should we not?" This is the real bed. Imitating the real bed a carpenter manufactures a particular bed. The painter, in his painting of this bed, imitates not the real bed as it is but the appearance of the bed. He is an "imitator who is concerned with what is begotten three removes from nature. And the tragedian, since he is an imitator, will then be one whose nature is third from the King and from truth, and all other imitators will be like him" (595–606). And this gives Plato one reason for expelling all imitative artists, who deal with appearances, from his utopian republic.

The philosopher, or at least the Platonic philosopher, deals with reality and truth, whereas the rhetorician deals with appearances and opinion, and hence to Plato rhetoric is a sham and a snare. The philosopher's instrument for the discovery of truth is dialectic, the argument between two people, the Socratic method illustrated in Plato's dialogs. Dialectic proceeds by reason and reveals truth. "Dialectic, and dialectic alone, goes directly to the first principle and is the only science which does away with hypothesis in order to make her ground secure" (533–534). It is concerned with truth, not with opinion.

In the *Gorgias* Plato shows Socrates using the dialectical method in three separate arguments: first with Gorgias, then with Polus, then with Callicles, a politician. He first seeks from Gorgias a definition of rhetoric. Under cross-questioning Gorgias states that rhetoric deals with discourse, with words, which relate to the best of human things.

Gor. That good, Socrates, which is truly the greatest, being that which gives to men freedom in their own persons, and to individuals the power of ruling over others in their several states.
Soc. And what would you consider this to be?

Gor. What is there greater than the word which persuades the judges in the courts or the senators in the council, or the citizens in the assembly, or at any other political meeting? . . .

Soc. Now I think, Gorgias, that you have very accurately explained what you conceive to be the art of rhetoric; and you mean to say, if I am not mistaken, that rhetoric is the artificer of persuasion. . . .

Gor. The definition seems to me to be very fair, Socrates; for persuasion is the chief end of rhetoric.

Socrates then asks if rhetoric is the only art which brings persuasion, if all teachers do not persuade men of that which they teach, if arithmetic and arithmeticians do not teach and therefore persuade us of the properties of number, and thus traps Gorgias into admitting that "arithmetic as well as rhetoric is an artificer of persuasion." Perhaps the real Gorgias would have pointed out that the arithmetician uses rhetoric to persuade about arithmetic, which is a subject not an artificer of persuasion. But Plato consistently belittles the greatest men of his age to enhance the figure of Socrates in his dialogs. Certainly Aristotle saw the fallacy and avoided it as we shall see later.

Gorgias, in taking up the argument again, says, "I answer, Socrates, that rhetoric is the art of persuasion in courts of law and other assemblies, as I was just now saying, and about the just and the unjust."

Plato is not too unfair in attributing to Gorgias this narrow limitation of the field of rhetoric. It was a limitation maintained by some rhetoricians for hundreds of years. Plato was also fair in putting into the mouth of Gorgias a defense of rhetoric which is echoed by Aristotle, Cicero and Quintilian: "Rhetoric should be used like any other competitive art, not against everybody . . . the rhetorician ought not to abuse his strength any more than a pugilist or master of fencing. . . . Suppose a man to have been trained to be a skilful boxer . . . he in the fullness of his strength goes and strikes his father or mother; but that is no

reason why trainers or fencing masters should be held in detesta-
tion. For they taught their art for a good purpose, to be used
against enemies and evildoers, in self defence not in aggression.
. . . But not on this account are the teachers bad, neither is the
art in fault or bad in itself: I should rather say that those who
make a bad use of the art are to blame. And the same argument
holds good for rhetoric."

But Plato was not satisfied to view rhetoric as a skill or instrument or weapon which could be put to good or bad use. He
asked rhetoric to have a high moral purpose and condemned
rhetoric because it does not. Hence he shows Gorgias answering
Yes to the following questions: "Then, when the rhetorician is
more persuasive than the physician, the ignorant is more persuasive
with the ignorant than he who has knowledge? . . . And the
same holds of the relation of rhetoric to all the other arts; the
rhetorician need not know the truth about things; he has only to
discover some way of persuading the ignorant that he has more
knowledge than those who know?"

But Gorgias is not so ready to admit that the rhetorician may
be "as ignorant of the just and unjust, base and honorable, good
and evil, as he is of medicine and the other arts." He states that
if a pupil does not know the truth of these things, he will have
to learn these things as well as rhetoric from his teacher.

Soc. Say no more, for there you are right; and so he whom you
make a rhetorician must either know the nature of the just and
the unjust already, or must be taught by you.

Gor. Certainly. . . .

Soc. And he who has learned medicine is a physician? He who
has learned anything whatever is that which his knowledge
makes him?

Gor. Certainly.

Soc. And in the same way, he who has learned what is just is
just?

Gor. To be sure.

And having swallowed that fallacy, Gorgias is thought to be defeated in the argument, for he has been made to contradict himself. If the teacher makes his pupil just by teaching him the nature of justice, then the pupil could not make an unjust use of rhetoric and the analogy of rhetoric and boxing is exploded (448–460).

In the second argument, the one with Polus, a pupil of Gorgias, Socrates gives his own adverse opinion of rhetoric. First of all rhetoric is not an art at all but "an experience in producing a sort of delight and gratification . . . a flattery and of an ignoble sort, because it aims at pleasure without any thought of the best. . . . An art I do not call it, but only an experience, because it is unable to explain or to give a reason of the nature of its own applications. And I do not call any irrational thing an art." In modern parlance Socrates is asserting that rhetoric is not an exact science.

Moreover, says Socrates, "Rhetoric is a ghost or counterfeit of politics." It simulates justice as sophistic simulates statesmanship and personal adornment simulates gymnastic and cookery simulates medicine. These spurious experiences or habits aim to give the appearance of justice, statesmanship, beauty, and health, not the reality. Hence Socrates cannot find enough hard words to describe the sham, deceitful, knavish, false, illiberal, spurious arts.

But, says Polus, "Are the good rhetoricians meanly regarded in states under the idea that they are flatterers? Have they not great power in states? Are they not like tyrants? They kill and despoil and exile anyone they please."

Now the *Gorgias* was probably written not more than ten years after Socrates had been impeached by an orator, a poet, and a demagogue and had been convicted and condemned by an Athenian jury. Plato knew only too well that rhetoricians, like tyrants, could kill, and he did not approve.

So Socrates is made to deny that rhetoricians have real power in states because real power is a good and a benefit to its possessor. But one who kills another unjustly is to be pitied, not envied, for the doing of injustice is the greatest of evils. "Yes, indeed, Polus, this is my doctrine; the men and women who are gentle and good are also happy, as I maintain, and the unjust and evil are miserable." Hence the claim that Gorgias had made that rhetoric conveyed the greatest good of man, "the power of ruling over others in states," is challenged and, to Plato's satisfaction, refuted. Gorgias's second claim that rhetoric, as the other greatest good of man, gives to men freedom in their own persons is met by Socrates by the following line of reasoning.

Soc. In my opinion, Polus, the unjust or doer of unjust actions is miserable in any case, . . . more miserable, however, if he be not punished and does not meet with retribution, and less miserable if he be punished and meets retribution at the hands of gods and men.

Polus points out that Socrates is alone in so believing. But Socrates is quite willing to be alone in his certainty of the truth in the face of the universal opinion that he is in error. He drives ahead in his contentions: "I maintained that he . . . who has done wrong and has not been punished, is, and ought to be, the most miserable of all men; and that the doer of injustice is more miserable than the sufferer; and he who escapes punishment, more miserable than he who suffers. . . . Well, Polus, if this is true, where is the great use of rhetoric? . . . Then rhetoric is of no use to us, Polus, in helping a man to excuse his own injustice, or that of his parents and friends, or children or country; but may be of use to anyone who holds that instead of excusing he ought to accuse—himself above all . . . so the wrongdoer may suffer and be made whole" (461–481).

Callicles, at the beginning of the third argument, is sure that Socrates must be joking. "For if you are in earnest and what you say is true, is not the whole of human life turned upside down?"

Socrates says he repeats only what philosophy tells him and philosophy is always true.

To which Callicles answers, "Philosophy is an elegant accomplishment . . . but if a man carries philosophy into later life, he is necessarily ignorant of those things which a gentleman and a person of honor ought to know; he is inexperienced in the laws of the state, and in the language which ought to be used in the dealings of man with man, whether private or public, and utterly ignorant of the pleasures and desires of mankind and of human character in general. . . . He flies from the busy center and the market place, in which, as the poet says, men become distinguished; he creeps into a corner for the rest of his life, and talks in a whisper with three or four admiring youths, but never speaks out like a freeman."

This man of the world, this Callicles, is an outspoken man. He says, according to Socrates, what the rest of the world thinks but does not like to say. He believes "that luxury, intemperance, and license, if they be supplied with means, are virtue and happiness." He believes that the strong are superior to the weak and should take what they want. Only the cowardly praise temperance and justice. Plato does not caricature the power politician in his portrait of Callicles. The Athenian embassy to the Melians, as reported by Thucydides (v.xvii), exhibits with like outspokenness the unabashed face of self-interest and asserts that might makes right.

But Callicles, shrewd worldling that he is, is not a dialectician, and Socrates has little trouble in getting him tangled in self-contradictions. So he admits that through rhetoric "a man may delight a whole assembly and yet have no regard for their true interests," and the flute playing, the choral art, dithyrambic poetry, harp playing, tragedy, and rhetoric have been invented for the sake of pleasure.

Soc. Then now we have discovered a sort of rhetoric which is addressed to a crowd of men, women, and children, freemen and slaves. And this is not much to our taste, for we have described it as having the nature of flattery.

Cal. Quite true.

Soc. Very good. And what do you say of that other rhetoric which
addresses the Athenian assembly and the assemblies of freemen
in other states? Do the rhetoricians appear to you always to
aim at what is best, and do they seek to improve the citizens
by their speeches, or are they too, like the rest of mankind, bent
upon giving them pleasure, forgetting the public good in the
thought of their interest, playing with the people as with children, and trying to amuse them, but never considering whether
they are better or worse for this?

Cal. I must distinguish. There are some who have a real care of
the public in what they say, while others are such as you
describe.

Soc. I am contented with the admission that rhetoric is of two
sorts: one, which is a mere flattery and disgraceful declamation;
the other, which is noble and aims at the training and improvement of the souls of the citizens, and strives to say what is
best, whether welcome or unwelcome, to the audience; but
have you ever known such a rhetoric; or if you have, and can
point out any rhetorician who is of this stamp, who is he?
(502–503.)

Callicles knows of none living, but suggests that Themistocles,
Miltiades, and Pericles were good men who aimed to improve
the citizens. But to Socrates even they failed to distinguish between the satisfaction of those desires which make men better and
the satisfaction of those which make men worse. He says, "Will
not the true rhetorician who is honest and understands his art
have his eyes fixed on these [temperance and justice] in all the
words which he addresses to the souls of men? . . . Will not his
aim be to implant justice in the souls of his citizens and take
away injustice, to implant temperance and take away intemperance, to implant every virtue and take away every vice?" (504.)

And the men of the world are silenced by the moral urgency
and religious fervor of Socrates. Both before Socrates and since,

of course, men of the world have consistently used rhetoric as well as all other instruments of power to satisfy their desires and to attain their ambitions, quite unrestrained by considerations of temperance and justice. But since Socrates even the men of the world have been constrained to give at least lip service to the ideal that rhetoric should be moral and should endeavor to make virtue and truth prevail. And Quintilian was not the least of the ancient teachers of rhetoric who urged that the public speaker must be a good man (1.Proem 9; 11.xx.4; xii.i.1).

In the *Phaedrus,* a later dialog than the *Gorgias,* Plato returns to his attack on Sicilian and Athenian rhetoric but in addition outlines his plan of a noble rhetoric which aims at improving the souls of the citizens, not with flattery, and deals with knowledge and truth, not with opinion and appearances.

Whereas the *Gorgias* was concerned entirely with political and legal rhetoric practiced in the law courts and public assembly, the *Phaedrus* deals for the most part with the rhetoric of praise and blame, and the examples are drawn from speeches praising and blaming love. Phaedrus shows Socrates a speech by Lysias urging the paradox that a young man should accept as a "lover" one who does not really love him. Socrates remarks on the disorderly structure, repetitious style, and lack of definition and then delivers a better speech on the same theme. Then after these two speeches condemning love and blaming lovers Socrates recognizes his error.

Phaedr. What error?

Soc. It was foolish, I say,—to a certain extent impious. . . . For if Love be, as he surely is, a divinity, he cannot be evil. Yet this was the error of both the speeches. There was also a simplicity about them which was refreshing; having no truth nor honesty in them, nevertheless they pretended to be something, hoping to succeed in deceiving the manikins of earth and gain celebrity among them (242).

In like manner in the *Symposium* Plato urges the claims of truth. Agathon has praised Love most highly, attributing to him all virtues. Socrates admires the speech, comparing it to the speeches of Gorgias, but professing his own simplicity. "For I imagined that the topics of praise should be true. . . . Whereas I now see that the intention was to attribute to Love every species of greatness and glory, whether really belonging to him or not, without regard to truth or falsehood, for the original purpose seems to have been, not that you should really praise Love, but only that you should appear to praise him" (198).

And in the *Phaedrus* Socrates goes about purging himself of wrongdoing in slandering Love by recanting in another speech which shall tell the truth, that the lover ought to be accepted, not the nonlover.

After Socrates has delivered his eloquent speech in praise of love, he and Phaedrus fall to discussing the rules of writing and speaking.

Soc. In good speaking should not the mind of the speaker know the truth of the matter about which he is going to speak?
Phaedr. And yet, Socrates, I have heard that he who would be an orator has nothing to do with true justice, but only with that which is likely to be approved by the many who sit in judgment; not with the truly good or honorable, but only with opinion about them, and that from opinion comes persuasion, and not from truth.

After showing that without knowledge of his subject an orator may make himself ridiculous, Socrates adds, "But perhaps rhetoric has been getting too roughly handled by us, and she might answer: What amazing nonsense you are talking! As if I forced any man to speak in ignorance of the truth! Whatever my advice may be worth, I should have told him to arrive at the truth first and then come to me. At the same time I boldly assert that mere knowledge of the truth will not give you the art of persuasion." Phaedrus adds, "And there is reason in the lady's defense of herself."

Socrates then reiterates that rhetoric is "a mere routine and trick, not an art." He then proceeds to say, "Lo! a Spartan appears and says that there never is nor ever will be a real art of speaking which is divorced from truth." And he adds of the orator, "He will never be able to speak about anything as he ought to speak unless he have a knowledge of philosophy."

Soc. Is not rhetoric, taken generally, a universal art of enchanting the mind by arguments, which is practiced not only in courts of law and in public assemblies, but in private houses also, having to do with all matters, great as well as small? . . .
Phaedr. I should rather say that I have heard the art confined to speaking and writing in law suits and speaking in public assemblies—not extended farther.

Here we have contrasted the conventional restricting of rhetoric, which Plato had attributed to Gorgias, and Plato's own wider view that rhetoric has to do with all subjects in all places.

Socrates then goes on to show that the rhetorician uses his ability to make the same thing appear just at one time and unjust at another. "He makes the same things appear to his hearers like and unlike, one and many, at rest and in motion." And since "it is clear that error slips in through resemblances . . . then he who would be a master of the art must understand the real nature of everything; or he will never know either how to make the gradual departure from truth into the opposite of truth which is effected by the help of resemblances, or how to avoid it. He then, who being ignorant of the truth aims at appearances, will only attain an art of rhetoric which is ridiculous and not an art at all" (260–262).

It is noteworthy that Plato is not here urging the public speaker always to speak the truth. He must know the truth so that he may persuade men the more skillfully—for their own good, of

course—of that which is not the truth and that he may avoid
being tricked by an opponent into accepting a falsehood as true.
The speaker's need to know the truth is prudential as well as
moral. To Plato the end justified the means. In his dialogs the
high moral purpose of Socrates is a constant justification for his
use of any fallacious trick of reasoning or any misrepresentation
of facts that may be effective in winning converts to his moral
(or religious) sense of what was philosophically real and true.
"Truth," as always in Plato, means true philosophical knowledge of the reality of Platonic "ideas" laid up in heaven, and this
knowledge is to be arrived at by the processes of dialectic.

After insisting that the speaker must know the truth, Socrates
takes up the speech of Lysias and his own speech as examples
of bad and good rhetoric. Love is the subject of each speech. But
love is an uncertain topic, like justice and goodness, concerning
which people are not agreed. In speaking on such debatable
topics one should define his terms; as Socrates started by defining
love, whereas Lysias started at the end instead of at the beginning, because he omitted a definition. Moreover his own speech
involved two important principles of speaking. So he says to
Phaedrus: "First, the comprehension of scattered particulars in
one idea; as in our definition of love, which whether true or false
certainly gave clearness and consistency to the discourse; the
speaker should define his several notions and so make his meaning clear. The second principle is that of division into species
according to the natural formation, where the joint is, not breaking any part as a bad carver might. Just as our two discourses
alike assumed, first of all, a single form of unreason; and then,
as the body which from being one becomes double and may be divided into a left side and right side, each having parts right and
left of the same name . . . after this manner the speaker proceeded to divide the parts of the left side and did not desist until he
found in them an evil and left-handed love which he justly re-
viled; and the other discourse leading us to the madness which

lay on the right side, found another love, also having the same name, but divine, which the speaker held up before us and applauded. . . . I am myself a great lover of these processes of division and generalization; they help me to speak and think. . . . And those who have this art, I have hitherto been in the habit of calling dialecticians" (264–266).

So, to Plato, the noble rhetorician must be a logician as well as a philosopher. Or perhaps the term philosopher would cover both, because the philosopher uses dialectic to discover and disseminate the ideal truth. Nowadays what little logic is taught is comprised in rhetoric as part of spoken or written composition. The lack of instruction in logic is one of the most serious blemishes in modern education. Certainly a rhetoric which fails to make the fullest use of logic is a shadowy thing.

Plato's next constructive contribution to a noble or "real" art of rhetoric was the insistence that the speaker must understand his hearers. He must not only know the truth of the subject under discussion but must also understand what we would call the psychology of the audience.

Socrates says, "Oratory is the art of enchanting the soul, and therefore he who would be an orator has to learn the difference of human souls . . . they are so many and of such a nature, and from them come the differences between man and man. Having proceeded this far in his analysis, he will next divide speeches into their different classes: . . . 'Such and such persons,' he will say, 'are affected by this or that kind of speech in this or that way,' and he will tell you why. The pupil must have a good theoretical notion of them first, and then he must have experience of them in actual life, and be able to follow them with all his senses about him, or he will never get beyond the precepts of his masters. But when he understands what persons are persuaded by what arguments, and sees the person about whom he was speaking in the abstract actually before him, and knows that it is he, and can say to himself, 'This is the man or this is the character who ought to have a certain argument applied to him in order to convince him of a certain opinion'; . . . he who knows all this and knows also when he should speak and when he should refrain, and when he should use pithy sayings, pathetic appeals, sensational effects, and all the other modes of speech which he has learned; . . . when, I say, he knows the times and seasons of all these things, then and not till then, he is a perfect master of his art" (271).

And at the end of the *Phaedrus* he has Socrates sum up in honest rhetorical fashion what he has said about the nature of the art: "Until a man knows the truth of the several particulars of which he is writing or speaking, and is able to define them as they are, and having defined them again to divide them until they can be no longer divided, and until in like manner he is able to discern the nature of the soul, and discover the different modes of discourse which are adapted to different natures, and to arrange and dispose them in such a way that the simple form of speech may be addressed to the simpler nature, and the complex and composite to the more complex nature—until he has accomplished all this, he will be unable to handle arguments according to rules of art, as far as their nature allows them to be subjected to art, either for the purpose of teaching or persuading; . . . such is the view which is implied in the whole preceding argument" (277).

Plato's demand that the speaker or writer should be a practicing psychologist does not seem unreasonable to us today. Psychology seems to us to be newer and fresher than logic and attracts many more students in colleges. The teacher of speaking or writing should certainly be familiar with such books as Hollingworth, *The Psychology of the Audience.*

Plato in demanding that the speaker be a psychologist, was, of course, again asserting that he should be a philosopher. For to Plato the knowledge of the soul could be the attainment only of the philosopher. Thus in recapitulation we can see that Plato set up requirements for the noble rhetoric which only a philosopher could fulfill, thus:

The philosopher knows the truth.

The philosopher is a master of dialectic, the instrument for the discovery and dissemination of truth.

The philosopher understands the nature of the soul.

The philosopher knows the nature of justice and temperance and virtue, and is alone fitted to make them prevail.

Philosophy is thus the only true rhetoric.

False rhetoric, to Plato, was false because:

It is based on opinion and appearances instead of philosophical truth and reality.

It uses specious and emotional appeals to the ignorant multitude instead of dialectical demonstrations to the intellectual.

It is ignorant of the nature of the soul.

It is a nonmoral instrument of persuasion instead of being an instrument of righteousness.

As Everett Lee Hunt summarized his attitude, "Plato never viewed rhetoric abstractly, as an art of composition, as an instrument which could be used or abused; he always considered it as a false impulse in human thought. . . . The ideal rhetoric sketched in the *Phaedrus* is as far from the possibilities of mankind as his Republic was from Athens." [3]

But it influenced Aristotle, Cicero, and Quintilian and cannot be ignored today. Plato's noble rhetoric had its noblest fruit in the tradition of Christian preaching, which was based on it and on Cicero and received its greatest impetus from St. Augustine's treatise on preaching, the *De doctrina Christiana*.[4] It has its place in the City of God if not in Athens.

[3] "Plato and Aristotle on Rhetoric and Rhetoricians," in *Studies in Rhetoric and Public Speaking in Honor of James Albert Winans*, p. 42.

[4] Baldwin, *Medieval Rhetoric and Poetic*, pp. 51–73, gives an analysis of St. Augustine.

Aristotle

Aristotle did not agree with Plato that true rhetoric had to be an instrument of righteousness and that all other rhetoric was ignoble. Instead, he tried to understand the nature, aims, and uses of rhetoric in the phenomenal world in which we live. Great classifier and systematizer of human knowledge, he approached rhetoric as he approached ethics, logic, psychology, politics, physics, biology, or astronomy—in a scientific spirit.

He was, moreover, thoroughly familiar with the philosophy of Plato. He came to Athens about 368 B.C. at the age of seventeen and for the next twenty years was closely associated with Plato's Academy until Plato's death about 348 B.C. In part his rhetoric is derived from Plato's views as stated in the *Gorgias* and the *Phaedrus* and in much greater part is a reaction away from Plato.

In the *Rhetoric* he characteristically places in the opening chapters his theoretical discussion of the nature, aims, and uses—his definition and division—of rhetoric. Most of what I shall quote from the *Rhetoric* is from this section.

In his opening paragraph Aristotle claims a close kinship between rhetoric, the art of public speaking, and dialectic, which he considers as the art of logical discussion. He claims rhetoric to be an art in the face of Plato's denials:

"Rhetoric is the counterpart of dialectic. Both alike are concerned with such things as come, more or less, within the general ken of all men and belong to no definite science. Accordingly all men make use, more or less, of both; for to a certain extent all men attempt to discuss statements and to maintain them, to defend themselves and attack others. Ordinary people do this either at random or through practice and from acquired habit. Both ways being possible, the subject can plainly be handled systematically, for it is possible to inquire the reason why some speakers succeed through practice and others spontaneously; and every one will at once agree that such an inquiry is the function of an art."

After condemning current treatises on rhetoric for devoting themselves exclusively to appeals to the feelings and neglecting persuasion through an effort to use logical argument, he continues:

"It is clear, then, that rhetorical study, in its strict sense, is concerned with the modes of persuasion. Persuasion is clearly a sort of demonstration, since we are most fully persuaded when we consider a thing to have been demonstrated. . . . The true and the approximately true are apprehended by the same faculty; it may also be noted that men have a sufficiently natural instinct for what is true, and usually do arrive at the truth. Hence the man who makes a good guess at truth is likely to make a good guess at probabilities."

Here we have a conception of "truth" far different from Plato's ideal forms laid up in heaven. These ideal forms Aristotle did not believe in. He did believe, as we shall see later, in scientifically demonstrated truths, about which there is no debate, and in such contingent and approximate truths as give us the best guide to action at any given moment and about which we do debate.

Continuing with his discussion, closer to Gorgias than to Plato, Aristotle next formulates the fourfold function of rhetoric. As Baldwin summarizes it, the function is "first and foremost to make truth prevail by presenting it effectively in the conditions of actual communication; second, to advance inquiry by such methods as are open to men generally; third, to cultivate the habit of seeing both sides and of analyzing sophistries and fallacies; and finally, to defend oneself and one's cause." [5]

As Aristotle himself puts it more fully: "Rhetoric is useful (1) because things that are true and things that are just have a natural tendency to prevail over their opposites, so that if the decisions of judges are not what they ought to be, the defeat must be due

[5] Baldwin, *Ancient Rhetoric and Poetic,* p. 9.

to the speakers themselves, and they must be blamed accordingly. Moreover, (2) before some audiences not even the possession of the exactest knowledge will make it easy for what we say to produce conviction. For argument based on knowledge implies instruction, and there are people whom one cannot instruct. Here then we must use, as our modes of persuasion and argument, notions possessed by everybody, as we observed in the *Topics* when dealing with a popular audience. [In the *Topics* he said, "When we have counted up the opinions held by most people, we shall meet them on the ground not of other people's convictions but of their own" (1.ii).] Further, (3) we must be able to employ persuasion, just as strict reasoning can be employed, on opposite sides of a question, not in order that we may in practice employ it in both ways (for we must not make people believe what is wrong), but in order that we may see clearly what the facts are, and that, if another man argues unfairly, we on our part may be able to confute him. No other of the arts draws opposite conclusions: dialectic and rhetoric alone do this. Both these arts draw opposite conclusions impartially. Nevertheless, the underlying facts do not lend themselves equally well to the contrary views. No; things that are true and things that are better are, by their nature, practically always easier to prove and easier to believe in. Again, (4) it is absurd to hold that a man ought to be ashamed of being unable to defend himself with his limbs, but not of being unable to defend himself with speech and reason, when the use of rational speech is more distinctive of a human being than the use of his limbs. And if it is objected that one who uses such power of speech unjustly might do great harm, that is a charge which may be made in common against all good things except virtue, and above all against the things that are most useful, as strength, health, wealth, generalship. A man can confer the greatest of benefits by a right use of these, and inflict the greatest of injuries by using them wrongly."

Thus Aristotle assigns to the public speaker the rather difficult task of making truth prevail among the generality of men as they are and of defending truth and himself against attack, using means of proof similar to those used by dialectic. But he comforts us with the assurance that it is easier to make the truth prevail than to make error prevail.

In the next paragraph he reverts to his objections against those who would restrict rhetoric to pleadings in the law courts and those who would define it as an artificer of persuasion. "It is clear, then, that rhetoric is not bound up with a single definite class of subjects, but is as universal as dialectic; it is clear also that it is useful. It is clear, further, that its function is not simply to succeed in persuading, but rather to discover the means of coming as near success as the circumstances of each particular case allow. In this it resembles all arts. For example, it is not the function of medicine simply to make a man quite healthy, but to put him as far as may be on the road to health." And he concludes his first chapter, "We must make as it were a fresh start, and before going further define what rhetoric is."

Chapter 2 opens with the definition, "Rhetoric may be defined as the faculty of observing in any given case the available means of persuasion." Or as Bishop Welldon translated it, "Rhetoric may be defined as the faculty of discovering all the possible means of persuasion in any subject." [6]

"There are these three means of effecting persuasion. The man who is to be in command of them must, it is clear, be able (1) to reason logically (*logos*), (2) to understand human character (*ethos*) and goodness in their various forms, and (3) to understand the emotions (*pathos*)—that is, to name them and describe them, to know their causes and the way in which they are excited. It thus appears that rhetoric is an offshoot of dialectic and also of ethical studies. Ethical studies may fairly be called political; and for this reason rhetoric masquerades as political science,

[6] J. E. C. Welldon, translation of the *Rhetoric*, London, 1886.

and the professors of it as political experts—sometimes from want of education, sometimes from ostentation, sometimes owing to other human failings. As a matter of fact, it is a branch of dialectic and similar to it, as we said at the outset. Neither rhetoric nor dialectic is the scientific study of any one separate subject; both are faculties for providing arguments."

Aristotle, in the foregoing, is in substantial agreement with Plato, who makes Socrates condemn rhetoric as "the ghost or counterfeit of politics" (*Gorgias* 463). With this difference: He believes that some public speakers erroneously pretend that rhetoric is political science, but that in its real nature rhetoric is, like dialectic, a faculty for providing arguments—a faculty, of course, which is essential to a statesman. In allying dialectic and rhetoric Aristotle parts company with Plato, who maintained that dialectic reveals truth and is as different as possible from rhetoric, which is an ignoble means of flattering the rabble.

Again he is both agreeing and disagreeing with Plato when he urges the importance of the speaker's character. Plato urges the necessity of absolute justice, temperance, and goodness as requirements of the speaker who would use the noble rhetoric. Aristotle urges that since "we believe good men more fully and more readily than others," the speaker should speak in such a way as to seem good. In Book II he says of the speaker, "His own character should look right and he should be thought to entertain the right feelings toward his hearers. . . . There are three things which inspire confidence in the speaker's own character—the three, namely, that induce us to believe a thing apart from any proof of it: good sense, good moral character, and good will" (II.i).

Aristotle is not urging a hypocritical assumption of goodness by an evil man. But as he had already said, "All good things can be abused save virtue alone." The good speaker must not hide his light under a bushel. If he is a good speaker as well as a good man, then he should exhibit his good sense, good morals, and good will to his audience. The art of rhetoric should teach him how.

When Aristotle names appeals to the emotions as a second mode of persuasion, his notion resembles somewhat Plato's plea for a psychology of the audience. He is, however, much closer to the writers of those treatises on rhetoric which he condemns for including little else.

"The emotions," Aristotle says, "are those feelings that so change men as to affect their judgements, and that are also attended by pain or pleasure. . . . Let us now proceed to analyze the subject before us." This he analyzes in eleven chapters of Book II.

Of these modes of persuasion Aristotle considered the most important to be the third, the proof of a truth or apparent truth by means of persuasive arguments. In an earlier treatise on logic, the *Prior Analytics,* he had written, "Every belief comes either through syllogism or from induction" (II.xxiii). And in the *Rhetoric* he shows how the public speaker can use persuasive arguments from these logical processes of deduction and induction in forms especially adapted to a popular audience, which he calls enthymeme and example. "I call the enthymeme a rhetorical syllogism, and the example a rhetorical induction. . . . When we base the proof of a proposition on a number of similar cases, this is induction in dialectic, example in rhetoric; when it is shown that, certain propositions being true, a further and quite distinct proposition must also be true in consequence, whether invariably or usually, this is called syllogism in dialectic, enthymeme in rhetoric" (I.2).

In this connection he makes an exceedingly important distinction between degrees of proof. First there is the scientific demonstration, the infallible sign or complete proof. "Suppose it were said, 'The fact that she is giving milk is a sign that she has lately borne a child.' Here we have an infallible kind of sign, the only kind that constitutes a complete proof, since it is the only kind that, if the particular statement is true, is irrefutable" (1.ii.18). As he says in the *Topics*, "It is a demonstration when the premises from which the reasoning starts are true and primary, or are such that our knowledge of them has come through premises which are primary and true" (1.i).

He points out in the *Rhetoric* that dialectic and rhetoric have little to do with such scientific demonstrations. Dialectic and rhetoric both deal with matters that call for discussion, with the regular subjects of debate. And we do not debate matters that have been settled. "The duty of rhetoric is to deal with such matters as we deliberate upon . . . in the hearing of persons who cannot take in at a glance a complicated argument or follow a long chain of reasoning. The subjects of our deliberation are such as seem to present us with alternative possibilities. About things that could not have been, and cannot now or in the future be, other than they are, nobody wastes his time in deliberation. . . . The enthymeme and the example, then, must deal with what is in the main contingent. . . . Most of the things about which we make decisions, and into which therefore we inquire, present us with alternative possibilities. For it is about our actions that we deliberate and inquire, and all our actions have a contingent character. Hardly any of them are determined by necessity. Again conclusions that state what is merely usual or possible must be drawn from premises that do the same" (1.2).

Hence he concludes that rhetorical and dialectical arguments must be drawn for the most part not from necessary premises, but from what is usually true, that is from probabilities—or as he says in the *Topics* "from opinions which are generally accepted" (1.i).

Many more conclusions have been scientifically demonstrated in our day than in the day of Aristotle and hence can be used as premises whence we can draw further necessary conclusions. But in the realm of human affairs it is as true as ever it was that we discuss and deliberate and argue for the most part only those questions which may issue in at least two ways. We must choose one of the ways to follow in action. We may choose rightly or wrongly, but choose we must. So in discussion and argument our students must be warned that they cannot "prove" that they are right in the sense of "scientifically demonstrate." They can "prove" only in the sense of pointing out the conclusion which has the strongest support from probabilities. Such a conclusion Aristotle calls "approximately true." Approximate truth is a very human kind of truth, far from the "real" truth that only Socrates and Plato could perceive.

The body of Aristotle's *Rhetoric* fulfills the promises of the first three chapters. The rest of Book I includes suggestions as to the kind of information and special knowledge the speaker will need in practicing each of the three kinds of rhetoric—forensic, epideictic, and deliberative—and deals with generally accepted opinions about happiness, expediency, virtue, good, justice, pleasure, and the like, for these generally accepted opinions furnish the premises and lines of argument which the speaker must be competent to use when he seeks to persuade an audience. Book II presents (1) a popular psychology of the emotions to guide the speaker in rousing or allaying the emotions of his audience, (2) a shrewd analysis of the characteristic mental and moral attitudes of men at different times of life and under different circumstances to guide the speaker in his efforts to adapt his arguments to his audience, and (3) an examination of the modes of proof by means of argument, inductive and syllogistic, confirmatory and refutative, sound and fallacious, that are likely to win an audience. Book III deals with style and arrangement, considered for their persuasiveness. "For it is not enough to know *what* we ought to say; we must also say it *as* we ought; much help is thus afforded towards producing the right impression of a speech" (III.1).

One clear note runs all through Aristotle's philosophy of rhetoric. "It is the hearer that determines a speech's end and object." First, the speaker should speak in such a way as to show his good sense, good morals, and good intentions towards his hearers. Second, he should speak in such a way as to arouse or allay the emotions of the hearers in order to make them more favorable to the cause he advocates. Third, he should speak in such a way as to make his cause seem to be logically demonstrated to his hearers, and he does this by basing his deductive and inductive arguments on premises which the hearers have observed to be usually true or which agree with what they in general believe. If a speaker is discussing a problem with a few well-informed and intelligent people, he will use strict logical processes and will seek to persuade them by dialectic. If he addresses a large and popular audience, he will base his persuasive arguments on notions possessed by most people. He will use rhetoric. In any event he will adapt his methods to his audience.

Teachers and learners of the arts of speaking and writing today will find this constant attention to the audience, in the widest sense of the word which includes readers as well as hearers, to be the most fruitful thought in Aristotle's *Rhetoric*. In twenty-four centuries customs, institutions, laws, means of communication have changed greatly, but the speaker or the writer today has, as in the past, one object—to make his sense of the truth prevail in the minds and hearts of his audience, by means of words, composed for this purpose, in speech or in writing. His aim is communication, not self-expression.

This Aristotelian attention to the audience as the controlling factor in communication is or can be fruitful today because a great part of our teaching and student speaking and writing displays a marked lack of attention to the audience. It is, perhaps, quite natural that this should be so. Young people are likely to be even more self-centered and self-obsessed than their elders. The rhetoric of childhood is largely centered on acquiring candy by the application of temper tantrums. Children come to rely on their nuisance value to gain their ends. Young people in schools and colleges still have far to go before they realize themselves as members of society or, as Aristotle said, "political animals." But difficult as it is to shift the attention of school and college students from the use of language as primarily an instrument of self-expression in their antisocial world to its use as a means of communication in a civilization, the teacher of speaking and writing is largely responsible for inducing the student to take the step.

Aristotle the philosopher has demonstrated that communication with an audience is essentially the end and aim of all rhetoric, both spoken and written. But he does not tell us how we as teachers are to get our pupils so to consider it. Nor does he show us how to teach our pupils to be effective communicators of their sense of truth to any given audience. Aristotle the philosopher lectured on rhetoric and wrote the most important of philosophical treatises on rhetoric. He taught rhetoric, but as Jebb states (p. 10), he did not succeed in training public speakers. No one ever could become a public speaker just by reading Aristotle's *Rhetoric*. His understanding of rhetoric would be enhanced, but his command over it as a means to an end would not. Teachers today should read and meditate Aristotle's *Rhetoric*, but they are not advised to use it as a textbook in college classes. For practical help in training young people to communicate effectively through speech and writing teachers must go to those who have successfully practiced and have successfully taught others to practice the arts of spoken and written communication. As was said at the beginning of this chapter, we can hope to receive such help from such ancient speakers, writers, and teachers as Gorgias, Isocrates, Cicero, and Quintilian. Hence, we shall now turn from the philosophers, moral and scientific alike, exalted and penetrating as they are, and listen to the rhetoricians, practical and unphilosophical as they frequently are. In the remainder of this chapter we shall see what the rhetoricians thought of the definition, division, uses, and aims of rhetoric. How rhetoric was practiced and taught will occupy the rest of this book.

Isocrates

Isocrates, "the old man eloquent" of Milton's tenth sonnet, is said to have written an *Art of Rhetoric,* but it has not survived.[7] We can, however, gather from passages in his speeches a good idea of what he conceived to be the nature, uses, and importance of rhetoric in education and in civil life. I have already introduced Isocrates as a teacher whose views on the relative importance of nature, art, and exercise were sane and well balanced, a teacher who emphasized the importance of the practical against the theoretical preoccupations of the philosophers, and emphasized a well-rounded education for a speaker against the narrow views of some teachers of forensic rhetoric.

The fullest statements of his philosophy of rhetoric occur in the *Antidosis,* written when he was eighty-two years old. Like Plato's *Apology of Socrates,* which it echoes, it was written to be read— not intended for public delivery. In this defense of his life and teaching he adopts the fiction of a court scene and defends himself against a fictitious indictment.

"Here in the indictment my accuser endeavors to vilify me, charging that I corrupt young men by teaching them to speak and gain their advantage in the courts contrary to justice" (30).

His first answer is that in his own practice and in his teaching he has been concerned, not with the forensic rhetoric of the law courts, but with a nobler political rhetoric:

"There are no fewer branches of composition in prose than in verse. For some men have devoted their lives to researches in the genealogies of the demigods; others have made studies in the poets; others have elected to compose histories of wars; while others have occupied themselves with dialog, and are called dialecticians. It would, however, be no slight task to attempt to

---

[7] Fragments remain. See *Isocratis Orationes,* edited by Benseler-Blass (1879), II, 275.

enumerate all the forms of prose, and I shall take up only that which is pertinent to me, and ignore the rest.

"For there are men who, albeit they are not strangers to the branches which I have mentioned, have chosen rather to write discourses, not for private disputes, but which deal with the world of Hellas, with affairs of state, and are appropriate to be delivered at the Pan-Hellenic assemblies—discourses which, as everyone will agree, are more akin to works composed in rhythm and set to music than to the speeches which are made in court. For they set forth facts in a style more imaginative and more ornate; they employ thoughts which are more lofty and more original, and, besides, they use throughout figures of speech in greater number and of more striking character. All men take as much pleasure in listening to this kind of prose as in listening to poetry, and many desire to take lessons in it, believing that those who excel in this field are wiser and better and of more use to the world than men who speak well in court" (45–47).

This passage describes quite fairly Isocrates' contributions to rhetoric. First he understands rhetoric to be discourse including all the arts of prose, written as well as spoken. He deals with it as a form of literature, not merely, as Aristotle did later, as the art of persuasive public speaking. His own "speeches" were not intended to be delivered before an audience, but were pamphlets or literary essays on subjects of wide interest and importance addressed to cultivated readers of subsequent ages as well as his own age. Hence his second but allied contribution to a philosophy of rhetoric, his emphasis on beauty of expression and such adornment as is appropriate to artistic prose. This is the eloquence Milton imitates in *Areopagitica*.

Isocrates preferred to call himself a philosopher rather than a sophist or rhetorician, and his school a school of philosophy. He does not usually talk about "rhetoric," but about the "art of discourse" (*Antidosis* 253). The art of discourse may, therefore, be as broad as the whole or the "philosophy of discourse" (*Panegyricus*

10). The Greek word translated as "discourse" is *logos,* the "word," wide and deep in significance. As M. H. Roberts points out, "The noun *logos* is an ablaut derivative of the verb *legein* 'to choose, to gather, to lay in order, to put into speech, to discourse.' A *logos* is the substance of a speech or announcement, a selection, gathering, organization of thought. . . . *Logos* is used in Greek in a multitude of senses such as a story, myth, proverb, discussion, reason, principle, proposition." [8] Norlin says that *logos* "is both the outward and the inward thought; it is not merely the form of expression, but reason, feeling, and imagination as well; it is that by which we persuade others and by which we persuade ourselves; it is that by which we direct public affairs and by which we set our own house in order; it is, in fine, that endowment of our human nature which raises us above mere animality and enables us to live the civilized life. The art of discourse may, therefore, be as broad as the whole life of civilized man; and this is just what Isocrates insisted that it should be." [9]

In an eloquent and justly famous passage in the *Antidosis* Isocrates voices his broad concept of the nature and use of discourse or rhetoric: "We ought to think of the art of discourse just as we think of the other arts, nor show ourselves intolerant toward that power which, of all the faculties which belong to the nature of man, is the source of most of our blessings. For in the other powers which we possess, we are in no respect superior to other living creatures; nay we are inferior to many in swiftness and in strength and in other resources; but, because there has been implanted in us the power to persuade each other and to make clear to each other whatever we desire, not only have we escaped the life of wild beasts, but we have come together and founded cities and made laws and invented arts; and, generally speaking, there is no institution devised by man which the power

[8] Murath H. Roberts, "The Science of Idiom: A Method of Inquiry into the Cognitive Design of Language," PMLA, LIX. I (March, 1944), 292.

[9] Norlin, *Introduction* to his Loeb Library translation of Isocrates.

of speech has not helped us to establish. For this it is which has laid down laws concerning things just and unjust, and things honourable and base; and if it were not for these ordinances we should not be able to live with one another. It is by this that we confute the bad and extol the good. Through this we educate the ignorant and appraise the wise; for the power to speak well is taken as the surest index of a sound understanding, and discourse which is true and lawful and just is the outward image of a good and faithful soul. With this faculty we both contend against others on matters which are open to dispute and seek light for ourselves on things which are unknown; for the same arguments which we use in persuading others when we speak in public, we employ also when we deliberate in our thoughts; and, while we call eloquent those who are able to speak before a crowd, we regard as sage those who most skilfully debate their problems in their own minds. And, if there is need to speak in brief summary of this power, we shall find that none of the things which are done with intelligence take place without the help of speech, but that in all our actions as well as in all our thoughts speech is our guide, and is most employed by those who have the most wisdom" (253-257).[10] That this passage represents the considered views of Isocrates is attested to by the fact that he quotes it verbatim from an earlier speech, the *Nicocles* (5-9), where he concluded even more vigorously: "Therefore, those who dare to speak with disrespect of educators and teachers of philosophy deserve our opprobrium no less than those who profane the sanctuaries of the gods."

We who teach rhetoric today should be vastly heartened by this stirring defense, even though we recognize that much of what Isocrates taught as the art or philosophy of discourse is now taught, if at all, in other departments within the division of the humanities or in the faculties of philosophy or of political science. There are, however, distinct advantages in teaching all the humanities as parts of one unified, focused, and integrated program

[10] See Jaeger, *Paideia*, III, 143.

as Isocrates taught them. When taught separately as descriptive sciences such studies as ethics, politics, logic, and literature may become just something to know. When properly integrated with rhetoric as Isocrates saw the matter, they are more likely to find useful application to private or public affairs.

That humanistic training in the art of discourse is educationally superior to a training in pure science he was convinced. But he never took an extreme position or condemned mathematical or logical studies. But unless a boy was planning a professional career in science he would be better prepared for life by a liberal education with an integrating focus on a broad and humane rhetoric.

"I believe," said Isocrates in the *Antidosis,* "that the teachers who are skilled in disputation and those who are occupied with astronomy and geometry and studies of that sort do not injure but, on the contrary, benefit their pupils, not so much as they profess, but more than others give them credit for. . . . For while we are occupied with the subtlety and exactness of astronomy and geometry and are forced to apply our minds to difficult problems, and are, in addition, being habituated to speak and apply ourselves to what is said and shown to us, and not to let our wits go wool-gathering, we gain the power, after being exercised and sharpened on these disciplines, of grasping and learning more easily and more quickly those subjects which are of more importance and of greater value. I do not, however, think it proper to apply the term 'philosophy' to a training which is no help to us in the present either in our speech or in our actions, but rather I would call it a gymnastic of the mind and a preparation for philosophy. It is, to be sure, a study more advanced than that which boys in school pursue, but it is for the most part the same sort of thing; for they also when they have laboured through their lessons in grammar, music, and the other branches, are not a whit advanced in their ability to speak and deliberate on affairs, but they have increased their aptitude for mastering greater and more serious studies" (261–267).

But on what grounds could Isocrates affirm that rhetoric, the art of discourse, was more practical and of more immediate use in life than the sciences or dialectic? Nowadays the shoe is on the other foot. He found his ground in the philosophical position that exact knowledge of the future is impossible, that the problem of practical life is that of making plans for the future, that the art of weighing the probabilities and uncertain contingencies of the future and forming reasonable judgments as to courses of action is the art of discourse. At the beginning of his career, in *Against the Sophists,* he wrote, "It is manifest to all that foreknowledge of future events is not vouchsafed to our human nature, but that we are so far removed from this prescience that Homer, who has been conceded the highest reputation for wisdom, has pictured even the gods as at times debating among themselves about the future—not that he knew their minds but that he desired to show us that for mankind this power lies in the realms of the impossible" (2). Isocrates held to this philosophy all his life and gave the most explicit statement in the *Antidosis.* "My view of this question is, as it happens, very simple. For since it is not in the nature of man to attain a science by the possession of which we can know positively what we should do or what we should say, in the next resort I hold that man to be wise who is able by his powers of conjecture to arrive generally at the best course, and I hold that man to be a philosopher who occupies himself with the studies from which he will most quickly gain that kind of insight" (271).

Having thus defended "opinion" against the strictures of Plato, having attacked Plato's claims of "knowledge," and having given Aristotle a fruitful lead toward his rhetoric of probabilities and approximate truth, Isocrates proceeds in the *Antidosis* to outline a practical morality of rhetoric as a defense against Plato's attacks in the *Gorgias.*

"I consider that the kind of art which can implant honesty and justice in depraved natures has never existed and does not now exist, and that people who profess that power will grow

weary and cease from their vain pretensions before such an education is ever found. But I do hold that people can become better
and worthier if they conceive an ambition to speak well, if they
become possessed of the desire to be able to persuade their hearers,
and, finally, if they set their hearts on seizing their advantage—I
do not mean 'advantage' in the sense given to that word by the
empty minded, but advantage in the true meaning of that term;
and that this is so I think I shall presently make clear.

"For, in the first place, when anyone elects to speak or write
discourses which are worthy of praise and honour, it is not conceivable that he will support causes which are unjust or petty
or devoted to private quarrels, and not rather those which are
great and honourable, devoted to the welfare of man and our
common good; for if he fails to find causes of this character,
he will accomplish nothing to the purpose. In the second place,
he will select from all the actions of men which bear upon his
subject those examples which are most illustrious and most edify-
ing; and, habituating himself to contemplate and appraise such
examples, he will feel their influence not only in the preparation
of a given discourse but in all the actions of his life. It follows,
then, that the power to speak well and think right will reward
the man who approaches the art of discourse with love of wisdom and love of honour.

"Furthermore, mark you, the man who wishes to persuade
people will not be negligent as to the matter of character; no,
on the contrary, he will apply himself above all to establish a
most honourable name among his fellow-citizens; for who does
not know that words carry greater conviction when spoken by
men of good repute than when spoken by men who live under
a cloud, and that the argument which is made by a man's life is of
more weight than that which is furnished by words? Therefore,
the stronger a man's desire to persuade his hearers, the more
zealously will he strive to be honourable and to have the esteem
of his fellow-citizens" (274–278).

Aristotle later did not deny that the speaker's reputation for honor influences an audience in his favor, but with his strictly logical view of rhetoric, he insisted that the creation of the appearance of honor by the speech itself was all that was intrinsic to the art of rhetoric. We are indebted more to Aristotle than to Isocrates for a logical and scientific understanding of our art, but to Isocrates we owe a broad view of rhetoric as the art of discourse, written as well as spoken, literary as well as oratorical, applicable to private as well as to public affairs, and in Isocrates we find the earliest, noblest example of the teacher of rhetoric, the teacher who is master of the art he teaches, who is devoted to the true advantage of his pupils, who envisages education in rhetoric as the training of young people to take their place in a human society where all transactions are conducted through the medium of language.

For forty years Isocrates was the most influential teacher in Athens. His pupils came from all parts of Hellas.[11] The list includes an amazing number of honorable and useful statesmen and generals, orators and historians, who had received their education in his school,[12] some studying with him for three or four years. The list prompted Cicero to write: "Then behold! there arose Isocrates, the master of all rhetoricians, from whose school, as from the Horse of Troy, none but leaders emerged." [13]

The strong influence of Isocrates on Cicero, both in his style and in his philosophy of rhetoric, is testified to by Jebb,[14] Blass,[15] and Hubbell.[16]

---

[11] Blass, *Die attische Beredsamkeit,* II, 17 ff.
[12] Dionysius of Halicarnassus *Critique on Isocrates* i.
[13] *De oratore* ii.xxii.94.
[14] Jebb, *Attic Orators,* II, 32 ff., 69.
[15] Blass, *Die attische Beredsamkeit,* II, 212 ff.
[16] Hubbell, *The Influence of Isocrates on Cicero, Dionysius, and Aristides.*

III. THE SCHOOLS

CICERO'S THEORY and practice of rhetoric was solidly based on first-hand study of the rhetorical writings of Plato and Aristotle as well as on the art of discourse of Isocrates. But unlike them all, he did not teach in a school. Few Roman teachers of rhetoric save Quintilian attained his breadth and depth of philosophy of rhetoric. None attained his eminence as a speaker. Although many teachers were in their day famous as speakers, all of them spent most of their time and energy teaching boys in schools.

But the practice and the true meaning of rhetoric in Roman times was determined by the school training. Hence, before I undertake to explain the teaching of ancient rhetoric in those areas controlled by the Roman Republic and Empire, I wish to establish very briefly the nature of the schools in which it was taught. These Roman schools differed from the Greek schools of the sixth and fifth centuries B.C., which are most familiar to us from the writings of Plato, Isocrates, and Aristotle, and from the sympathetic interpretation of Werner Jaeger's *Paideia*. They were, however, practically identical with the Hellenistic Greek schools of their own epoch. These did not so much imitate the Greek schools as take over their methods with little or no modification.[1] The most noteworthy change was that they taught Latin as well as Greek grammar, literature, and rhetoric, whereas the Greek schools for the most part carried on instruction in Greek only.

This Greco-Roman educational program was not only homo-

[1] Marrou, *Histoire de l'éducation dans l'antiquité*, p. 359.

geneous, but widespread and long-lived. It was fully accepted in Rome by the middle of the second century B.C.[2] Juvenal records its extension to the north by the end of the first century: "Today the whole world has its Greek and Roman Athens: eloquent Gaul has trained the pleaders of Britain, and distant Thule talks of hiring a rhetorician" (*Satire* xv.110). In the late fourth century Ausonius memorializes in a poem, the *Professores,* his former colleagues who had taught Greek and Latin grammar and rhetoric at Bordeaux. It was this Greco-Roman system which was revived and taken over by the humanists of the sixteenth century.[3]

According to this system, instruction was carried on in three stages: primary, secondary, and advanced, as Apuleius, writing in the second century, clearly states: "In the feasts of the Muses the first cup is poured by the literator, who teaches us to read. Then comes the grammaticus, who adorns us with different sorts of knowledge. Finally the rhetor places in our hands the weapons of eloquence" (*Florida* 20). Suetonius, in his brief vita, records that the poet Persius had an education following this conventional sequence, for he "studied until the twelfth year of his age at Volaterrae, and then at Rome with the grammarian Remmius Palaemon and the rhetorician Verginius Flavus." Marrou, in the following summary, indicates that this sequence was typical: "In Rome, as in the Greek-speaking countries, there were three successive steps in instruction. Normally these corresponded to the three types of school taught by three special teachers. At seven the child entered the primary school, which he quit at eleven or twelve for the school of the grammaticus. When he was of age to receive the toga virilis, about fifteen, he passed to the school of the rhetor. The advanced studies normally lasted till he was about twenty, although they might be prolonged." [4]

The primus magister, as St. Augustine calls him (*Confessiones*

[2] Gwynn, *Roman Education from Cicero to Quintilian,* p. 40.
[3] D. L. Clark, *John Milton at St. Paul's School,* p. 4.
[4] Marrou, *Histoire de l'éducation dans l'antiquité,* p. 360.

13), took children when they knew nothing and taught them the three R's. In this primary school, boys, and some girls as well, sat on backless benches or forms, memorized the alphabet backward and forward, learned to write with a stylus on wax tablets held on the knee and with a reed pen on papyrus. Before they exercised themselves in reading connected passages, they read and memorized moral maxims of one or two verses. After the third century they habitually used the *Disticha Catonis,* attributed to the schoolmaster Dionysius Cato, which became one of the most popular schoolbooks of the Middle Ages and the Renaissance. The children also studied arithmetic through fractions and weights and measures. This primary instruction was well beaten in. As Juvenal reminds us "presenting the hand to the ferule" was equivalent to "going to school" (*Satire* 1.15). In fact, the ancient primary school [5] was almost the exact equivalent of the Elizabethan petty school and the first and second forms of the grammar school.

Some children continued their schooling in the *ludus literarius,* or grammar school, but many could have gone no farther than the primary school. The Romans were not ironical in calling grammar school a "game" (*ludus*). In their practical way they considered all games as exercises preparing young people for the activities of war and peace which they must confront as adults. The elementary exercises of the grammar school, which I shall discuss in some detail in a later chapter, were planned to prepare a boy for subsequent advanced instruction in rhetoric and ultimately for an active life in public affairs. The master of the school was usually called, both in Latin and Greek, the grammaticus. Jullien endeavors to define his major function by calling him "professor of literature." [6]

The school of the grammaticus, or the grammar school, was concerned with much more than we think of as grammar. Seneca (*Epistolae* 88) and Cicero (*De oratore* 1.187) both indicate that

---

[5] *Ibid.:* for the Greek schools, pp. 200–222; for the Roman, pp. 359–368.

[6] Jullien, *Les Professeurs de littérature dans l'ancienne Rome.*

the grammaticus taught not only correctness of language, the meaning of words, and correct accent and delivery, but also the interpretation of the historians and the poets. Quintilian (i.iv) concurs and goes on to point out that the grammaticus edits and emends texts [7] and establishes the canon of a poet, accepting the authentic and rejecting spurious attributions. "Nor is it sufficient to have read the poets only; every class of writers must be studied, not simply for matter, but for words, which often receive their authority from writers." Quintilian adds that the professor of literature must also know music, if he is to teach meter and rhythm, and also some astronomy, if he is to explain many passages in the poets.

Gwynn, indeed, points out that in theory, at least, the grammar school was devoted to teaching all of the seven liberal arts—"a regular curriculum of studies, not yet clearly defined in all its parts, but certainly including literature, rhetoric, dialectics, arithmetic, geometry, astronomy, and music." [8] It is clear, however, that the language arts of the trivium predominated. As Marrou points out, the mathematical arts were for the most part taught by special teachers in special schools.[9]

The persistence of grammar-school practices is witnessed by Donatus, whose grammar was standard throughout the Middle Ages. Aelius Donatus was teaching in Rome about 350. He was the teacher of St. Jerome. His *Ars grammatica* deals with the voice, letters, syllables, metrical feet, accents, punctuation marks, the parts of speech, the defects and excellencies of language, poetical license in forms and syntax, and the figures of rhetoric. A more advanced and later grammar is that of Priscian, who was teaching Latin in Constantinople around 515. The extant works of Priscian include treatises on the eight parts of speech, an extremely elaborate commentary on Virgil; others are on the meters of Terence,

---

[7] For the story of textual criticism, see Marrou, *Saint Augustin et la fin de la culture antique,* pp. 21–23.

[8] Gwynn, *Roman Education from Cicero to Quintilian,* p. 85.

[9] Marrou, *Histoire de l'éducation dans l'antiquité,* p. 378.

on accents, on weights and measures; and he made a close translation of the elementary rhetorical exercises attributed to Hermogenes. A woodcut in the *Margarita philosophica* (1503) shows
Lady Grammar opening the narrow gate to the Tower of Knowledge in order to enable two children to enter the lower room
where sits a figure labeled "Donatus." "Priscian" sits in the school-
room on the floor above.

The basic method of the grammaticus as professor of literature
was the explanatory lecture or praelectio. According to Quintilian
(i.viii) he read the text aloud expressively, and analyzed it, explaining the hard words, idiomatic usages, references to myth and
history, parts of speech, syntax, the rhythms of prose and prosody
of verse, figures of speech, and the moral lessons to be learned.
The pupils then took turns reading aloud to the professor, expressively but with manly dignity, Quintilian hopes, not in sing-
song nor in the manner of an actor. The professor then quizzed
each boy, in elaborate detail, on the scansion of the verse and
parsing of all parts of speech. The purpose of this study was to
form the pupil's style by imitation of the language of the classics
and to give him models of good conduct to imitate and of bad
conduct to shun.

The ancient Greco-Roman grammar school also gave instruction in the writing and speaking of themes or elementary rhetorical exercises. Suetonius informs us in *On Grammarians* that
in the early days the grammaticus often taught rhetoric as
well and wrote treatises on both grammar and rhetoric. "It
was this custom, I think, which led those of later times also,
although the two professions had now become distinct, nevertheless either to retain or to introduce certain kinds of exercises suited
to the training of orators, such as problems, paraphrases, addresses,
character sketches and similar things: doubtless that they might
not turn over their pupils to the rhetoricians wholly ignorant and
unprepared" (iv). Quintilian considered such teaching of rhetorical exercises in the grammar school, save for the most ele-

mentary, as encroachment on the preserves of the professor of rhetoric (ii.iv.1–3). But the practice continued and became standard procedure.

Instruction in the advanced school of rhetoric, like instruction in the grammar school, was primarily devoted to the language arts of the trivium—grammar, logic, and rhetoric. The professor of rhetoric did not, of course, teach formal grammar, but he criticized his student's style, spoken and written, for correctness and clearness as well as for appropriateness and use of embellishment. He did not teach logic as a formal discipline, but the boys had a thorough workout in applying logical proof in confirmation and rebuttal and in detecting fallacies.

The rhetoric taught in most schools from the recorded beginnings in Greek-speaking Sicily to the end of the Roman Empire was primarily the rhetoric of a pleader in a law court. In its most utilitarian aspects this rhetorical training did, with more or less success, prepare boys for professional careers as advocates.[10] Training in rhetoric also helped a boy to participate in the debates of a legislative assembly and make appropriate speeches on such occasions as festivals and funerals. And for hundreds of years training in rhetoric prepared boys for future careers as Christian preachers.

Actually training in rhetoric did much more. It gave the only introduction possible to a variety of literary and cultural pursuits such as the composition of poems, letters, histories, dialogs, and philosophical essays. In a narrow sense, the professor of rhetoric was training orators. In a broader view, he was preparing young gentlemen to practice all the arts of discourse, which, according to Isocrates, teach how to think well and live well while they teach how to speak well, for "none of the things which are done with intelligence are done without the help of speech" (*Antidosis* 257). Thus in the Greco-Roman schools education was almost exclu-

---

[10] Parks, *The Roman Rhetorical Schools as a Preparation for the Courts under the Empire*, pp. 96–97.

sively education in rhetoric, which the ancients considered an adequate preparation for life for free men, whom custom debarred from handicrafts and all activities involving manual dexterity.

The educational methods of the professor of rhetoric were similar to those of the professor of literature, but on an advanced scale of difficulty. First, he grounded his pupils in the complicated theory of rhetoric by making them memorize the precise definitions and the elaborate classifications and subclassifications formulated in the precepts of rhetoric and embodied in textbooks, such as the *Ad Herennium,* and in the professor's own lectures.

The professor's next step was to analyze the models for imitation by means of the praelectio. But instead of explicating poems and some histories as did the grammaticus, he concentrated on the rhetorical virtues of the great classical orations of the past, as Quintilian explains (ii.v), pointing out how the orators had gone about finding arguments, ordering them for presentation to a given audience, and clothing them with proper language. It was also expected that he would furnish in his own speeches models for his pupils to follow.

Finally the professor of rhetoric led his pupils to apply the precepts and imitate the models in their own themes. These themes or exercises might be of a general or philosophical nature (theses) such as, "Should a man marry?" Or they might be of a more specific nature, simulating the actual debates in assembly or courtroom. These exercises (called melete in Greek and *declamatio* in Latin) were of two sorts. The exercise called suasoria advised someone, usually a character from poetry or history, to do something or not do it, as "Should Cato marry?" The controversia argued pro or con on the issues of a fictitious or hypothetical legal case, somewhat like the moot-court cases argued in some American law schools. The legal-minded Romans emphasized controversiae more in their schools than did the Greeks.

Suetonius in his work *On Rhetoricians* points out how in the early days rhetorical exercises were taught in grammar schools and also points out that in the early days the professors of rhetoric taught exercises in the composition of theses, which in the later empire were regularly taught in the grammar school: "The pupils would . . . show that some practices in everyday life were expedient and necessary, and others harmful and unnecessary. Frequently they defended or attacked the credibility of fables. This type of thesis the Greeks called destructive and constructive. Finally these exercises went out of use and gave place to the controversia" (1). It was doubtless the growing popularity of the declamatory exercises of suasoria and controversia in the schools of rhetoric that tended to displace the thesis.[11] But in the grammar schools, at least, exercises in the composition of theses never went out of use so long as Roman rhetoric was taught.

In practice the school system which I have so briefly summarized was not always so tidy as it was in theory. As Suetonius has told us, in the early days the grammaticus frequently taught rhetoric as well as grammar. It is clear that many boys went to grammar school with little or no training in elementary school, for Ausonius sings of the grammaticus Ammonius that he "taught the first elements to rude boys." He also mentions Nepotianus who taught both grammar and rhetoric at the University of Bordeaux (*Professores* x, xv).

Nevertheless, the precepts of rhetoric as they became formulated in the second century B.C. were but slightly modified in imperial times. And the ingrained traditionalism of the schoolmasters and professors led them to use the same methods and assign the same themes for hundreds of years.[12] Hence, although my treatment of ancient rhetoric is admittedly nonhistorical,[13] I do not believe that the arrangement of my material will cause any significant distortion of the doctrines of the ancient rhetoricians, which I now recommend to those who have read thus far.

[11] The story is told in detail in Bonner, *Roman Declamation*, pp. 1–26.
[12] Marrou, *Histoire de l'éducation dans l'antiquité*, pp. 380–386.
[13] The history is compactly summarized by M. L. Clarke, *Rhetoric at Rome; a Historical Survey*.

IV. THE PRECEPTS
OF RHETORIC

No ASPECT of ancient rhetoric is so well known today as its precepts and rules. This is only natural, for although the precepts were delivered for the most part orally to the students in the professors' lectures, they survive to this day in many written textbooks, treatises, and compendiums. Indeed, many of the surviving treatises, including the *Rhetoric* of Aristotle, represent the professor's lecture notes released by him for publication or taken down by students who subsequently published them. Since many of the precepts of ancient rhetoric are still valid and continue to afford useful guidance to the modern student who wishes to improve the effectiveness of his communication, it is also only natural that they appear with little change as the rules and principles taught by modern textbooks on composition and public speaking.

True, the ancients by no means believed that rules alone could train even a talented boy to become an accomplished speaker. The rules must be supplemented by the imitation of models and by practice exercises in writing and speaking. But, none the less, the rules and precepts were of the greatest importance and the boys must have them at their tongues' ends. Cato's Stoic view, "Hold to your matter and the words will come (*rem tene, verba sequentur*)," [1] was in effect a sturdy rear-guard action against the victorious forces of Greek literature and Greek rhetoric. Even

[1] In Halm, *Rhetores Latini Minores*, p. 374.

Cato surrendered and learned Greek in his old age. Quintilian says of him, indeed, that he was the first Roman to write on the art of rhetoric (iii.i.19).

The art of rhetoric (*ars, techne*) aimed to present the general principles of effective public speaking in a systematic form as a guide to the students who were learning to write and speak. The precepts or rules of the art were thought to have especial validity because they were discovered, not devised. They were based firmly on experience. The precepts were sound because they formulated the practices of great speakers of the past. Cicero's statement of this view in the *De oratore* is famous: "I believe the force of all the precepts is this, not that orators by following them have gained distinction for eloquence, but that certain men have observed what men of eloquence have done of their own accord and have deduced the precepts therefrom. Thus eloquence is not born of the theoretical system (*artificium*); rather, the system is born of eloquence. None the less I do not reject the precepts. They are indeed, although less necessary to oratory, yet a proper part of a liberal education" (i.xxxii.146).

Certainly the precepts of rhetoric, as well as its practice, occupied Cicero all his life. He went on from his youthful treatise, *De inventione,* written probably between 85 and 80 b.c., through his justly famous essays, *De oratore, Orator,* and *Brutus,* to his latest treatise, *De partitione oratoria,* published late in 46 b.c. The last is the most systematic of Cicero's treatments of rhetoric, and I shall imitate its analysis and sequence. Moreover I believe it represents most accurately of all surviving ancient treatises those details of rhetorical theory most useful to young students in the schools of rhetoric. Cicero wrote it for the instruction of his own son, Marcus, aged nineteen, when the boy was preparing to go to Athens for advanced study.

Although I shall present ancient rhetorical precepts within the framework of the *De partitione oratoria* I shall not restrict myself to Cicero's personal opinions nor to the opinions of any other writer. What I shall attempt is a simple—but not oversimplified —exposition of traditional doctrine. As Quintilian sagely remarks, "It has seemed safest to follow the majority of writers, and so reason seems to dictate" (III.iv.II). And I shall quote from a variety of writers, seeking always for wisdom and felicity of expression. I shall aim not at completeness or even fullness, or at a history of the development of rhetorical theory. I shall set as my unattainable ideal those qualities Cicero himself stipulates for the statement of facts in a speech—that it be clear, convincing, and agreeable (*De partitione oratoria* II.31).

In his *De partitione oratoria,* or "The Classification of Rhetoric," Cicero divided his subject logically into three aspects: (1) the speaker's resources as a speaker (*vis oratoris*); (2) the speech itself as something with a beginning, middle, and end (*oratio*); and (3) the speech situation (*quaestio*), which treats of the nature of the case and the audience.

The five subdivisions of the *vis oratoris* had been well established long before the time of Cicero. Crassus in the *De oratore* describes the five parts as commonplaces in his schooldays: "Since the speaker's resources are subdivided into five parts, he ought first to find out what he should say; then to dispose and arrange what he has found, not only in an orderly way, but with a certain weight and judgment; then to clothe and adorn his matter with language; then to secure it in his memory; and finally to deliver it with dignity and grace" (I.xxxi.142).

In the conventional idiom of the treatises on rhetoric we find the five parts named as follows:

(1) *Inventio:* "To find out what he should say."
(2) *Dispositio:* "To dispose and arrange what he has found."
(3) *Elocutio:* "To clothe with language."
(4) *Memoria:* "To secure it in his memory."
(5) *Pronuntiatio* or *actio:* "To deliver it."

This terminology and analysis was well established in the first century B.C. It is implicit in Aristotle. It flourished under the Roman Empire. It survives in the fifth-century treatise of Martianus Capella and was habitual in the rhetorical treatises of the Middle Ages and the Renaissance.[2]

The speech itself (*oratio*), the second main aspect of ancient rhetoric, was in turn conventionally divided into parts, but the number of the parts was sometimes increased by making subdivisions coordinate. Thus Aristotle in the *Rhetoric* impatiently asserts, "A speech has two parts. You must state your case, and you must prove it" (III.13). But the division into six parts offered by the *Ad Herennium* was followed by many writers in classical and postclassical times. It runs thus:

(1) *Exordium:* An opening to render the audience attentive and friendly.

(2) *Narratio:* A statement of facts colored in the speaker's favor.

(3) *Divisio* or *partitio:* A forecast of the main points the speaker plans to make.

(4) *Confirmatio:* Affirmative proof.

(5) *Confutatio:* Refutation or rebuttal.

(6) *Conclusio* or *peroratio:* Conclusion.

Cicero in his *De partitione oratoria* makes four parts by including *partitio* with *narratio* and by treating *confirmatio* and *confutatio* under one category (1.4; II.33–51). He thus agrees with Aristotle, who in the *Rhetoric* grants that forensic speeches at least may have four parts (III.13). Recalling Quintilian's warning, "Excessive subdivision is a fault into which many rhetoricians have fallen" (III.xi.22), I shall follow the fourfold division in my discussion.

The third major aspect of rhetoric which Cicero treats in the *De partitione oratoria* he calls "the question" (*quaestio*). I have translated this freely as "the speech situation," because it includes a discussion not only of the matter at issue and the speaker's in-

[2] *Ad Herennium* 1.3; *De inventione* vi; Quintilian III.iii; Martianus Capella, *De nuptiis* v.442. See D. L. Clark, *John Milton at St. Paul's School*, pp. 10–14, for the Ramian developments of the Renaissance.

tention, but also the adaptation of the speech to the particular audience addressed. The *quaestio* may be of either of two kinds. It may be a general discussion (*quaestio infinita*), also called a thesis. It may, on the other hand, deal with particular persons or occasions (*quaestio finita*); this Cicero calls *causa,* frequently translated as "case" in the legal sense. The *causa* is subdivided into the familiar categories based on Aristotle: forensic (*genus judiciale*), epideictic (*genus demonstrativum*), and deliberative (*genus deliberativum*). Quintilian agrees with this fundamental analysis and cites a number of other rhetoricians in support of it (iii.v.5–18). Thus we see that ancient rhetoric, like ancient Gaul, was divided into three. The *partitio* being established, we may take up the parts one at a time and discuss them one at a time.

The Five Resources of the Speaker

INVENTIO

Of the five parts into which the speaker's resources were anciently divided, *inventio,* or the art of finding out what the speaker or writer should say, is not only the first in time but the first in importance. And the first task is to investigate the facts. As Quintilian points out, since an orator speaks on any subject, he is bound to deal with some on which he is not informed. If he does not know, he studies for the occasion and then speaks (ii.xxi. 14–15). Antonius, in Cicero's *De oratore,* emphasizes this point and warns that the fictitious cases sometimes argued in the schools did not afford adequate training in investigating the facts. "Our first precept is this. The speaker must investigate the facts thoroughly. This is not taught in the schools, for the cases assigned to the boys are easy. 'The statute forbids a foreigner to ascend the wall, a foreigner ascends, he repulses the enemy, he is prosecuted' " (ii.xxiv.99–101). In such a school case, he points out, there are no facts to investigate. Whereas in the forum there are wills, evidence of witnesses, contracts, agreements, decrees, and lives and characters of the parties to a suit—all to be investigated. Lawyers who undertake too many cases often lose and incur reproach. "For no one can speak, without disgrace, on a subject which he has not mastered."

It is not surprising that the schools of rhetoric failed to give much, if any, training in the investigation of facts, for ancient rhetoricians, following Aristotle (1.2), considered that the establishing of facts by the testimony of witnesses or on the evidence of contracts or other documents lay outside the art of rhetoric. The speaker would, of course, use these and other nonrhetorical means to persuasion, but he was expected to learn from experience in the courts. Likewise the art of interrogating witnesses, according to Quintilian, was not taught in the schools; but the student could learn a great deal from imitating the Socratic dialogs (v.vii.28).

Within the art of rhetoric, however, there was much for the schools to teach the student about rhetorical invention, or the art of discovering arguments. So the student was taught first how to determine the main character and the main issues of the case he was preparing to argue. The hinge, as it were, upon which a case turns was called by Roman rhetoricians the status from the Greek stasis. I shall retain the Latin word, using it in its technical sense, rather than confusing the discussion by translating it.

Both Cicero and Quintilian follow the tradition in believing that the status of a case can be determined by asking questions. They favored the following three: whether a thing is, what it is, of what kind it is (*an sit, quid sit, quale sit*). Does the case turn on a question of fact, of definition, or of quality? [3] Quintilian analyzes Cicero's defense of Milo as an example. First (fact): Did Milo kill Clodius? Yes, fact admitted. Second (definition): Did Milo murder Clodius? No. Clodius lay in wait and attacked Milo. Therefore, the killing was not premeditated. It must be defined as self-defense, not as murder. Third (quality): Was the act good

[3] Cicero *Orator* 15; *De oratore* II.xxiv.26. Quintilian III.vi.80.

or bad? Good, because Clodius was a bad citizen, and the republic was better off with him dead (III.vi.93). As Cicero puts it in the *De oratore*, "Let the student first seek out the nature of the case, never obscure, whether a thing was done, what was the quality of the act, and what name it should have. Once this is ascertained, good sense at once perceives what constitutes the case, that is, that without which there would be no dispute (II.xxx.132).

Some earlier writers made it much more complicated. The *Ad Herennium*, for instance, classified states as general, legal, and judicial (I.xi.13). In his *De inventione*, Cicero had four ratiocinatory states and five legal (1). Such analysis indicates a preoccupation with the forensic rhetoric of the law courts. But Quintilian points out that all disputes, in the law courts or out, may profitably be studied by means of the status of fact, the status of definition, and the status of quality:

"When these are explored there are no more questions to ask. These include both definite and indefinite questions. One or more of these questions will be dealt with in any demonstrative, deliberative, or judicial theme. These questions cover all judicial cases whether they turn on reason or on law. There is no judicial dispute which is not to be settled with the aid of definition, consideration of quality, or conjecture as to fact" (III.vi.81–82).

Status, as a method of analyzing the issues implicit in any subject upon which one is to think, write, or speak, was usually taught in the schools of Greece and Rome in connection with the composition of speeches on the fictitious legal cases called controversiae. As Quintilian points out, however, it is not restricted to the study of legal cases. It is helpful in exploring all material in court or out. Any student who has had constant drill in status, either in factual or fictitious themes, will develop a habit of going to the heart of any problem. He has a technic at his command for getting on the road promptly, staying on the road, and arriving at a destination. He is taught how to discover the one thing he, in relation to his material, has to say.

Once the speaker has investigated and so far as possible mastered the facts involved in his case, and has determined the status or issue on which the case turns, he should seek to discover all possible means to persuade his audience. Aristotle in the *Rhetoric* points out that the means of effecting persuasion are three: "Of the modes of persuasion furnished by the spoken word there are three kinds. The first kind depends on the personal character (*ethos*) of the speaker; the second on putting the audience in a certain frame of mind; the third on the proof, or apparent proof, provided by the words of the speech itself. Persuasion is achieved by the speaker's personal character (*ethos*) when the speech is so spoken as to make us think him credible. . . . Secondly, persuasion may come through the hearers, when the speech stirs their emotions (*pathos*). Our judgments when we are pleased and friendly are not the same as when we are pained and hostile. . . . Thirdly, persuasion is effected through the speech itself when we have proved a truth or an apparent truth by means of the persuasive arguments suitable to the case in question" (1.2).

In his *Rhetoric* Aristotle develops this analysis with great fullness, devoting the second book to *ethos* and *pathos* and pointing out in detail how to go about creating a favorable impression on the hearers and rousing or allaying their emotions. "There are three things which inspire confidence in the orator's own character —the three, namely, that induce us to believe a thing apart from any proof of it: good sense, good moral character, and good will. . . . It follows that any one who is thought to have all three of these good qualities will inspire trust in his audience. . . .

"The emotions are all those feelings that so change men as to affect their judgments, and that are also attended by pain or pleasure. Such are anger, pity, fear and the like, with their opposites. We must arrange what we have to say about each of them under three heads. Take, for instance, the emotion of anger: here we must discover (1) what the state of mind of angry people is, (2) who the people are with whom they usually get angry, and

(3) on what grounds they get angry with them. It is not enough to know one or even two of these points; unless we know all three, we shall be unable to arouse anger in any one. The same is true of the other emotions" (II.1).

No other ancient writer on rhetoric ever gave anything like so full a treatment of the psychology of the audience as did Aristotle. As Philodemus, a contemporary of Cicero, remarks, "In regard to *pathe* and *ethe* which move juries, the most important part is to know how these emotions are aroused and allayed. This alone, judging that it is none of their business, the rhetors have not borrowed from Aristotle, though they have borrowed everything else." [4]

But Cicero in his *De oratore* does consider an investigation of character and the emotions as well as of proof in his treatment of *inventio,* although he falls far short of the fullness of Aristotle. Antonius has been explaining that first he investigated the facts and then determined the status. "Next I consider most carefully two other points, the one how to win favor for myself or those for whom I plead, the other how to sway the minds of my hearers in the direction I desire. Thus the whole art of speaking rests on three things to bring about persuasion, that we prove what we allege to be true, that we win the favor of the audience, that we arouse in their minds whatever feelings our cause may require" (II.xxvii.114–115). This analysis he repeats almost immediately: "The three things which alone have the power to persuade: that the minds of the hearers be won over, instructed and moved (*conciliare, docere, movere*)" (II.xxviii.121). [5]

But the student of oratory is still to be instructed in detail how to go about discovering or inventing arguments which will win over his audience, prove his case and move to action. On the school level, at least, the art was based on what were called the places of argument. Thus in the *De partitione* Cicero informs his son that

---

[4] "The *Rhetorica* of Philodemus," translated by H. M. Hubbell, *Transactions of the Connecticut Academy of Arts and Sciences,* XXIII, 338.

[5] Quintilian III.v.2: "ut doceat, moveat, delectet."

arguments are derived from the places (*ex locis*). Anticipating our question, Cicero Junior asks, "What do you mean by 'places'?" And Cicero Senior replies, "The places in which arguments lurk" (ii.5). In the *De oratore* Cicero has Antonius advise sending the student to a teacher who will "show him the seats and as it were homes of all arguments and will illustrate them briefly and define them in proper terms" (ii.xxxix.162). Quintilian follows along when he speaks of "the seats of arguments (*sedes argumentorum*) where they lurk and whence they are to be sought" (v.x.20). These "places" are also called "topics" from the Greek word *"topos"* meaning "place."

Clearly the doctrine of the "places" or "topics" of argument is based on a metaphor. One goes looking for arguments in some "places" of the mind as one looks for a book on a shelf or a letter in a pigeonhole. In practice the student was taught to ask certain questions. As Quintilian puts it: "In regard to everything that is done the question arises, Why? or Where? or When? or How? or By what means?" (v.x.32.) And the ancient student of rhetoric in seeking answers to these questions was guided, as is the modern student of newspaper reporting, to those "places" where information and arguments may be found. The places pointed to by Quintilian's questions were cause, place, time, manner, means.

Let me give a few other simple examples. One of the most important of the places or topics of argument is that of cause and effect. The teacher trains the student to ask, "What might have caused the effect we are investigating? What effects might result from this situation?" Other important places or topics of argument are similarity and dissimilarity. "What is it like? What is it different from?" Two very important places are definition and division. "What is it? What are its parts?"

In the *De partitione oratoria* (ii.7) Cicero lists as places of argument: definition, contrast, similarity, dissimilarity, consistency, inconsistency, conjunction, repugnancy, cause and effect, distribution as of genus and species, or of past and present time, or of magnitude (as more, equal, or less).[6] Quintilian gives a fuller and slightly different list. He discusses—each with rather full subdivision—causes, place, time, resources, means, definition, genus, species, differentia, property, division, order of events, similarity, dissimilarity, contraries, consequences, conjugates, and comparatives (v.x.32–94).

In addition to these places or topics of argument that are applicable to the investigation of all sorts of situations, hence called commonplaces or common topics, there are special places for special situations. Thus, for the forensic rhetoric of the law courts there are the places of justice and equity and their opposites; for epideictic rhetoric there are the places of virtue and vice, for the speaker must answer the question, In what respects is my subject praiseworthy? In deliberative rhetoric there are the places of possibility, honor, and expediency.

Then there are the places applicable to the investigation of persons rather than of things. Of a person one asks concerning his parents, race, nation, sex, age, education, fortune, social standing (v.x.23–31).

Like many another schoolboy before and since, Cicero Junior in the *De partitione oratoria* seems to have found all this heap of places a bit confusing. So he asks, "Shall we then derive arguments from all these places?" And his father wisely advises: "By no means. We shall examine and question them all. But we shall use our judgment and always reject the weak ones and sometimes omit those of too general application or of too little relevance (iii.8). Also in his *Orator* Cicero urges that the wise speaker will run rapidly over the places of argument and use only the apt ones (xiv.47). Quintilian adds that the best are those which have their origin in the case at issue (ii.iv.32).

In the *De oratore* Cicero represents Antonius as making a pertinent remark, beautifully turned, on the selection of arguments: "As to the arguments which are useful and trustworthy, if they are

[6] Cicero gives a fuller treatment in *De oratore* ii.xxxix–xl.162–173.

numerous, as often happens, I think that those of least weight, or closely resembling those of greater weight, should be set aside and excluded from the speech. For when I collect arguments for my cases, I make it a practice not to count them, but to weigh them" (ii.lxxvi.309).[7]

The origin of the topics is to be found in logic. On the very first page of his *Rhetoric* Aristotle indicates that he considered the introduction of logical arguments into a discussion of rhetoric to be his own contribution, earlier treatises being devoted almost exclusively to the rousing of the feelings. His first sentence— "Rhetoric is the counterpart of Dialectic"—points out that the art of public speaking uses the same modes of argument as does the art of logical discussion. These modes he had treated fully in his *Topics,* to which he refers in his *Rhetoric* and from which he draws much of his material. In the *Topics* he treats hundreds of sources of arguments. Cicero in his own treatise on logic, the *Topica,* simplified the topics under seventeen main heads and many subdivisions.

For the student of rhetoric in antiquity, as today, the value of the places of argument is that in endeavoring to find answers to the questions posed, the student begins to see relationships amongst the data of his knowledge and experience. In a word, he begins to think. Or in terms of public speaking, he begins to discover means to logical persuasion. As treated in *inventio* the process was analytical and exploratory. When ancient rhetoric took up the places of argument in the doctrine of proof and refutation in the composition of the speech itself, the process was reversed. The student then was taught to synthesize the arguments he had found into a close-knit fabric of proof and apparent proof of his case. The means for securing this synthesis were the technics of inductive and deductive reasoning adapted to the speech situation.

In our schools and colleges today we need more of the tradition

[7] Selection of arguments from the *sedes argumentorum* may be considered as a function of *dispositio* as well as *inventio.* See Wagner, "The Meaning of *Dispositio*" in *Studies in Speech and Drama,* pp. 285 ff.

of *inventio* in our own teaching of oral and written composition. Practice in the use of status and of the places of argument can be as fruitful now as in the past. Our students deserve more training in the preparation of their themes. They would need far less correction after the theme is spoken or written.

Moreover, the tradition of rhetorical invention should by no means be restricted to school instruction in public address or written communication. It is fundamental to the preparation of course papers, master's essays, or doctoral dissertations. Outside university life it is fundamental to the preparation of editorials, magazine articles, biographies, historical essays, and political pamphlets.

DISPOSITIO

When Cicero in *De oratore* stated that after finding out what he should say, the speaker should next "dispose and arrange what he has found, not only in an orderly way, but with a certain weight and judgment" (i.xxxi.142), he suggests a two-fold aspect of *dispositio* which he enlarges on later. There the speaker, now Antonius, says: "Now I return . . . to the order and arrangement (*collocatio*) of facts and places of argument. The methods of doing this are two, the one arising from the nature of cases, the other contributed by the judgment and prudence of the speaker" (ii.lxxvi.307).

The first of these methods, arising from the nature of all cases, is the familiar division of any speech into *exordium,* statement of facts, proof and refutation, and peroration. This division, says Antonius, is prescribed by the nature of oratory. I shall treat it in the section on the speech itself (*oratio*) as Cicero does in the *De partitione oratoria* and as Martianus Capella does in the *De nuptiis.*

There remain many problems of sequence: problems not basic for all speeches but growing out of the strategy involved in marshaling arguments to win over a given audience at a given time in a given case. The speaker needs all his prudence and judgment to

decide rightly many problems of sequence. Should a given argument be introduced in his *exordium,* presented in the midst of
his speech, or reserved for his peroration? Should he rebut his
opponent's argument before or after presenting his own? Would
it be more expedient to present his proposition first and then support it, or to present his evidence in such a way as to prepare the
way for the acceptance of his proposition?

In answering such questions as these, Antonius in the *De
oratore* observes: "And because, as I have often said, there are
three methods of bringing people over to our opinions—instructing their minds, winning their favor, moving their emotions—only
one of these methods should we openly profess, so that we should
seem to desire nothing but to instruct. The other two methods,
like blood in the body, should be diffused throughout our speech"
(ii.lxxvii.310). In amplifying this figure he points out that, though
the *exordium* and peroration are the parts of a speech most appropriate for arguments based on *ethos* and *pathos,* appeals to the
emotions may be advantageously introduced as digressions after
the statement of facts, or after the confirmation, or after the refutation, or in any part of the speech whatever.

Antonius next considers the strategy of placing arguments in
the sequence of a speech and urges against saving the strongest
argument for the last: "For the situation requires that the expectations of the audience should be met as quickly as possible. If their
expectations are not satisfied at the beginning, a great deal more
effort must be put into the rest of the speech, for a case is in a bad
way which does not appear to be strengthened when it is first
stated. . . . So in the speech the strongest argument should come
first . . . some of the outstanding arguments may be reserved for
the peroration, and the arguments of moderate strength—for bad
arguments should be given no place at all—may be thrown together in the midst" (313–314).

This advice on arrangement is necessarily general for reasons
which Quintilian aptly states in the preface to Book vii: "The

whole of this book will be devoted to arrangement, which, if it could be taught by rules applicable to all subjects, would not have been attained by so few speakers. But as legal cases have been and will be of infinite variety and as no one case throughout the ages has been found exactly like another, the pleader must exercise his sagacity, his vigilance, his invention, his judgment, and look to himself for counsel. Yet I do not deny that there are some things which can be taught, and these I shall not pass by."

The things which can be taught about *dispositio,* which he defines as "the distribution of things and their parts in advantageous places," Quintilian discusses quite properly in connection with particular cases, actual or fictitious. Thus to show that one side may find it expedient to state one point first and the other side to state another he uses as illustration the speeches of Demosthenes and Aeschines in the trial of Ctesiphon. The point that it is good strategy to descend from the general to the particular he illustrates with a controversia frequently argued in the schools of declamation. With an analysis of another complicated school case he demonstrates that in defending a client who has the letter of the law against him but equity in his favor the speaker should first attack the legal position of the opposition and conclude with the appeal to equity because judges listen to nothing more readily.

Likewise he distinguishes between accusation and defense when he states that an accuser might open with a strong argument, conclude with the strongest, and put the weaker in the middle, but that the defense must first attack the strongest argument of the accusation.

"Attacks on the past life of the accused must generally be refuted first, that the judge may begin to listen favorably; but Cicero, in the *Pro Vareno,* has postponed such considerations to the conclusion, being guided not by what is expedient generally, but by what was expedient on that occasion" (VII.i.12). The status of the case, he also shows, helps to determine the sequence of the arrangement. Thus Cicero in the *Pro Milone* first admits that

Milo killed Clodius, next asserts it was self-defense, not murder, and finally develops the basic status that the act was good. But in the *Pro Rabirio* the sequence is reversed: if he had killed Saturninus, he would have acted rightly; but he did not kill him. Throughout his book on arrangement Quintilian shows that the most expedient disposal of the arguments cannot be determined until the student or professional speaker has mastered his facts, has determined the status of the case, and has invented and chosen the arguments which can be used in support of his cause.

So far the discussion of arrangement by Cicero and Quintilian is clearly based on the judicial rhetoric of the law courts, the most important aspect of rhetoric to the Romans. But what of epideictic and deliberative rhetoric? Do the same principles apply? In the *De partitione oratoria* Cicero says No. The method of arrangement must be adapted to the purpose of the speech. In epideictic speeches, which aim primarily to give pleasure, the sequence may be chronological, from genus to species, from large to small, or the reverse. Or it may follow any other plan which may contribute variety. In deliberative speeches the *exordium* may be short or absent because deliberative bodies have more interest in the subject of discussion than do judges and juries. There may be very little statement of facts because deliberation looks to the future, not the past. Finally the speaker will not always be able to keep to the arrangement he had planned to use. He must be responsive to the ears of his hearers and change what they reject (vi.12–15. Cf. Aristotle *Rhetoric* iii.13).

Hence it is understandable that teachers and textbooks could not state sound precepts for expedient arrangement save in the most general terms. The methods could be learned only by trial and error in the composition of many exercises under the guidance of a wise and experienced teacher. But in the elementary exercises in rhetoric the beginning student was bound to an inflexible formula for handling the *inventio* and *dispositio* of each of his themes. There are no indications that many teachers in advanced schools of rhetoric were as competent as Quintilian to carry into the school the flexible adaptation of structure to circumstance practiced by so skillful a pleader as Cicero. Hence we can understand why so few speakers and writers of any age have excelled in the judicious arrangement of their material.

ELOCUTIO

Crassus, in *De oratore,* states that the third task of a speaker is "to clothe and adorn his matter with language." This art of putting proper words in proper places is with us called "style." No other aspect of rhetoric or poetry in antiquity received so much attention in surviving treatises. Aristotle gave almost all of Book III of his *Rhetoric* to style (*lexis*). Almost half of the *Ad Herennium* is devoted to style (*elocutio*). Cicero devotes at least one third of the *De oratore* and all of the *Orator* to style. Quintilian devotes Books VIII and IX to style. Dionysius of Halicarnassus and Demetrius and "Longinus" devoted whole treatises to style.[8] By the late Middle Ages rhetoric had come to mean style alone.[9]

In general the Greek and Roman writers of antiquity analyzed style according to three different principles. First, style was shown to involve two different aspects of language: words and sentences. Diction, selection of words (*electio verborum*) usually received less attention than the arrangement of words in sentences (*compositio verborum*)—in Greek *synthesis*—what we usually call sentence structure or sentence movement.[10] A more fruitful analysis is that of the virtues or graces of style which the teacher endeavored to inculcate. Aristotle in the *Rhetoric* felt that all the virtues of style could be included under clearness or under appropriateness (III.12). But most of his followers made four virtues of style: correctness, clearness, embellishment, and appro-

---

[8] Dionysius of Halicarnassus *De compositione verborum;* Demetrius *De elocutione;* "Longinus" *De sublimitate.*

[9] D. L. Clark, *Rhetoric and Poetry in the Renaissance,* p. 47.

[10] Aristotle *Rhetoric* III.2–12.

priateness.[11] A third analysis of the types or kinds of style seems to have arisen later than Theophrastus.[12] Most writers agree that styles may be classified as grand, medium, and plain, although Demetrius in the *De elocutione* gives four: elevated, smooth or elegant, plain, and forcible (II–V).

Since the virtues of correctness, clearness, embellishment, and appropriateness may be attained by means of both words and sentences, I shall follow the analysis according to virtues in my discussion. Moreover the types or kinds of style may be fruitfully discussed as aspects of appropriateness to the speaker, the audience, and the subject.

Correctness. To the Roman correctness in the use of language was *latinitas*. To the Greek it was *hellenismos*.[13] Most people today think that the duty of an English teacher is to teach the correct use of English. Then, as now, the teaching of correctness was the duty of the child's parents, his nurse, and his elementary school teachers. Hence it is only natural that textbooks of rhetoric may mention correctness but dismiss the subject, as does the *Ad Herennium* (IV.xii.17),[14] on the ground that it belongs to the school of the grammaticus. Likewise, Antonius in the *De oratore* says: "Of purity of language I do not suppose that any account is expected of me. For we do not attempt to teach public speaking to anyone who does not know how to speak, nor do we hope that one who cannot speak correctly will learn to speak eloquently (*ornate*). . . . Let us therefore omit it as easy to learn but necessary in practice. It is taught to boys in the grammar school" (III.x.38).

But Quintilian in Book I does not hesitate to discuss correctness as one of the functions of grammar. It has two parts. One teaches the boy how to avoid faults in the use of single words [barba-

---

[11] Cicero *De oratore* 1.144; Quintilian VIII. *Proem* 31 and VIII.i.1 and III.x.37.
[12] See two articles by Hendrickson in *American Journal of Philology*, XXV (1904), 125, XXVI (1905), 249.
[13] Smiley, *Latinitas*, Chapter I.
[14] Aristotle discusses correctness briefly in the *Rhetoric* III.5.

risms]. The other teaches him how to avoid faults in grammatical agreement of words in a sentence [solecisms] (i.v).

What is correct? Standards of correctness in the use of language were to a degree uncertain in antiquity, as they are today. Quintilian lists four criteria: (1) reason derived from study of analogy and etymology; (2) antiquity; (3) the authority of the best authors; and (4) custom—not what the majority say, but the "consensus of the educated."[15] To Quintilian, as to Horace,[16] good current usage was the best criterion for establishing correctness in language. "For it would be almost ridiculous to prefer the language which men have spoken to the language which they now speak" (i.vi).

But the grammaticus not only taught correctness in grammar, spelling, and punctuation; he also read and interpreted the poets and historians.[17] As soon as their poems became generally available, Virgil, Horace, Ovid, Lucan, Statius, Persius, and Martial became school authors and were read, explicated, and memorized in the grammar schools in their own lifetimes or soon after.[18] They were to remain school authors for many hundreds of years. St. Augustine in the fourth century was intimately familiar, as a former schoolmaster should be, with Virgil, Terence, Cicero, Horace, Lucan, Persius, Ovid, Catullus, Juvenal, and Sallust.[19] John Milton read most of them at St. Paul's School in the seventeenth century.[20] Where Latin is studied they are still school authors. As school authors they became the norm, the law and arbiters of correctness in language ruling above Quintilian's preference for the best current linguistic usage. St. Jerome felt that

[15] i.vi. For the quarrel between the analogists and anomalists, see Gwynn, *Roman Education from Cicero to Quintilian*, pp. 35–36.

[16] . . . *usus . . . arbitrium est et jus et norma loquendi. Epistle to the Pisos*, 71–72.

[17] Cicero *De oratore* 1.187; Suetonius, *On Grammarians*, 4. See also the discussion in Jullien, *Les Professeurs de littérature dans l'ancienne Rome*, p. 213.

[18] Gwynn, *Roman Education from Cicero to Quintilian*, p. 156.

[19] Marrou, *Saint Augustin et la fin de la culture antique*, pp. 18–19.

[20] D. L. Clark, *John Milton at St. Paul's School*, pp. 100–125.

even though Virgil and Terence were pagan poets, they were necessary for children to read for their "pure Latin" (*Epistolae* 21). John Colet in his statutes for St. Paul's School (1518) insisted that the school should teach "the olde laten spech and the varay Romayne tong which in the tyme of Tully and Salust and Virgill and Terence was usid, whiche also seint Jerome and seint ambrose and seint Austen and many hooly doctors lernyd in theyr tymes." [21] So we can readily understand that Latin was taught as a dead language as early as the days of Jerome and Augustine.[22] That language was correct which was vouched for by the Best Authors of the Best Period.

Clearness. "Style to be good must be clear," says Aristotle, "as is proved by the fact that speech which fails to convey a plain meaning will fail to do just what speech has to do" (*Rhetoric* III.2). He suggests that clearness is attained by using words which are current and ordinary, by introducing metaphors drawn from kindred and similar things, and by avoiding redundancy. In his discussion of correctness or purity of language he includes several caveats which subsequent writers have included amongst the aids to clearness: using specific rather than general words, avoiding ambiguous terms unless you want to deceive, avoiding overlong suspensions of thought through misuse of parentheses (*Rhetoric* III.5).

Early Roman rhetoric tends to treat clearness as it did correctness—as something essential, but preliminary to, or outside of, oratory. Thus the *Ad Herennium* defines it but does not analyze or exemplify (IV.17–18). And Antonius in the *De oratore* dismisses it as a minimal essential (III.x.38).

Quintilian, on the other hand, has the highest opinion of clearness (*perspicuitas*). "To me," he says, "clearness is the first virtue of style." To attain clearness he advises against the following friends of obscurity: the use of obsolete and local or provincial words; overlong sentences and overlong suspensions; ambiguity,

[21] Lupton, *A Life of John Colet*, p. 278.
[22] Marrou, *Saint Augustin et la fin de la culture antique*, p. 14.

vagueness, and circumlocution; overcondensation; perverse ingenuity in the use of words with occult meanings which the hearer is expected to puzzle out. "Let there be proper words in proper places, let not the conclusion of the sense be too long postponed, let there be nothing lacking and nothing superfluous. Thus our language will be commended by the learned and clear to the unlearned. . . . We must bear in mind that the judge is not always so keenly attentive as to dispel the obscurity of our language and throw the light of his intellect on the darkness of our speech. On the contrary. Many things will distract his thoughts unless what we say is so clear that our words will strike into his mind, like sun in the eyes, even though he is inattentive. Hence our care must be, not that he will be able to understand us, but that it be impossible for him to misunderstand" (viii.ii.22–24).

As members of the same family of languages Greek, Latin, and English are sufficiently similar to make the suggestions of Aristotle and Quintilian of value today. The communication of plain meaning clearly is exceedingly difficult.

Embellishment. Having asserted that no one ever admired an orator for merely speaking good Latin or ever praised a speaker because the audience could understand what he said, Crassus, in the *De oratore,* bursts forth: "Whom, then, do men tremble to hear? Whom do they admire when he speaks? To whom do they cry out their applause? Whom do they think to be a god, so to speak, among men? Those who speak elegantly (*distincte*), clearly (*explicate*), copiously (*abundanter*), brilliantly (*illuminate*)—in words and matter produce in their prose almost the rhythms of verse. They are those who speak with what I call embellishment (*ornate*)" (iii.xiv.53).

Quintilian fundamentally agrees: "By polish and embellishment (*cultu atque ornatu*) of style the orator commends himself; whereas by other means he courts the approval of the learned, by this the applause of the multitude, for he fights not only with stout but also with dazzling weapons. In his defense of Cornelius, if Cicero had limited himself merely to instructing the judge, to speaking to the purpose and in pure and clear Latin, would he have caused the Roman people to testify their admiration not only by acclamation but by bursts of applause? It was the loftiness, brilliance, and weight of his eloquence that drew forth the thunder of approbation" (viii.iii.2–3).

Quintilian goes on to point out that embellishment of style is not merely an end in itself. It contributes to winning cases: "For those who listen with pleasure are more attentive and more prone to believe. They are frequently captivated with pleasure and carried away with admiration. . . . Cicero was right when he wrote in a letter to Brutus, 'Eloquence which excites no admiration I account unworthy of the name.' Aristotle also thinks that to excite admiration is one of our greatest objects." [23]

Aristotle also insists that the use of embellishment must be controlled by appropriateness to the speaker, the audience, and the circumstances. Moreover, "A writer must disguise his art and give the impression of speaking naturally, not artificially. Naturalness is persuasive, artificiality is the contrary" (iii.2). And following the lead of Isocrates, he condemns all excess and recommends "a falling short rather than an overdoing of the effects aimed at." [24] And Quintilian praises a style whose embellishment is manly, noble, and chaste, free from effeminate smoothness or a complexion counterfeited by paint. He likes flowering fruit trees and praises an orchard or olive grove, carefully pruned and planted in orderly rows, which seems to him to be an appropriate symbol for tastefully embellished prose. "True beauty is never separated from utility" (viii.iii.11).

Naturally enough, countless writers and speakers in antiquity, intoxicated by the sound of their own voices, failed to observe these restraints. They enjoyed and practiced the devices of artistic

[23] "Admiration" is to be taken in its etymological sense "to wonder at." The letter to Brutus does not survive. Aristotle *Rhetoric* iii.2. Also *Poetics* 21–22.

[24] Atkins, *Literary Criticism in Antiquity*, I, 129, 149; Isocrates *To Nicocles* 33; Aristotle *Rhetoric* iii.3.

prose for their own sake. They cultivated their flowers of rhetoric, they laid on their gayest colors, they brightened their language with dazzling lights. *Flores, colores, lumina* in rhetorical contexts are synonyms of *exornatio,* which Thomas Wilson, in his *Arte of Rhetorique* (1560), correctly defined as "a gorgious beautifying of the tongue." [25] The flowers, colors, and lights are the embellishments which distinguish the art prose of the orator or man of letters from the plain prose of everyday life.

In his distinguished treatise on the art prose of antiquity, Eduard Norden points out three postulates which remained constant from the sixth century B.C. to the Renaissance: that embellished prose should be figurative, similar to poetry, and rhythmical.[26] Since the poetical coloring of embellished prose shows itself largely in the use of figures and in rhythmical sentence movement, I shall divide my discussion into two parts only.

The figures which were taught in the schools, analyzed by the critics, and employed by the orators and men of letters were in antiquity classified as tropes, figures of thought, and figures of language. Of these the tropes (*tropi, tropoi* in Greek) are the most familiar to us because they include metaphors and other figures of similarity. Quintilian defines a trope as "an artistic turning of a word or phrase from its proper signification to another" (VIII.vi.1). He admits that grammarians have disputed interminably about the nature and classification of tropes, but he offers a simple analysis based on the notion that tropes may involve both single words and words in combination, that some tropes are used to add to significance and others for embellishment alone. I shall follow Quintilian because his views have dominated subsequent theories on the figures.

His list starts with metaphor, the most important of tropes, with a side glance at simile. He proceeds to synecdoche and metonymy, which Aristotle had treated as aspects of metaphor

[25] Edited by G. H. Mair, p. 169.
[26] Norden, *Die antike Kunstprosa,* I, 50–55.

(*Poetics* 21, *Rhetoric* iii.2–4). Briefly he touches on antonomasia, which employs an epithet of a person instead of his name; onomatopoeia, which he says is much commoner in Greek than in Latin; catachresis, an artful impropriety; metalepsis, the use of one word for another which it suggests by association. Thence he proceeds to ornamental epithets: Allegory, which, he points out, is related to irony as both say one thing and mean another; periphrasis or circumlocution; hyperbaton, a transposition of words; and hyperbole or exaggeration (viii.vi).

The figures of thought (*figurae sententiarum*) and figures of language (*figurae verborum*) are next in order. As Quintilian admits that it is "not easy to tell the difference between tropes and figures" (ix.i.3), the modern student need not feel unduly stupid if he gets them confused at times. In an endeavor to keep meanings clear Quintilian gives two definitions of *figurae* (in Greek *schemata*). First, "A figure is a conformation of speech differing from the common and the ordinary." A few paragraphs later he says, "A figure is a form of speech given a new turn by art (*arte aliqua novata*) (ix.i.4, 14). Now the figures of thought deal with the conception of ideas, and the figures of language deal with their expression. All of the figures of thought depart somewhat from direct and ordinary patterns of thinking and meaning. They do not mean quite what they say. Thus a simple question asking for information is not a figure. But the rhetorical question, which does not ask for information but is designed to emphasize a point, is a figure of thought. "How long, Catiline, will you abuse our patience?"

Quintilian's list, which I prefer to the elaborate discussion of Cicero because of its relative simplicity, is as follows: (1) The rhetorical question (*interrogatio*), which I have just used as an illustration, with the following variations: the reply which sidesteps or evades a question asked; dissimulation, or replying in such a way as to seem not to understand the speaker; asking a question and answering it oneself. (2) Anticipation (*prolepsis*), which forestalls objections. (3) Hesitation (*dubitatio*), when the speaker pretends to be at a loss where to begin, or end, or what to say. (4) Consultation (*communicatio*), when the speaker asks the advice of the judge or pretends to take his opponent into his confidence, or otherwise endeavors to seem stupider than he is. (5) Simulation of any passion, as fear, sorrow, anger, and the like, in order to arouse the emotions of the audience. (6) Impersonation of characters (*prosopopoeia*). Here the speaker will compose lines as though spoken by his client, his opponent, the gods, his fatherland. A form of dramatic monolog or dialog adapted to pleading. (7) Apostrophe, which aims to divert the mind of the judge from the issue by turning away to address some other person or thing, real or imagined. (8) Illustration (*evidentia*), where the speaker gives a vivid word picture of an imagined scene as if it were before his eyes. (9) Irony, a rather full development of something contrary to what the speaker wishes to be understood. (Irony as a trope is shorter and simpler.) (10) Simulated reticence (*aposiopesis*), when the speaker breaks off in the middle of a sentence, but only after the audience has discovered what he means. (11) Mimicry (*ethopoeia*), an imitation of some person's manners in word or deed. (12) Pretended repentance for something said, or a transition managed by a pretended, "That reminds me." (13) Intimation (*emphasis*) of something latent, not expressed, when it would be unsafe or unbecoming to speak plainly.

In summing up his treatment of the figures of thought, all of which are devious devices for implying or suggesting what is not stated or proved, Quintilian points out that they should be used sparingly, for they betray themselves by their multiplicity. Their overuse may make the judge believe that the speaker mistrusts his own cause since he does not give it clear and vigorous support. For straightforward eloquence requires strength to win an audience, while doublings and turnings are the resources of weakness. If sparingly used, however, the figures of thought help to win audiences, for "The auditor delights to understand what is insinuated, applauds his own penetration, and plumes himself on another's eloquence" (ix.ii).

The figures of language (*figurae verborum,* in Greek *schemata lexeos*), are verbal patterns which depart in some ingenious way from the patterns of everyday speech. The most familiar examples today are parallelism, antithesis, and climax. The ancients also enjoyed word play and rhyme in prose much more than we do. The consensus of antiquity attributed the invention of the verbal figures to Gorgias of Leontini and named them Gorgian figures in his honor, but, as Norden points out,[27] the figures were in use in verse and in prose before his time. At least he made outstanding use of the figures of language and taught their use to his students, as Quintilian says: "To add grace to style by balance and antithesis was a great concern of the ancients. Gorgias practiced these devices immoderately, and Isocrates in his younger days was devoted to them. Cicero had great delight in them but set bounds to his indulgence in these verbal patterns, which are not displeasing unless used to excess, and gave dignity to what would otherwise have been trivial by the weight of his thought. For in itself the use of these devices is a flat and inane affectation, but when united with vigorous thought, it seems to be not forced but natural" (ix.iii.74).

The Gorgian figures of correspondence are these: (1) *parison,* an even balance in the members of a sentence; (2) *homoeoteleuton,* the use of like endings, rhyme; (3) *homoeoptoton,* the use of similar case endings in parallel constructions; (4) *isocolon,* parallelism, perfect equality in the balance of phrases and clauses.

Related patterns which Quintilian lists are: *paronomasia,* the bringing together of two or more words different in meaning but similar in sound, as in word play or alliteration; *hyperbaton,* the artful transposition of words; *antithesis,* which Quintilian translates as *contrapositio.*

[27] *Antike Kunstprosa,* I, 25–29.

Other figures of language which Quintilian lists are: repetition of words or phrases for effect; iteration of a thought by piling up different words of similar significance; pleonasm, or redundancy for amplification; asyndeton, which omits connective particles; polysyndeton, which repeats connectives; climax (ix.iii.66–100).

But examples are needful as well as definitions if the reader is to become fully aware of the effect of ancient patterned prose. Many of the patterns depend for their effect on the rich inflectional system of Latin and Greek and cannot be illustrated save in the ancient languages. Euphuism derived a good many of the figures of language, as well as tropes and figures of thought, from ancient rhetoric and ancient practitioners of the ornate styles.[28] C. S. Baldwin illustrates many of the ancient verbal patterns with selected sentences from De Quincey.[29] I shall quote as a brief example a passage from *The Encomium on Helen* by Gorgias, translated by LaRue Van Hook in an effort "to reproduce in English the effect of the original Greek":

"Embellishment to a city is the valour of its citizens; to a person, comeliness; to a soul, wisdom; to a deed, virtue; to a discourse, truth. But the opposite to these is lack of embellishment. Now a man, woman, discourse, work, city, deed, if deserving of praise, must be honoured with praise, but if undeserving must be censured. For it is alike aberration and stultification to censure the commendable and commend the censurable.

"It is the duty of the same individual both to proclaim justice wholly, and to declaim against injustice holily, to confute the detractors of Helen, a woman concerning whom there has been uniform and universal praise of poets and the celebration of her name has been the commemoration of her fame. But I desire by rational calculation to free the lady's reputation, by disclosing her detractors as prevaricators, and, by revealing the truth, to put an end to error."[30]

---

[28] *Ibid.*, I, 785 ff.   [29] Baldwin, *Medieval Rhetoric and Poetic,* pp. 42–49.

[30] First printed, with a discussion of the style of Gorgias, in *The Classical Weekly,* February 15, 1913, reprinted in *Isocrates* (Loeb edition, 1945), III, 55.

The Gorgian figures also come closer home. As C. N. Smiley has shown,[31] Lincoln made free use of antithesis, anaphora, alliteration, assonance, balanced clauses, similar endings.

Quintilian's final criticism of the figures may appropriately be quoted: "Although they are ornaments to language when they are judiciously employed, they are extremely ridiculous when introduced in immoderate profusion" (ix.iii.100).

In his encomium of embellishment, which I quoted at the beginning of the discussion of art prose, Crassus in the *De oratore* praised the eloquence of the orators who "produce in their prose almost the rhythms of verse" (iii.xiv.53). This statement should guide us in our study of the precepts of ancient sentence movement (*compositio verborum, synthesis*). First we should be aware constantly that ancient speakers and theorists of prose style were dealing with the spoken word or the written word addressed to the mind's ear. Seneca betrays the ear-mindedness of the ancients when he says, "Even when we write we are in the habit of punctuating" (*Epistolae* 11). For to him, as to the others, punctuation was a pause in speaking. Consequently it is only natural that the ancients conceived the sentence first as a rhythmical pattern and only second as a logical pattern. We should, then, learn from Crassus that although the rhythms of prose should be almost those of verse, they should never (or at least seldom) fall into the recognizable metric patterns of verse.

Cicero in *Orator* points out that Thrasymachus was the inventor of rhythmical prose and that Isocrates learned from him and practiced the device with greater skill (175). Norden says that rhythmical prose was written before Thrasymachus.[32] But the tradition passed on by Cicero suggests that rhythmical prose began to be practiced and taught as a conscious art in the generations before Aristotle. The earliest authoritative statement is that

[31] *Classical Journal* XIII (November, 1917), No. 2, 124.
[32] Norden, *Antike Kunstprosa,* I, 25–29.

of Isocrates in a surviving fragment of his *Rhetoric:* "Prose must not be merely prose, or else it will be dry; it must not be metrical, for then artifice is manifest; it must rather be compounded of all sorts of rhythms, of which the ones most commonly used should be the iambic and trochaic." [33] Following the lead of Isocrates, Aristotle makes these distinctions with great care: "The form of a prose composition should be neither metrical nor destitute of rhythm. The metrical form destroys the hearer's trust by its artificial appearance, and at the same time diverts his attention, making him watch for metrical recurrences. . . . On the other hand, unrhythmical language is too unlimited; we do not want the limitations of meter, but some limitation we must have, or the effect will be vague and unsatisfactory" (*Rhetoric* III.8).[34]

Dionysius of Halicarnassus affects to observe Aristotle's distinction between prose and verse, but he advocates prose so rhythmical as to be nearer verse than the best taste usually allows, either ancient or modern (*De compositione verborum* xvii–xviii). The ancients recognized two steps in the acquisition of a harmonious and rhythmical prose. The first step was negative—an avoidance of word patterns which create disharmony. The avoidance of hiatus, or the clash of vowels, was the first and perhaps the most important item of the negative step. Isocrates had condemned hiatus as halting and uneven, and after him theorists accepted the dictum that in artistic prose hiatus was to be avoided.[35] Quintilian was especially hostile to a hiatus involving ending one word and beginning the next with an *a* or *o*, although he sensibly remarks that it is better for an impromptu speaker to indulge in an occasional hiatus than to worry so much as to divert his attention from more important considerations (IX.iv.33–37).[36] Dionysius of Halicarnassus goes so far as to quote a whole ode of

---

[33] Atkins, *Literary Criticism in Antiquity*, I, 130.
[34] Cicero discusses rhythm in *De oratore* III.xlvii.182; *Orator* 212.
[35] Atkins, *Literary Criticism in Antiquity*, I, 130.
[36] See also *Ad Herennium* IV.18; Cicero *Orator* 150–155.

Sappho's to show that the smoothness of her style results from her studious avoidance of hiatus (*De compositione verborum* xxiii).

Other interferences with harmony which the ancients shunned were consonant clashes; undue repetition of similars, whether letters, words, inflections; and jingling rhymes.

Once the stumbling blocks to harmony had been removed, the literary artist could proceed to acquire rhythm in his handling of prose. In preparation for this, his first halting steps were taken when he was a boy in the *ludus literarius* under the grammaticus, with whom he learned to read the poets aloud with proper quantity and accent and to memorize many lines and whole poems. To drive these lessons home, his teacher had him perform exercises in the composition of correct verses in the various quantitative meters of Greek and Latin poetry. If he had special aptitudes for writing verse, he was on the way to becoming a poet. If not, he at least had his first preparation for the practice of that other harmony of rhythmical prose.[37]

Ancient rhetoric, like the modern rhetoric based on it, envisaged two typical sentence patterns: the loose and the periodic. The periodic Quintilian described as compact and of a firm texture (*vincta atque contexta*), the other looser (*soluta*) (ix.iv.19).

The distinction goes back to Aristotle, whose statement in the *Rhetoric* is full and clear: "The language of prose must be either free-running, with its parts united by nothing except the connecting words . . . or compact and antithetical. The free running style is the ancient one, e.g. 'Here is set forth the inquiry of Herodotus the Thurian.' Every one used this method formerly; not many do so now. By free-running style I mean the kind that has no natural stopping-places, and comes to a stop only because there is no more to say of that subject. This style is unsatisfying just because it goes on indefinitely—one always likes to sight a stopping-place in front of one: it is only at the goal that men

[37] Jullien, *Les Professeurs de littérature dans l'ancienne Rome,* pp. 236–240.

in a race faint and collapse; while they see the end of the course before them, they can keep going. Such, then, is the free-running kind of style; the compact is that which is in periods. By a period I mean a portion of speech that has in itself a beginning and an end, being at the same time not too big to be taken in at a glance. Language of this kind is satisfying because it is just the reverse of indefinite; and moreover, the hearer always feels that he is grasping something and has reached some definite conclusion; whereas it is unsatisfactory to see nothing in front of you and get nowhere" (III.9).

Demetrius follows Aristotle in making this distinction, even to citing Herodotus as an habitual user of the loose or free-running sentence (*De elocutione* 1.12).[38] Indeed it is a fair inference that the loose style was not considered as intrinsically inferior, but that it was more acceptable in historical and narrative prose, while the periodic was more characteristic of oratory.

Classical discussions of the oratorical period are so full, so complicated, and depend so much for their cogency and force on examples which exhibit the nuances of Greek and Latin metrics and rhythmics that I shall boldly condense and refer the student for a fuller treatment to the discussions of Cicero in the *Orator* and of Demetrius in *On Style*.

Briefly, then, the ancient *periodus,* unlike the modern periodic sentence which terminates when the syntax is complete, aimed at a rhythmic rounding off. Cicero calls the period *circuitus* (*Orator* 187); Quintilian prefers *ambitus* or *circumductum* (IX.iv.22). Aristotle says of the period and its rounding off: "A sentence should break off with the long syllable: the fact that it is over should be indicated not by the scribe, or by his period-mark in the margin, but by the rhythm itself" (*Rhetoric* III.8).

This rounded period was built up of shorter units of expression. The shortest are the *kommata* (Latin *incisa*); longer units built up of the shorter ones are the *kola* (Latin *membra*). Clearly the

[38] Also Cicero *Orator* 186.

modern marks of punctuation, the comma and colon, take their names from the units of expression which they were first devised to set off; the comma to set off brief and incomplete units, the colon longer units, and the period to mark the full stop at the end of the sentence. At least by the end of the fourth century the *Artes grammaticae* were teaching the use of marks of punctuation to indicate an opportunity for taking breath or a suitable pause in delivery at the termination of *kommata* or *kola*. Not until Isidore in the seventh century was it suggested that the points marked off the sense as well as the rhythm.[39]

The psychological effect on the hearer of the different types of period is best treated by Aristotle in the *Rhetoric:* "A period may be either divided into several members (*kola*) or simple. The period of several members is a portion of speech (1) complete in itself, (2) divided into parts, and (3) easily delivered at a single breath—as a whole, that is; not by fresh breath being taken at the division. A member is one of the two parts of such a period. By 'simple' period, I mean that which has only one member. The members, and the whole periods, should be neither curt nor long. A member which is too short often makes the listener stumble; he is still expecting the rhythm to go to the limit his mind has fixed for it; and if meanwhile he is pulled back by the speaker's stopping, the shock is bound to make him, so to speak, stumble. If, on the other hand, you go on too long, you make him feel left behind" (III.9).

There were many views as to which poetical meters supplied the most appropriate feet for use in prose rhythms. Isocrates had suggested iambic and trochaic. Aristotle thought differently. The iambic is too commonplace. The trochaic is too much like dancing. "There remains the paean, which speakers began to use in the time of Thrasymachus. . . . There are two opposite kinds of paean, one of which is suitable to the beginning of a sentence,

[39] Ong, "Historical Backgrounds of Elizabethan and Jacobean Punctuation Theory," PMLA (1944), 349–351, 353.

where it is indeed actually used; this is the kind that begins with a long syllable and ends with three short ones. . . . The other paean begins, conversely, with three short syllables and ends with a long one. . . . This kind of paean makes a real close: a short syllable can give no effect of finality, and therefore makes the rhythm appear truncated" (III.8).

Cicero also thought well of the paean and agreed that the conclusion of the period (*clausula*) was the proper place to introduce one or two metrical feet. By the prompting of nature, the ear, he says, recognizes "a certain rhythmical flow to the conclusion of the period (*certos cursus conclusionesque verborum*)" (*Orator* 178). In the Middle Ages the terminal rhythms became conventionalized as the three forms of the *cursus: cursus planus, cursus tardus,* and *cursus velox.*[40] But Cicero, with Quintilian concurring, considered a great number of different metrical feet appropriate to a variety of situations. The sound should fit the sense, and some aggressively poetical rhythms were more appropriate to panegyric than to forensic pleading (*Orator* 207–215).[41]

To demonstrate the importance of rhythmical sentence movement ancient critics and teachers sometimes dislocated the word order of artistic prose without changing the words. Thus Dionysius garbles fine prose and poetry to show what is lost by faulty *compositio* (*De compositione verborum* iv.84), as does "Longinus" (*De sublimitate,* xxxix). Cicero not only dislocates good prose by changing the order of the words, but also improves the prose of a careless writer by rearrangement (*Orator* 232–233). The same device can be used by the teacher of English prose to demonstrate the importance of word order to modern students. Lincoln's Gettysburg Address, for instance, can be garbled almost beyond recognition merely by transposing words and phrases within a sentence.

Quintilian recognizes the value of this practice in teaching stu-

[40] Albert C. Clark, *The Cursus in Mediaeval and Vulgar Latin.*
[41] See also Quintilian IX.iv.79–120.

dents, but in commenting on Cicero's revisions of the careless prose of Gracchus, he graciously remarks: "For Cicero that was becoming; but for ourselves, we may be content with the task of tightening the composition of our own sentences which we have loosely written. For why should we seek farther for examples of faults which we can find in our own prose?" (ix.iv.15.)

I quote the foregoing especially for its suggestion that the niceties of prose rhythm are most appropriately sought after in revision. With further suggestions on the value of writing as preparation for rhythmical speech Quintilian concludes his discussion with this timely warning: "I have not discussed this subject at length with the intention that the orator, whose language ought to move and flow, should waste his energies in measuring feet and weighing syllables. . . . Assiduous exercise in writing will give us sufficient command of prose rhythms to enable us to use them when we speak extemporaneously. Nor is it so much the feet that are to be regarded as the flow of the whole period. Just as those who make verses consider not the five or six individual feet that form the verse, but the metrical movement of the whole verse. . . . Therefore rhythmical sentence movement (*compositio*) in prose holds the same place as versification in poetry. The best judge of rhythm is the ear" (ix.iv.112–116).

In Roman imperial times the art of the rhythmical period was largely lost. Rhythms were shorter and more metrical than Cicero or Quintilian would have approved and were gained by forced word transposition and a straining for effect in the use of the figures of antithesis and balance and of sententious point.[42]

Appropriateness. That the style of prose should be appropriate as well as pure, clear, and embellished was the consensus of antiquity. Like the thoughts which it clothes, language should be appropriate to the speaker, to the audience, and to the subject. The following analysis offered in the *Rhetoric* by Aristotle was accepted with but slight modification and shift of emphasis by

[42] Norden, *Antike Kunstprosa,* pp. 277–300.

subsequent writers, including Cicero and Quintilian: "Your language will be appropriate if it expresses emotion (*pathos*), and character (*ethos*), and if it corresponds to its subject. 'Correspondence to subject' means that we must neither speak casually about weighty matters, nor solemnly about trivial ones; nor must we add ornamental epithets to commonplace nouns, or the effect will be comic. . . . To express emotion, you will employ the language of anger in speaking of outrage, the language of disgust and discreet reluctance to utter a word when speaking of impiety or foulness; the language of exultation for a tale of glory, and that of humiliation for a tale of pity. . . . This aptness of language is one thing that makes people believe in the truth of your story. . . .

"Furthermore, this way of proving your story by displaying these signs of its genuineness expresses your personal character. Each type of man, each type of disposition, will have its own appropriate way of letting the truth appear. Under 'class' I include differences of age . . . sex . . . or nationality. By 'disposition' I here mean those dispositions only which determine the character of a man's life" (III.7).

Appropriateness to the character (*ethos*) of the audience Aristotle considers under the heads of the three kinds of rhetoric. Thus the style of a speech will be adapted to the different audiences of forensic and judicial speeches and, as Aristotle suggests, the readers of epideictic speeches, which he classifies as written rather than spoken: "It should be observed that each kind of rhetoric has its appropriate style. The style of written prose is not that of spoken oratory, nor are those of political and forensic speaking the same. . . . The written style is more finished: the spoken better admits of dramatic delivery. . . . Thus strings of unconnected words, and constant repetitions of words and phrases, are very properly condemned in written speeches: but not in spoken speeches. . . .

"Now the style of oratory addressed to public assemblies (deliberative) is really just like scene-painting. The bigger the throng, the more distant is the point of view: so that, in the one and the other, high finish in detail is superfluous and seems better away. The forensic style is more highly finished; still more so is the style of language addressed to a single judge, with whom there is very little room for rhetorical artifices. . . . It is ceremonial (epideictic) oratory that is most literary, for it is meant to be read; and next to it forensic oratory" (III.12).

Quintilian is in substantial agreement on the importance of appropriateness in style when he says: "What does it avail if our language is pure Latin, significant and polished, embellished with figures and rhythm unless it is adapted to lead the judge to the conclusions we wish and confirm him in them?" (XI.i.1.) "On this subject," he continues, "Cicero briefly touches in the third book of the *De oratore,* nor may he be said to have omitted anything when he says, 'One kind of style is not suited to every case, or every audience, or every speaker, or every occasion.' In his *Orator* he says the same in not many more words" (XI.i.4).[43]

But Cicero, he remarks, was addressing experienced speakers who already knew the truth of the matter and hence could speak briefly, but he himself is writing also for learners and must consequently go into greater detail. I shall not quote Quintilian where he goes over much the same ground as Aristotle on appropriateness to the subject and the audience. But especially full and interesting is his discussion of the desirability of writing and speaking in a style appropriate to the character of the speaker—or rather that impression of his character which it may be expedient for the speaker to convey to his audience. For the speaker should do or say nothing unworthy of himself, but always, everywhere, and to all men act and speak honorably. First the speaker should not boast or speak arrogantly, or indulge in self-derision, which is the final and most ostentatious form of boasting. An impudent, noisy, and angry tone is unbecoming to all speakers and especially

---

[43] The references are to *De oratore* III.lv.210; *Orator* xxi.70–74.

reprehensible in older speakers who occupy positions of dignity. Other vices unbecoming to all speakers are grovelling adulation, studied buffoonery, immodesty, and a disregard of authority.

The style should, moreover, be fitting to the age and standing of the speaker. A bold and florid style is less becoming to an older man than a mild and precise style. Younger men may appropriately use a style more exuberant and daring. A simpler style is suitable for soldiers; an unembellished style for those who boast of being philosophers. Quintilian recognizes that he is discussing the same sort of decorum as that recommended for dramatic dialog when he says: "There is a great regard paid to character among the tragic and comic poets; for they introduce many and various persons." When he is writing speeches for others to deliver, an orator must be especially careful to adapt the style to the character of the person who will speak the words. So also must the declaimer adapt his style to the fictitious character whom he impersonates in a fictitious case in the declamation schools (ix.i.8–42).[44]

Cicero points out that there is a style appropriate to each of the literary forms as well as to oratory. Thus the style appropriate to the orator differs from the styles appropriate to the philosopher, the epideictic speaker, the historian, and the poet. Where the orator uses a vigorous and biting style, addressed to winning over a popular audience, the philosopher uses a style more expository, conversational, gentle, and academic. Whereas the advocate uses a style adapted to rousing and persuading an audience, the epideictic speaker aims in his style to soothe and delight with a freer use of figures and rhythm. The language appropriate to historical writing resembles that of epideictic in that it is smooth, flowing, and embellished in contrast with the vehement and brilliant style of the orator. The style of the orator is rhythmical, whereas that of the poet is metrical (*Orator* xix.62–66).

Lucius Annaeus Seneca voices the Stoic view of style (transla-

[44] For decorum in drama, see Horace, *Epistle to the Pisos* 101–178.

tion by Lodge in 1614): "Thou complainest that the Letters which I send thee, are not written over-curiously; but who is he that writeth in so an affected Style, but he that would write to insinuate? Such as my speech should be if we were sitting together, or if men walked out together, easie and without Art: such will I that my Epistles be, that they neither be extravagant nor affected. If it were possible that a man might understand that which I thinke, I had rather expresse it by signes, then by words. And if I should dispute likewise, I would not stampe upon the ground, nor cast my hands abroad, nor lift up my voice: I would leave that to Orators, and content myselfe to have made thee understand my conceit, without inriching my speech, nor neglecting it also. . . . Truely, I would not that my discourses which men hold of so great matters, should be dull and drie: for Philosophie renounceth not a happie and gentle spirit, yet will she not likewise that we imploy over-much affectation in our discourse. In briefe, see here what is the sum of our intention. Let us speake what we thinke, and thinke what we speake; let our speech be answerable to our life. . . . It is not necessarie that our words be pleasing, but that they profit" (*Epistolae* 75).

The Three Types of Style. When John Milton speaks of the "organic arts which inable men to discourse and write perspicuously, elegantly, and according to the fitted stile of lofty, mean, or lowly," [45] he shows his familiarity with the classification of styles that first appeared in the first century B.C., and shows also his awareness that the style should be appropriate ("fitted") as well as clear and embellished.

The ancients used a wide variety of words to describe the three types of style: the grand, the intermediate, and the plain. The lofty, elevated, magnificent, grand, sublime style is given appreciative and discriminating treatment by "Longinus" in his

[45] *Of Education,* in *The Works of John Milton* (Columbia ed.), IV, 286. See also D. L. Clark, "John Milton and the Fitted Stile," *Seventeenth-Century News,* Winter, 1953.

treatise best known by its Latin title, *De sublimitate*. According to him, the elevated style has its origin in the faculty of grasping great conceptions and in emotional intensity. Amplification is a rhetorical piling up through iteration. The elevated style, or sublimity, carries its hearer not to persuasion but to ecstasy (i.4). When one strives for elevation of style and fails, he achieves fustian or bombast, what the ancients called frigidity. In illustrating the theme that "great words issue from those whose thoughts are weighty" he quotes, amongst appropriate passages from Homer and Hesiod, verses from Genesis. "Thus too the lawgiver of the Jews, no common man, when he had duly conceived the power of the Deity, showed it forth as duly. At the very beginning of his laws, 'God said,' he writes— What? 'Let there be light, and there was light, Let there be earth and there was earth" (ix.9).

The usual view of the grand style was more rhetorical. Cicero, who called this style weighty, grand, emphatic (*gravis, grandis, vehemens*), thought it should be used to excite and move the audience to action. With Quintilian in agreement, he recommended it as especially useful in peroration (*Orator* xxi.68–69; Quintilian xii.x.61).

At the opposite extreme was what Milton called the lowly style. This plain, simple, unadorned style, says Cicero, is appropriate to the statement of facts and to proof. Demetrius favored it for letters. What he says is so timeless that I shall quote a few pertinent sentences: "We will next treat of the epistolary style, since it too should be plain. . . . The letter, like the dialog, should abound in glimpses of character. It may be said that everybody reveals his own soul in his letters. In every other form of composition it is possible to discern the writer's character, but in none so clearly as in the epistolary. . . .

"There should be a certain degree of freedom in the [sentence] structure of a letter. It is absurd to build up periods, as if you were writing not a letter but a speech for the law courts. A letter is designed to be the heart's good wishes in brief; it is the exposition of a simple subject in simple terms.

"Ornament, however, it may have in the shape of friendly bits of kindly advice, mixed with a few good proverbs. . . . But the man who utters sententious maxims and exhortations seems to be no longer talking familiarly in a letter but to be speaking from a pulpit.

"Since occasionally we write to States or royal personages, such letters must be composed in a slightly heightened tone. It is right to have regard to the person to whom the letter is addressed. The heightening should not, however, be carried so far that we have a treatise in place of a letter. So much with regard to letter writing and the plain style." [46]

The vice of the plain style is aridity, resulting from understatement and abruptness.

The mean or intermediate style was considered to be somewhere between the grand and the plain styles. In *Orator* Cicero describes it rather unflatteringly: "Between these two is interjected a mean or moderate style which uses neither the intellectual acumen of the latter nor the lightning flashes of the former. It is related to both but has the excellencies of neither" (v.21).

Other writers did not join Cicero in belittling the intermediate style, but praised it as the golden mean of the peripatetics. Dionysius of Halicarnassus praised it as elegant, smooth, and florid, using words "smooth as a maiden's face" (*De compositione verborum* 21–24). Demetrius says its elegance includes grace and geniality and is derived from the use of pleasantries, surprise, figures, smooth words, climactic order with a turn, point, and rhythm (*On Style* III.128–189).

[46] Demetrius, *On Style*, with English translation by W. Rhys Roberts, IV, 223–235. See Rhys Roberts' Introduction, pp. 257–274, for a discussion of the types of style and for identification of Demetrius as a grammaticus of the first century. Also Seneca *Epistolae* 75.

Quintilian waxes poetical and says it flows gently, "like a clear stream overshadowed on either side by banks of greenwood" (xii.x.60). Its attendant evil, says Demetrius, is affectation, a striving for effects. In the *Orator* Cicero admits the usefulness of the intermediate or charming style to please, delight, and win over an audience.

Demetrius is the only one of the ancients who discussed a fourth type of style—the forcible—in order to create a special place of honor for Demosthenes.[47] Cicero had been content with the assertion that Demosthenes had excelled in all three of the conventional types (*Orator* vi.23).

In summing up the three types of style and relating each to an appropriate function, Cicero states, with Quintilian concurring, that the plain style is for proving, the grand style for moving, the intermediate style for pleasing (*Orator* xxi.69; Quintilian xii.x.58).

MEMORIA (MEMORY)

Whether the public speaker learns by heart a speech he has written or prepares to speak extemporaneously after mastering the substance, he needs a well-trained and retentive memory. Hence all surviving treatises which pretend to completeness, from the *Ad Herennium* (iii.xvi.28ff.) on give at least a brief treatment of memory and usually expound an artificial technic of memory based on visual association.[48] Both Cicero and Quintilian tell the story of how Simonides of Ceos came to invent this art of memory (*De oratore* ii.lxxxvi.350 ff.; Quintilian xii.ii). Simonides, so it goes, was called from a banquet hall by an urgent message. No sooner had he gone outside than the roof of the hall fell in, killing and crushing all the guests so that it was impossible to recognize any of them. But Simonides was able to identify each guest for interment because he remembered

[47] Rhys Roberts, Introduction to Demetrius, *On Style*, p. 267.
[48] Grasberger, *Erziehung und Unterricht*, II, 131–138.

where each reclined at table. This led him to the discovery of the truth that memory is assisted by places or localities impressed on the mind. Cicero adds, "Like letters inscribed on a wax tablet."

Quintilian tells in some detail how the system works. The speaker familiarizes himself with a series of visual images such as the rooms of a house and furniture in each room. He then associates part of what he has written or planned with each chair, statue, or the like in a room. Then when he speaks he imagines that he is going into the vestibule of the house, for instance, and is reminded of the words or thoughts associated with it. As he imagines himself going through the other rooms in order, he is in turn reminded of other associated words and thoughts in the order which he had planned.

Quintilian points out that this system is more useful for keeping in mind a series of arguments which one plans to use in an extemporaneous speech than it is in learning a written speech by heart. But if a long speech is learned in parts which correspond with carefully arranged divisions of the *dispositio,* then one may more readily keep in mind the order of the parts which he has memorized separately. Moreover, "All sentences that have been well constructed will guide the memory by their sequence; for as we learn by heart verse more readily than prose, we learn periodic prose more easily than loose" (xi.ii.39).

He concludes his discussion of memory with the question "Whether those who are going to deliver a speech should learn it by heart word for word or whether it be sufficient to master merely the substance and order of particulars?" [49] He leaves the question unanswered, but his asking it indicates that there were two schools of thought. He himself favored writing and memorizing a speech if the speaker had a good memory and there were time. Otherwise it is safer, he claims, after grasping the substance, to give oneself freedom of expression.

[49] See the discussion in Baldwin, *Ancient Rhetoric and Poetic,* pp. 82–84.

PRONUNTIATIO (DELIVERY)

The importance of delivery to a public speaker is attested by the often repeated story of Demosthenes, who, when asked what was of first importance in oratory, replied, "Delivery," and gave the same reply when asked what was second and third.[50] Cicero, who liked the story so well that he repeated it thrice in three different treatises, says he liked even more the story of Aeschines at Rhodes. "Aeschines is reported to have read, at the request of the Rhodians, that outstanding speech he had delivered against Ctesiphon, in opposition to Demosthenes, and he was asked to read next day the speech Demosthenes had delivered in favor of Ctesiphon. And when he had read this too in a pleasing and powerful voice, and all expressed their admiration, 'How much more would you have admired it,' said he, 'if you had heard him deliver it himself.'" And Cicero, in agreement, declared, "Delivery is the one dominant power in oratory" (De oratore III.lvi.213).

We may well agree that training in voice and diction, gesture and facial expression, was of the greatest importance to the public speaker in antiquity as it is today. But then as now it is the sort of training that is least amenable to transmission in a written treatise. But, as Aristotle asserts, "The principles of good diction can be taught" (Rhetoric III.1). And they were taught in antiquity with success. Constant classroom and individual drill can accomplish what the textbook alone cannot.

That teachers of speech in antiquity had at least some success with stutterers is indicated by an interesting letter from Augustus to his wife concerning that ill-favored boy who later became the emperor Claudius: "Confound me, dear Livia, if I am not surprised that your grandson Tiberius could please me with his declaiming. How in the world anyone who is so unclear in his

[50] Philodemus Rhetoric IV.ii (Hubbell trans. p. 301); Cicero De oratore III.lvi.213; Brutus xxxvii.142; Orator xvii.56; Quintilian XI.iii.6.

conversation can speak with clearness and propriety when he declaims, is more than I can see." [51]

The Romans used two words to designate delivery, *actio* and *pronuntiatio,* which should indicate an analysis into the use of the voice and the use of gesture. The analysis exists, but the words were used more or less indiscriminately. Cicero seems to prefer *actio* as the term which includes voice and gesture (*De oratore* iii.lvi.213; *Orator* 55). The author of the *Ad Herennium* (iii.xi.19) and Quintilian (xi.iii.1) use *pronuntiatio,* although Quintilian adds, "It does not matter which term we employ."

All who discuss oratorical delivery from Aristotle on are given to referring to its similarity to acting. The public speaker should observe and imitate the technic of a good actor but should avoid a delivery which smacks too obviously of the stage.

Although many seem to have written on delivery, Quintilian's treatment is the fullest that survives and should give us an accurate picture of the more sensible teaching practices of antiquity. Quintilian divides his treatment into two parts: the training of the boy in the grammar school and his training in the school of rhetoric. In the grammar school the young boy must be carefully drilled in correct pronunciation and distinct utterance. He must be taught to avoid annoying mannerisms of posture and facial expression. As an exercise he may memorize declamatory passages from comedy and recite them with appropriate interpretive expression. When he is a little older he may memorize and recite selected passages from oratory. From well-planned gymnastic exercises he should acquire poise and grace of movement (i.xi).

In a later book Quintilian gives detailed advice for the training of the older student in the school of rhetoric. First the boys should be taught that physical robustness is one of the greatest aids to good delivery. They should use normal care in diet and exercise and should abjure wine and women. The boy should

[51] Suetonius *Life of Claudius* iv.6.

also practice daily exercises in the speaking of memorized passages of oratorical prose. Demosthenes is introduced as a favorite example. He increased his breathing capacity by reciting as many verses as possible on a breath while climbing a hill; when he practiced speaking, he rolled pebbles under his tongue that he might speak all the more freely when unencumbered; he practiced gesture and posture before a large mirror; he broke himself of a bad habit of shrugging by practicing with a spear suspended above his shoulder (xi.iii.54, 68, 130). These stories must have been the stock in trade of generations of teachers of speech. Plutarch and Libanius also tell them in their lives of Demosthenes.

According to Quintilian's doctrine, voice and diction, like literary style, should be pure, clear, embellished, and appropriate. Speech must be pure and correct Latin with no trace of the foreign or provincial. Speech must be clear through careful enunciation and observance of proper pauses. It should be embellished and can be if the voice has pleasing quality and is well controlled. Beauty of speech will be aided by careful avoidance of such vices as monotony, straining, excessive rapidity or slowness, panting, spraying saliva, chanting, and singing. Voice and diction will be appropriate if they are adapted to the subject of the speech. And he gives shrewd advice on how to use the imagination in simulating emotions the speaker does not feel. "In representing such feelings, the first requisite is to impress ourselves as much as possible, to conceive lively ideas of things, and to allow ourselves to be moved by them as if they were real; and then the voice, as an intermediate organ, will convey to the minds of the judges that impression which it receives from our own."

In his discussion of gesture and movement Quintilian gives detailed directions on how to use the head, eyes, eyebrows, nose (don't pick or rub it), lips, neck, shoulders, and hands. All of these directions are adjusted to the fact that the speaker is dressed in a toga, which restricts the movement of the left arm but leaves the right arm great freedom. Vices to be avoided include turning your back on the audience, excessive walking about, and such overuse of gesture as would suggest pantomimic dancing (xi.iii: voice, 1–64; gesture, 65–184).

The Speech

So far in this chapter we have considered the speaker's resources, the art of discovering arguments, arranging them in a persuasive sequence, clothing them in language, remembering them, and delivering them before an audience. Now we shall take up the speech itself, the skill in composition and delivery that will draw on all the speaker's resources.

In summarizing the traditional doctrine of the schools Crassus, remembering his youth, is represented in the *De oratore* as saying: "I had been taught that before we speak on the point at issue, the minds of the audience should be conciliated; next, our case should be stated; then the point in controversy should be established; then our allegations should be confirmed and those advanced against us refuted; and that at the conclusion of our speech what is in our favor should be amplified and expanded, what favors the adversary should be weakened and demolished" (i.xxxi.143).

This passage alludes to the traditional division of a speech into an *exordium,* statement of facts (*narratio*), proof (*confirmatio* and *refutatio*), and peroration, which Aristotle allowed for the forensic speeches of the law courts (iii.13–19). Cicero reverted to this fourfold division of the speech in *De partitione oratoria* (26 ff.). In his early *De inventione* Cicero, like the author of the *Ad Herennium,* had inserted a *divisio* after the *narratio* and had separated refutation from confirmatory proof (*De inventione* i.xiv–xix; *Ad Herennium* i.5).

EXORDIUM. The *exordium* is the proem, introduction, entrance, or beginning of the speech. Traditionally it had three aims: to make the audience well disposed (*benevolum*), attentive (*attentum*), and willing to receive information (*docilem*). These might be accomplished directly or by insinuation.[52]

Aristotle does not anchor his discussion to this formula, which prevailed through post-classical times, but he covers the ground and makes some interesting suggestions for adapting the *exordium* to the different audiences of the three kinds of rhetoric. Thus for epideictic rhetoric he says: "Introductions for speeches of display, then, may be composed of some piece of praise or censure, or advice to do or not to do something, or of appeals to the audience. . . . We must make the hearer feel that the eulogy includes either himself or his family or his way of life or something or other of the kind."

In forensic speeches he recommends giving the audience a foretaste of the theme as is done in the prolog of epic or drama. "This, then, is the most essential function of the introduction, to show what the aim of the speech is. . . . The introduction of political (deliberative) oratory will be made out of the same materials as those of the forensic kind, though the nature of political oratory makes them very rare . . . but you may have to say something on account of yourself or your opponents; or those present may be inclined to treat the matter more or less seriously than you wish them to. You may accordingly have to excite or dispel some prejudice, or make the matter under discussion seem more or less important than before."

For all types of speeches, says Aristotle, the speaker will need to seek the good will of his audience and remove prejudice from himself. "The appeal to the hearer aims at securing his good will or arousing his resentment, or sometimes at gaining his serious attention to the case, or even distracting it." Hence the speaker may gain attention by telling the members of his audience that they are about to hear something that is important, surprising, or

[52] See *Ad Herennium* 1.6; *De inventione* 1.20; *De partitione* 28; Quintilian IV.i.5.

agreeable. Indeed these bids for attention may be more needful later in the speech than in the introduction and should be so used. "Choose therefore any point in the speech where such an appeal is needed, and then say 'Now I beg you to note this point —it concerns you quite as much as myself.' . . . This is what Prodicus called 'slipping in a bit of the fifty-drachma show lecture whenever the audience began to nod.' "

Aristotle regretfully remarks that if audiences were not weak-minded no introduction save a statement of the subject would be necessary. "It is plain that introductions are addressed not to ideal hearers but to hearers as we find them" (III.14).

As Quintilian's discussion is based, in part at least, on Aristotle and adds little new, I shall make no effort to quote fully. What he does contribute, however, is some sound advice for the student: "Since it is not sufficient, however, to indicate to learners what enters into the nature of an *exordium* without instructing them also how an *exordium* may be best composed, I add that he who is going to speak should reflect what he has to say, before whom, at what time or place, under what circumstance, under what pre-possessions of the public; what opinion it is likely that the judge has formed previous to the commencement of the pleadings; and what the speaker has to desire or deprecate. Nature herself will lead him to understand what he ought to say first" (IV.i.52).

Discussing the composition of *exordia*, Antonius in the *De oratore* remarks: "It was then my practice to think last of what is to be spoken first, what *exordium* should I employ. For whenever I have been inclined to plan it first, nothing has occurred but what was bald, trifling, shopworn, or ordinary" (II.lxxvii.315).

This sensible practice, followed by many professional speakers and writers today, struck Quintilian as offensively illogical: "I do not agree with those who think the *exordium* is to be written last. . . . We ought certainly begin with what is naturally first" (III.ix.8).

We can agree with him more readily when he points out some

faulty practices in the schools, as, for instance, the bad habit of not telling in the *exordium* what the case is about just because the theme had been assigned and all the pupils in the room knew what it was about and the childish affectation of striving for such subtle and ingenious transitions from *exordium* to *narratio* that the audience fails to follow. That should come last in the *exordium* which is most readily linked to the next division of the speech. And the linking should be explicit. Quintilian also ridicules the silly schoolmaster who taught that no *exordium* should consist of more than four sentences.

STATEMENT OF FACTS (NARRATIO). "The statement of a case," says Quintilian, "is an exposition of what has been done, or is supposed to have been done, adapted to persuade" (IV.ii.31). As Quintilian suggests, the *narratio* need not be a chronological narrative. It may depart from a time sequence and be expository in design as well as in intention. And the "facts" need not be facts, but what the advocate thinks it expedient that the judges or jury should believe to be facts. And a liar needs a good memory if he succeeds in keeping his mendacious *narratio* self-consistent. And the aim of the *narratio* is not the disinterested aim we now hope for in history, but the persuasive aim of a pleader who wishes to influence people. And then, just to complicate matters, *narratio* was also used as a term to describe the narrating of illustrative myths, fictions, and anecdotes which a speaker might introduce as he might a metaphor or allegory to dissemble his argument through the medium of a symbol.

As Aristotle points out, only a forensic speech is likely to have a statement of facts because when we praise or dispraise in an epideictic speech the facts are likely to be known and need only coloring, and as deliberative speeches deal with what would be expedient in the future, there is not likely to be much past action to state (III.16).

Moreover, even in forensic oratory the *narratio* may be omitted if the facts are well known, especially if the judge views the facts with the same bias as the advocate. But if the judge views the well-known facts in a way hostile to the speaker's client, then the advocate should retell them with a favorable slant. As Quintilian says, "For a statement of facts is not made merely that the judge may comprehend the case, but rather that he may look upon it in the same light as ourselves" (iv.ii.21).

Isocrates seems to be responsible for the formula that was taught in the schools: a statement of facts should be brief, clear, and plausible. All writers repeat this formula whenever they discuss *narratio*.[53] "Of this specification I approve," say Quintilian, "though Aristotle differs from Isocrates in one particular, as he ridicules the direction about brevity, as if it were absolutely necessary that a statement should be long or short, and as if there were no possibility of fixing it at a just medium" (iv.ii.32). Probably Isocrates had meant only that the statement should be as brief as is consistent with persuasive effectiveness. Cicero, an avowed follower of Isocrates, makes the point clear in the *De oratore* that if brevity means using only the essential minimum, devotion to it may be detrimental in a *narratio* because it may make the statement obscure or less pleasant and persuasive (*De oratore* ii.lxxx.326).

There seems to have been no questioning in antiquity of the other two precepts, that the statement be clear and sound like the truth even when it was not true. There were, however, some precepts taught in the schools which were altogether too ironclad to suit Quintilian: "The following directions are commonly given respecting the statement of facts: that no digression is to be made from it; that we are to address ourselves constantly to the judge; that we are to speak in no character but our own; and that we are to introduce no argumentation; and some even add that we are not to attempt to excite the feelings. These precepts, doubt-

[53] Thus we find it in *Ad Herennium* i.ix.14–17, in Aristotle (*Rhetoric* iii.16), and in Cicero (*De inventione* i.xix; *De oratore* ii.lxxx.325; *De partitione oratoria* ix.31–32).

less, are in general to be observed, or, I may say, never to be departed from, unless the nature of our cause obliges us to disregard them" (iv.ii.103).

And he goes on for ten paragraphs to show in detail, with examples mostly from Cicero's speeches, just how violation of these precepts may add to the effectiveness of a *narratio*. Indeed in a passage of the *De partitione oratoria,* which Quintilian may have had in mind, Cicero urges a fourth requirement for the *narratio,* that it possess agreeableness or charm (*suavitas*): "And the *narratio* has agreeableness when it involves elements of wonder, suspense, and the unexpected, intermixed with emotional disturbance, dialog between persons, grief, anger, fear, joy, desire" (ix.32).

The relationship of the statement of facts to the proof Quintilian aptly states as follows: "What difference is there between proof and a statement of facts, except that a statement is a connected exposition of that which is to be proved, and proof is a verification of that which has been stated?" (iv.ii.79.)

Finally, as Aristotle suggests in the *Rhetoric,* it is not even necessary that all of the statement of facts be delivered between the introduction and the proof. The statement may be introduced piecemeal anywhere in the speech where it will do the most good (iii.16). But no schoolmaster would be likely to teach the young any such daring departure from conventional speech composition.

PROOF (CONFIRMATIO). When we consider proof in rhetoric, we must be careful to remember that rhetoric does not concern itself with scientifically demonstrated truths, about which there is no debate, but with such contingent and approximate truths as lead to differences of opinion. We do not argue or persuade in favor of the probability of a proposition in Euclid. We demonstrate. Hence the Latin use of *confirmatio* as the term for rhetorical proof is less misleading than our habitual use in English of the one word, *proof,* both for scientific demonstration and for persuasive argument used in support of the probability of one side of a debatable issue. Hence it is *confirmatio* and *refutatio,* not demonstration, that make up the third part of a speech, usually coming after an introduction and a statement of facts.

Aristotle points out in the *Rhetoric* that there are three modes of persuasion furnished by the spoken word: (1) the character of the speaker (*ethos*), who should speak as if he had good sense, virtue, and good will; (2) the rousing or allaying of the emotions (*pathos*) of the audience; and (3) "The proof, or apparent proof, provided by the words (*logos*) of the speech itself" (1.2). The influence of *ethos* and *pathos* in persuading an audience is pervasive. These appeals may be used in any or all parts of a speech, whereas the use of persuasive arguments to strengthen and corroborate a speaker's position in a debate belongs primarily in the *confirmatio.*

I have already discussed the differences between those proofs which lie outside the art of rhetoric, such as laws, witnesses, contracts, torture, and oaths, and those rhetorical arguments which are provided by the words of the speech itself. These nonrhetorical proofs may carry great weight in deciding a case. Moreover they may be given rhetorical treatment by the speaker, who may urge that a witness is unreliable, may impugn evidence given under torture, or may appeal from law to equity or vice versa (Aristotle *Rhetoric* 1.15; *Ad Herennium* ii.vi.9; Cicero *De oratore* ii. xxviii.116 and *De partitione oratoria* xiv.48–51; Quintilian v.i–vii).

The kinds of proof or persuasive arguments which do belong to the art of rhetoric are two: the enthymeme, including the maxim, and the example.

The enthymeme is a rhetorical adaptation of deductive logic. "I call the enthymeme," says Aristotle in the *Rhetoric,* "a rhetorical syllogism. . . . When it is shown that, certain propositions being true, a further and quite distinct proposition must also be true in consequence, whether invariably or usually, this is called a syllogism in dialectic and an enthymeme in rhetoric" (1.2).

On this statement Quintilian expands somewhat: "The enthymeme is called by some a rhetorical syllogism, by others a part of a syllogism, because the syllogism has always its premises and conclusion, and establishes by means of all its parts that which it has set out to prove, while the enthymeme is satisfied to let its proof be understood" (v.xiv.24).

Aristotle adds that the brevity of the enthymeme makes it easier to follow than the full syllogistic statement and hence better adapted to a popular audience. Enthymemes should be selected with the aid of the places of argument (*topoi*) (*Rhetoric* II.22).

We are all familiar with the syllogism which demonstrates the mortality of Socrates. *Major premise:* All men are mortal. *Minor premise:* Socrates is a man. *Conclusion:* Therefore Socrates is mortal. An enthymeme on Socrates might be, "Socrates as a man is bound to die"; or, "Socrates must share the inevitable fate of all men." In this instance the enthymemes may be said to be incomplete syllogisms which omit the statement of the major or minor premise. On the other hand an enthymeme may differ from a logical syllogism in drawing its conclusion, not from a major premise of universal application, but from one based on opinions generally, or frequently, accepted, or on premises of dubious validity. Thus as an example of an indication from which no necessary conclusion can be drawn, Quintilian quotes Hermagoras, "Atalanta is not a virgin, because she strolls through the woods with young men" (v.ix.12). But Atalanta undoubtedly got herself talked about because there are always some people who would accept the unexpressed major premise that girls who wander in the woods with young men are less likely to be virgins than girls who stay at home. The argument of the enthymeme is based, not on a universal, but on a probability.

"Of probability," says Quintilian, "there are three degrees: one which rests on very strong grounds, because that to which it is applied generally happens, as 'that children are loved by their parents'; a second, somewhat more inclined to uncertainty, as 'that he who is in good health today will live until tomorrow'; a third, which is only not repugnant to credibility, as 'a theft committed in a house was committed by one of the household.' . . . But all probability, on which the far greater part of reasoning depends, flows from sources of this nature, whether it is credible that a father was killed by his son; that a father committed incest with his daughter; and again, whether poisoning be credible in a step-mother, or adultery in a man of licentious life; also, whether it be credible that a crime was committed in the sight of the whole world, or that false testimony was given for a small bribe, because each of these crimes proceeds from a peculiar cast of character, generally, not always. Otherwise all reasoning about them would be absolute certainty, and not mere probable argument" (v.x. 16, 19).

Whether all these arguments from probability are strictly to be called enthymemes is itself debatable.[54] What might be considered a form of enthymeme Quintilian defines as an epicheirema: "But the epicheirema differs in no respect from the syllogism, except that the syllogism has a greater number of forms, and infers truth from truth; while the epicheirema is generally employed about probabilities." Consequently, as he implies, the epicheirema, not the syllogism, will be the deductive argument most used by the public speaker. "For if it were always possible to prove what is disputed by what is acknowledged, there would scarcely be any work for the orator in the matter" (v.xiv.14).

Refutation of deductive arguments, whatever their form, Aristotle discusses in the *Rhetoric* under two headings. One can offer a counter enthymeme, that is draw an opposite conclusion from the premises of the adversary; or one can raise objections, that is adduce exceptions to the premises of the adversary. It is not enough to refute by showing that the adversary's conclusions are unnecessary. They must also be shown to be improbable. All arguments, save demonstrations, can be refuted (II.25).[55]

[54] Cope, *Introduction to Aristotle's Rhetoric*, p. 103.
[55] See also Quintilian II.iv.18; Cicero *De inventione* 1.42–78.

As philosopher and logician, Aristotle is exceedingly interested in apparent enthymemes, fallacies, which he discusses in the *Rhetoric* in connection with enthymemes and their refutation, but his fullest treatment is in *Prior Analytics* (ii.26–27) [56] and the *Sophistical Refutations,* where he justifies the study of fallacious reasoning: "It is the business of one who knows a thing, himself to avoid the fallacies in the subjects which he knows and be able to show up the man who makes them" (1).

No other writer on rhetoric has paid so much attention to the public speaker's use of logical processes in argument as Aristotle, who, indeed, had introduced logic into rhetoric. That subsequent writers were not merely ignorant or inattentive is shown by Quintilian's ironical conclusion to his rather full discussion of the use of deductive reasoning in rhetoric: "It seems to me that I have gone through the sacred ritual of those who deliver precepts on rhetoric. But one must exercise judgment in using the precepts. For though I do not think it unlawful to use syllogisms occasionally in a speech, yet I should by no means like it to consist wholly of syllogisms, or to be crowded with a mass of epicheiremata and enthymemes, for it would then resemble the dialogs and disputations of logicians, rather than oratorical pleading. . . . For what true orator has ever spoken in such a way? In Demosthenes himself are to be found few traces of slavish adherence to the rules. Yet the Greeks of our day . . . bind their thoughts as it were in chains, connecting them in an intricate series, proving what is undisputed, confirming what is admitted" (v.xiv.27, 32).

And in his last book Quintilian repeats his warning against slavish use of logic in oratory. Logic, he says, "concerns the orator if it be his business to know the exact significations of terms, to clear ambiguities, to disentangle perplexities, to distinguish falsehood from truth, and to establish or refute what he may desire; though, indeed, we shall not have to use these arts with such exactness and preciseness in pleadings in the forum, as is observed

[56] Digested by Cope, *Introduction to Aristotle's Rhetoric,* pp. 269 ff.

in the disputations of the schools; because the orator must not only instruct his audience, but must move and delight them . . . and has need of energy, animation, and grace" (xii.ii.10–11. See also vii.iii.14).

Both Aristotle in his *Rhetoric* (ii.18–26) and Quintilian (v.viii–xiv) in their discussion of syllogism and enthymeme as aids to proof give full development of the places of argument which, with status, has been discussed under *inventio*. They show with examples how the arguments thus discovered and selected may be brought to bear in a speech to confirm and refute. So does Cicero, but in the *De oratore* he attacks logic as helping only to test truth, not to discover it (ii.xxxviii.157). And in the *De partitione oratoria* he ignores deductive logic, relating the finding of arguments, not to syllogism and enthymeme, but to the status of the case: (1) conjecture as to fact (*an sit*); (2) definition (*quid sit*); and (3) quality, good or bad, of the action (*quale sit*). Probability he discusses fully under the first head of conjecture as to fact. He follows the analysis furnished by the places of argument. Thus under the topic of person, he seeks probabilities under the subheads: youth (youth is more likely to be self-indulgent), age, nature, fortune, and the like. "As to probabilities, in some cases they carry weight singly of themselves, in some, even if they seem thin of themselves, they carry weight if combined" (xi.40).

In all his discussion of argument from probabilities there is nothing incompatible with the doctrine explained by Aristotle and Quintilian. It is significant, however, that in a treatise written for the instruction of his nineteen-year-old son in the rudiments of argument, he refrained from using the exact terminology as well as the exact methods of logic. The late Latin compend of Martianus Capella, who usually shows a Ciceronian influence, is likewise silent on syllogism and enthymeme, although of course he treats both in his treatise on logic. Like Cicero he bases his theory of rhetorical proof on the places of argument alone. To be sure, Cassiodorus in the late sixth century, basing his treatment on

Fortunatianus (late fourth century), in turn based on Quintilian, does give the doctrine of syllogism, enthymeme, epicheirema.[57] But I surmise that few boys in the schools of rhetoric were taught the doctrine of confirmation and refutation according to a formal study of syllogism and enthymeme.

"The maxim," Aristotle states in the *Rhetoric*, "is part of an enthymeme." It is, he adds, a statement of a general kind about courses of practical conduct to be chosen or avoided. He treats maxims (*gnome*) quite seriously and suggests that they carry a good deal of weight: "One great advantage of maxims to a speaker is due to the want of intelligence of his hearers, who love to hear him succeed in expressing as a universal truth the opinions which they hold themselves about particular cases." They have an added advantage: "If the maxims are sound, they display the speaker as a man of sound moral character" (II.20–21).

There are two kinds of maxim: the maxim proper or simple unsupported epigrammatic statement which seems true because common and familiar, and the statement which needs the support of a reason. This latter, even in its expression, is an enthymeme. Thus, "There is no man among us all is free," is a maxim. When a reason is added, "For all are slaves of money or of chance," it becomes an enthymeme (II.21).

This second variety Quintilian calls *sententia cum ratione* and mentions as one form of enthymeme. He gives no further separate consideration to it. In his treatment of figures of style, between hyperbole and trope, he discusses *sententiae* as striking thoughts. "Such thoughts were far from common among the ancients, but in our day are used to excess" (VIII.v.2). The maxim and related proverb were both used as themes for development in the elementary exercises in rhetoric taught in the grammar schools. Perhaps their use in schoolboy themes weakened their force in professional public speaking. Perhaps illiterate audiences were less

[57] Cassiodorus, *Secular Letters*, On Rhetoric, 12–15, in *An Introduction to Divine and Human Readings*, trans. with introduction and notes by L. W. Jones (New York, 1946), pp. 155–158.

common in the time of Quintilian than in the time of Aristotle.

The second kind of proof belonging to the art of rhetoric is the example. In the same passage where he defined enthymeme as a rhetorical syllogism Aristotle defined an example as a rhetorical induction. But the rhetorical example does not move from particular to general as does a logical induction. Nor does it move from universal to particular as does a deduction. It moves instead from particular to particular in the same class or order. "When two statements are of the same order, but one is more familiar than the other, the former is an example" (i.2).

From Aristotle's own illustrations we are assured that examples were used as confirmation in oratory long before his time. But his analysis in the *Rhetoric* is so clear and has been followed by so many subsequent writers that I shall follow it here: "This form of argument has two varieties; one consisting in the mention of actual past facts, the other in the invention of facts by the speaker. Of the latter, again, there are two varieties, the illustrative parallel and the fable" (ii.20).

Cicero, in the *De partitione oratoria,* teaches the same classification, preferring to use the term *exemplum* especially for the historical parallel: "The greatest support of a probability is furnished by first an example, then the introduction of a parallel case (*similitudo*); sometimes a fable, even if it be incredible, nevertheless influences people" (xi.40).

"The most important of these proofs," says Quintilian, referring to those based on similarity, "is that which is most properly termed example, that is to say, the adducing of some past happening or supposed happening, adapted to persuade the hearer" (v.xi.6).[58]

"As an instance of the mention of actual facts," says Aristotle, "take the following. The speaker may argue thus: 'We must prepare for war against the king of Persia and not let him subdue Egypt. For Darius of old did not cross the Aegean until he had

[58] See also Cicero *De inventione* i.xxx.49; *Ad Herennium* iv.lxix.62.

seized Egypt; but once he had seized it, he did cross. And Xerxes, again, did not attack us until he had seized Egypt'" (II.20).

Aristotle also in the *Rhetoric* (I.2) illustrates the use of the example from history by an argument against giving Dionysius a bodyguard. This Quintilian borrows from him and condenses: "As if a speaker, for example, on remarking that 'Dionysius requested guards for his person, in order that, with the aid of their arms, he might make himself tyrant,' should support his argument with the example, 'Pisistratus secured absolute power in the same manner'" (v.xi.8). Quintilian also points out that arguments from example must be either from things similar, dissimilar, or contrary, and illustrates with samples of each of these kinds extracted from the speeches of Cicero.

Aristotle remarks that it is hard to find parallels from actual past events, however valuable they are when found. But at some time during the reign of Tiberius a professor named Valerius Maximus made it easy with the publication of a work called *The Memorable Deeds and Sayings,* in nine books. It is a collection of rhetorical *exempla,* interspersed with moral maxims, for the most part from Roman history, arranged like a commonplace book under headings to facilitate ready reference. For example, Book I deals with religion, auspices, omens, prodigies, and marvels. Book v gives *exempla* of clemency, gratitude, duty, affection, patriotism. Book ix illustrates lust, cruelty, anger, perfidy, and like themes. In his preface Valerius announces that his purpose is to save his readers the trouble of going to historical sources to search out illustrative anecdotes. As he presents them, they are readily available for use by the professor of rhetoric and his students.[59]

Aristotle listed the illustrative parallel or analogy as the first of the two kinds of invented example. His own illustration is drawn from Socrates: "Public officials ought not to be selected by lot.

[59] Duff, *A Literary History of Rome in the Silver Age,* pp. 65–81. For pedagogical use of commonplace books, see D. L. Clark, *John Milton at St. Paul's School,* pp. 217–226.

That is like using the lot to select athletes, instead of choosing those who are fit for the contest; or using the lot to select the steersman from a ship's crew, as if we ought to take the man on whom the lot falls, and not the man who knows most about it" (1.20).

Quintilian, as usual, draws most of his illustrations from the speeches of Cicero. But he points out the need to avoid false analogies. It takes judgment to make sure that we are making a proper comparison. The following he approves, "As rowers are inefficient without a steersman, so are soldiers without a general." But a similitude improperly drawn may backfire, thus, " 'As a new ship is more serviceable than an old, so is it with friendship; as we praise a woman generous with her money, so should we praise one generous with her body.' The similitude is in the words 'old' and 'generous,' but there is a great difference between ships and friendship and between money and modesty" (v.xi.25–26). As we need to be careful in our own use of analogies, so in refutation should we be alert to attack the false analogies of our adversaries.

"Instances of fable," says Aristotle, "are that of Stesichorus about Phalaris, and that of Aesop in defense of the popular leader," and he tells the stories with appreciation of their humor as well as of their aptness: "When the people of Himera had made Phalaris military dictator, and were going to give him a bodyguard, Stesichorus wound up a long talk by telling them the fable of the horse who had a field all to himself. Presently there came a stag and began to spoil his pasturage. The horse, wishing to revenge himself on the stag, asked a man if he could help him do so. The man said, 'Yes, if you will let me bridle you and get on your back with javelins in my hand.' The horse agreed, and the man mounted; but instead of getting his revenge on the stag, the horse found himself the slave of the man. 'You too,' said Stesichorus, 'take care lest, in your desire for revenge on your enemies, you meet the same fate as the horse. By making Phalaris military dictator, you have already let yourself be bridled. If you let him get on your backs by giving him a bodyguard, from that moment you will be his slaves.' "

Then Aristotle tells how Aesop defended the demagogue by the fable of the fox caught in the cleft of a rock. The fox was infested with dog ticks which sucked his blood. A benevolent hedgehog offered to remove the ticks, but the fox declined the kind offer on the ground that his ticks were already full of blood and had ceased to annoy him much, whereas if they were removed, a new colony of ticks would establish themselves and thus entirely drain him of blood. " 'So, men of Samos,' said Aesop, 'my client will do you no further harm; he is wealthy already. If you put him to death, others will come along who are not rich, and their peculations will empty your treasury completely' " (ii.20).

Quintilian is rather scornful of fables, or at least he is less amused by them than Aristotle. "They are," he says, "adapted to attract the minds of rustic and illiterate people." He refers to the fable of the revolt of the members of the body against the belly which is said to have been used by Menenius Agrippa to reconcile the people to the senate, a story well known to readers of *Coriolanus*.

In summing up the relative value of different sorts of *exempla* Aristotle says: "Fables are suitable for addresses to popular assemblies; and they have one advantage—they are comparatively easy to invent, whereas it is hard to find parallels among actual past events. . . . But while it is easier to supply parallels by inventing fables, it is more valuable for the political speaker to supply them by quoting what has actually happened, since in most respects the future will be like what the past has been."

He advises, moreover, that examples be used as supplementary evidence after an enthymeme rather than before: "If they follow the enthymemes, they have the effect of witnesses giving evidence, and this always tells. For the same reason, if you put your examples first you must give a large number of them; if you put them last, a single one is sufficient" (ii.20).

The fictitious rhetorical example readily expanded into story and branched off from speechmaking, finding its destiny as a literary form with traces of its rhetorical origin.

PERORATION. Ancient discussions of the peroration, epilog, or conclusion are, like a good peroration itself, in general brief. Let me then briefly gather together all such statements as have before been rehearsed. All who discuss the peroration agree that in it the speaker should recapitulate, enumerate, or sum up the arguments by which he has endeavored to prove his case.[60] Quintilian warns that the enumeration should be as brief as possible, running over only the principal heads, "For if we dwell upon them, we will have not an enumeration but a sort of second speech" (vi.i.i). Cicero in the *De partitione* also warns against the childishness of too elaborate or verbatim repetition. An enumeration should be used only if important points may have escaped the memory of the audience or if the speaker may strengthen his argument by a brief recapitulation (xvii.59–60).

Aristotle has a higher regard for the value of recapitulation or at least speaks more affirmatively: "Finally you have to review what you have already said. Here you may properly do what some wrongly recommend in the introduction—repeat your points frequently so as to make them easily understood. What you should do in your introduction is to state your subject, in order that the point to be judged may be quite plain; in the epilogue you should summarize the arguments by which your case has been proved. The first step in this reviewing process is to observe that you have done what you undertook to do. You must, then, state what you have said and why you have said it" (iii.18).

These remarks seem to me to be the only possible source for the old rule-of-thumb precept for making a speech, "Tell 'em what you're going to tell 'em. Tell 'em. Then tell 'em what you've told 'em."

[60] The question is discussed in Aristotle *Rhetoric* iii.18; *Ad Herennium* ii.xxx.47; Cicero *De inventione* i.lii–lv. 98 ff. and *De partitione oratoria* xvii.59–60; Quintilian vi.i.1–8.

As to the second function of the peroration—and indeed the third and fourth, as well—there seems to be less unanimity, though most writers manage to cover much the same ground. Cicero in *De partitione oratoria* names amplification as the second, but includes appeals to the feelings (xv.52–58). Quintilian names appeals to the feelings, but gives full discussion to methods of amplifying them (vi.i.9–53). And Aristotle in his *Rhetoric* makes separate headings of conciliating the audience, amplification, and appeals to the feelings (iii.18).[61]

"The prosecutor has to rouse the judge," says Quintilian, "while the defendant's business is to soothe him." But, he adds, the reverse is sometimes true. So many of his precepts encourage restraint on the speaker's part in his efforts to rouse the feelings of the audience that one can be quite sure that he had suffered through many speeches that concluded with rant, bombast, and hysteria. Many of his stories of appeals that misfired so badly as to elicit laughter instead of tears are quite funny. He blames the absurdities on bad teaching in the schools.

But even successful appeals should be brief. "Yet our supplications for pity should not be long; as it is observed, not without reason, nothing dries sooner than tears" (vi.i.27). Cicero, in his *De inventione,* quotes this from the rhetorician Apollonius (i.lvi.109). He seems to have liked it well enough to improve on it when he urges brevity of emotional appeal in the *De partitione oratoria:* "Tears dry quickly, especially those shed for the adversities of others" (xvii.57).

Quintilian also seems aware of Cicero's views when he says: "It is admitted among all orators that a recapitulation may be made with advantage even in other parts of the speech, if the cause be complex and require to be supported by numerous arguments; while nobody doubts that there are many short and simple causes in which a recapitulation is unnecessary" (vi.i.8. Cicero *De partitione oratoria* xv.53).

[61] *Ad Herennium* gives amplification and appeals to the feelings as second and third; *De inventione* has rousing anger and pleas for pity.

The same is true of appeals to the feelings: "But all those addresses to the feelings, though they are thought by some to have a place only in the exordium and the peroration, in which indeed they are most frequently introduced, are admissible also in other parts, but more sparingly" (vi.i.51).

Quintilian perorates eloquently in the peroration of his discussion of peroration: "In the peroration, if anywhere, we may call forth all the resources of eloquence. For if we have treated the other parts successfully, we are secure of the attention of the judges at the conclusion, where, having passed the rocks and shallows on our voyage, we may expand our sails in safety; and, as amplification forms the greatest part of a peroration, we may use language of the greatest magnificence and elegance. It is then that we may shake the theater, when we come to that with which the old tragedies and comedies were concluded, *Plaudite,* 'Give us your applause.' "

Aristotle concludes the last page of his *Rhetoric,* devoted appropriately to his discussion of the peroration, with a magnificent asyndeton of four words, which, in an inadequate language such as English, can be translated only by four sentences: "I have done. You have heard me. The facts are before you. I ask for your judgment."

The Speech Situation

As I have already said, the third major aspect of rhetoric, after the speaker's resources and the speech itself, is the question or speech situation, which includes a discussion of the nature of the matter at issue, the speaker's intentions, and the adaptation of the speech to the particular audience addressed. Cicero, in the *De inventione,* attributed to Hermagoras the distinction between the thesis (*quaestio infinita*) and the cause (*quaestio finita*). The thesis is a general question, unlimited by considerations of time, place, or persons. The classical example is, "Should a man marry?"

The cause, or case in the legal sense, is a question limited by considerations of a particular time, place, and person. "Should Cato marry Marcia?" The cause is divided into three kinds: epideictic, deliberative, and judicial.

When Cicero discusses the analysis in the *De inventione,* he asserts that only the cause is the business of the orator. Let the philosophers enjoy their discussions of theses (i.vi.8). But as he acquired age and experience, Cicero changed his mind about the value and use of the thesis. In the *De oratore* he ridicules the schoolmasters who rule out the thesis or general question from oratory, "not knowing that all controversies can be related to the essence and nature of a general question. . . . Indeed, there is no cause in which the debatable issue turns on the persons involved in the suit and not on arguments related to such general questions" (ii.xxxi.133–134).

Cicero's fullest and strongest statement is that in the *Orator:* "Whenever he can, the orator will divert the controversy from particular persons and circumstances to universal abstract questions, for he can debate a genus on wider grounds than a species. Whatever is proved of the whole is of necessity proved of the part. A question thus transferred from specific persons and circumstances to a discussion of a universal genus is called a thesis. Aristotle used to have young men argue theses as an exercise, not to teach them the exact style of philosophical disputation, but the ample style of oratory" (xiv.45–46).

Quintilian refers with approval to Cicero's mature discussions of the thesis and uses Cicero as a witness against professors who hold different views. "Moreover in inquiries that relate to an individual, though it is not enough to consider the general question, yet we cannot arrive at the decision of the particular point without discussing the general question first. For how will Cato consider whether he himself ought to marry unless it be first settled whether men ought marry at all?" (iii.v.5–16.)

In the *De partitione oratoria* Cicero analyzes the thesis, which he here calls *propositum* and *consultatio,* in a way that is exceedingly fruitful and interesting. In a thesis, he points out, one may discuss matters of learning and knowing on the one hand and matters of acting and doing on the other. In discussing matters of knowing one should follow the usual procedure of first investigating the status of the question: (1; *an sit*) "Does justice exist in nature, or is it based on custom?" (2; *quid sit*) "Is justice to be defined as what is beneficial to the greatest number?" (3; *quale sit*) "Is it expedient to live justly?" The thesis must also consider questions of justice, utility, and equity in terms of degrees, of more and most, of less and least.

The thesis which discusses questions of making, doing, or acting is itself of two kinds, says Cicero. The first kind considers the theory of duty: "How should a state be administered? How should a man conduct himself in poverty? How should one pay respect to his parents?" The second kind considers how one may obtain or avoid something: "How win fame? How avoid envy? How oratory calms minds, consoles and assuages, diminishes desire; or the opposite?" One discovers arguments in the same places and arranges them in support of a thesis according to the same methods indicated for other types of question (61–68).

Thus Cicero, in enlarging on the thesis as a legitimate literary form adapted to the discussion of many questions not related to the law courts or the senate, was enabled to find a place for a number of his own literary works, including all his discussions of the nature, value, and use of oratory and his essays on duty, politics, philosophy, friendship, old age, and the nature of the gods. By the very nature and variety of his own interests he was forced, almost as Isocrates was, to take a broad view of rhetoric or the philosophy of the word and to include a great deal that Aristotle's narrow view of rhetoric excluded.

As a school exercise, thesis flourished for centuries.[62] "Should a

[62] Bonner, *Roman Declamation,* pp. 2–11.

man marry?" was debated in the English grammar schools of the seventeenth century.[63]

The limited question (*quaestio finita*) or cause was the only one treated by Aristotle and in practice the only one given full consideration in treatises on rhetoric. The three kinds of cause, as I have stated more than once before, were the epideictic, the deliberative, and the judicial. The three kinds had been practiced and discussed long before Aristotle, but the clearness of his philosophical statement established it as a norm for subsequent writers. Aristotle gives his analysis of the three kinds at the very beginning of his *Rhetoric* (1.3). Cicero in the *De partitione oratoria*—and I follow this plan—gives it at the end, after he has discussed all aspects of all kinds of public speaking. Then and then only does he discuss the differences in aim and method of the three kinds.

EPIDEICTIC. The first kind that I shall discuss is that called by Aristotle the epideictic. Baldwin translates the word as "occasional," the kind of speech that "adorns an occasion." He adds, "The kind of oratory Aristotle means is the oratory of the Gettysburg Address, of most other commemorative addresses, and of many sermons." [64] Rhys Roberts, in his version of Aristotle's *Rhetoric*, translates it as "the ceremonial oratory of display." I prefer not to translate it but to allow the meaning of this technical term to become apparent as the discussion progresses.

Aristotle said that "Rhetoric falls into three divisions, determined by three classes of listeners to speeches." The hearer of epideictic, he states, is an observer or onlooker because he is present, not to decide anything as to the justice of past happenings or the expediency of proposals for the future. If this observer decides anything, he merely decides on the orator's skill and virtuosity. "The ceremonial oratory of display either praises or censures some-

[63] D. L. Clark, *John Milton at St. Paul's School*, p. 246.
[64] Baldwin, *Ancient Rhetoric and Poetic*, p. 15 and note.

body. . . . The ceremonial orator is, properly speaking, concerned with the present, since all men praise or blame in view of the state of things existing at the time, though they often find it useful also to recall the past and to make guesses at the future. . . . Those who praise or attack a man aim at proving him worthy of honour or the reverse, and they too treat all other considerations with reference to this one. . . . Those who praise or censure a man do not consider whether his acts have been expedient or not, but often make it a ground of actual praise that he has neglected his own interest to do what was honourable" (1.3).

In a later chapter Aristotle takes up epideictic in some detail, "We now have to consider virtue and vice, the noble and the base, since these are the objects of praise and blame." He goes on to give a summary account of the noble and of virtue which must be understood if the speaker is to know on what grounds to argue. He points out also that virtue may not always be absolute in time and place. A man should be praised for those qualities or actions which are esteemed by the audience.

"The forms of virtue are justice, courage, temperance, magnificence, magnanimity, liberality, gentleness, prudence, wisdom." And he discusses each briefly as being useful to others and hence noble. The vices are opposites of the virtues. They are the things of which men feel ashamed.

If our hero is not so virtuous as he should be, or our villain so base, Aristotle suggests, "We are to assume, when we wish to praise a man or blame him, that qualities closely allied to those which he actually has are identical with them; for instance, that the cautious man is cold-blooded and treacherous, and that the stupid man is an honest fellow or the thick-skinned man is a good-tempered one. . . . Those who run to extremes will be said to possess corresponding good qualities; rashness will be called courage, and extravagance generosity" (1.9).

This cynical advice scandalized Quintilian, who quotes it with the following caveat: "This, however, the real orator, that is a good man, will never do, unless he is led to it by considerations of public good" (iii.vii.25). Other points which I have quoted from Aristotle he repeats with approval.

Among the places of argument most useful to the epideictic speaker, says Aristotle, is amplification (*auxesis*), which magnifies and heightens the effect. "Where we take our hero's actions as admitted facts, our business is simply to invest these with dignity and nobility" (1.9).

Quintilian believed that this aspect of epideictic may account for the Roman name for it—*demonstrativum*. "Praise and blame demonstrate the nature of anything (*quale sit quidque*)" (iii.iv. 14).[65] Or as he says in another context, the speeches of praise and blame turn most often on the status of quality (iii.vii.28). He agrees that the proper business of such speeches is to amplify and embellish. It is the characteristic embellishment of epideictic which he has in mind when he says that it has more of ostentation than demonstration as usually practiced (iii.iv.13). The showy inflated style of encomium is characterized by aggressive rhythm and a wealth of figures.

This stylistic exuberance of epideictic leads Cicero to omit it from his discussion in his *Orator,* as remote from the conflicts of the forum. He admits, however, the value of exercises in epideictic for the student. "It is indeed the wet nurse, as it were, of that orator we are educating. . . . By her his vocabulary is increased and a freer license in sentence structure and rhythmical arrangement is enjoyed." He dwells on the sophistic origin of the form in the stylistic extravagances of Gorgias and Thrasymachus and the more restrained artistry of Isocrates. "So I wish that those who do not esteem Isocrates would allow me to be mistaken along with Socrates and Plato. The mellifluous style, then, flowing with free rhythms, characterized by sententious point and ringing words, belongs in epideictic oratory. It is, we said, appropriate for the

[65] *Genus demonstrativum* is the name for epideictic in *Ad Herennium* i.ii.2, *De inventione* i.v.7, and Martianus Capella v.468.

sophists, better fitted for a dress parade than for a battle, not out of place as a school exercise, but despised and rejected by the forum. But since eloquence brought up on such nourishment will later on become robust and ruddy, I did not think it off the subject to devote a few words to what we may call the cradle of the orator. But this belongs to the school and to the parade. Let us now go to the front where the battle rages" (37–42).

Later in his life, in the *De partitione oratoria,* Cicero took a broader view of epideictic rhetoric, although he had chosen to discuss only one form of it, that devoted to praise and dispraise. "For there is no kind of rhetoric which can produce more copious oratory or can do more service for the state or can afford the speaker better opportunities to discourse on virtues and vices." He goes on to point out that the study and practice of epideictic oratory results in teaching the student better conduct. "The principles which guide us in praising or dispraising are valuable, not only for good public speaking, but also for honorable living" (69–70). And at the end of the section he has Cicero Junior say, "You have taught me briefly, not only how to give praise, but how to endeavor that I may be justly praised myself" (83).

The difficulty of keeping epideictic in a tight compartment isolated from other kinds of rhetoric is put clearly in Aristotle's statement, "To praise a man is in one respect akin to urging a course of action. The suggestions which would be made in the latter case become encomiums when differently expressed" (1.9).

But encomium from the earliest times had had a deliberative intention. Like the poetical encomium of Pindaric hymns, the prose encomiums of Isocrates, such as the *Evagoras,* praised the great in order to offer a noble example for others to follow in their own efforts to achieve virtue and nobility in their own lives.[66]

DELIBERATIVE. The rhetoric devoted to urging an audience to do or not to do something, as expedient or inexpedient in the future,

[66] Jaeger, *Paideia,* III, 86.

Aristotle in his *Rhetoric* thought of as political, although he grants that private counselors utilize the same rhetorical means as do speakers who address public assemblies (1.3). But it was Isocrates who pointed out the broader implications of deliberation when he said in *Antidosis,* "The same arguments which we use in persuading others when we speak in public we employ also when we deliberate in our thoughts" (257).

Since Roman rhetoricians habitually use the term deliberative (*genus deliberativum*), I shall prefer it to Aristotle's term political as a name for the rhetoric which persuades or dissuades in regard to future action.

Aristotle, who tends to restrict his discussion to political debate, first points out that the political orator does not offer counsel concerning things which exist inevitably or things which occur naturally or accidentally. "Clearly counsel can only be given on matters about which people deliberate, matters namely that ultimately depend on ourselves" (1.4). The debatable subjects which depend on our action he lists as finance, war and peace, national defense, imports and exports, and legislation, about which the political speaker should be well informed.

He next discusses the nature of happiness, because happiness is the aim and end determining what people choose or avoid. This discussion is not idealistic. It describes what most people in the audience will agree is happiness, based on the possession of such goods as friends, wealth, good children, happy old age, health, beauty, strength, fame, and virtue. These are the ends that all the world desires. "Deliberation seeks to determine not ends but means to ends," Aristotle adds (1.6). People will deliberate what is the most useful or expedient means of attaining the ends which all agree are good. Or if "the people agree that two things are both useful but do not agree about which is the more so, the next step will be to treat of relative goodness and relative utility" (1.7).

Finally the political orator must understand the form of government under which people live: democracy, oligarchy, aristocracy, monarchy. "The most important and effective qualification for success in persuading audiences and speaking well on public affairs is to understand all the forms of government and to discriminate their various customs, institutions, and interests. For all men are persuaded by considerations of their interest, and their interest lies in the maintenance of the established order" (1.8). Or we might add today, "or its overthrow."

Aristotle concludes that he has dealt with ethics and politics "only to the extent demanded by the present occasion; a detailed account of the subject has been given in the Politics" (*Rhetoric* 1.8; *Politics* iii, iv).

Cicero, in the *De partitione oratoria,* takes very much the same ground as Aristotle. The end sought by deliberation is utility—something desired by the audience. The steps to be taken by the pleader are these. First he asks, Is the suggested course of action possible? If it is not possible there is no debate. If the course is possible, deliberation can go forward. Second he asks, Is the course of action necessary? This is to be understood in the sense of indispensable to security or liberty, for if it can be shown to be necessary, we need not consider whether it be honorable or useful. And if a course of action be considered of the greatest importance it may be deemed virtually necessary. Next can the proposed course of action be shown to be useful or expedient in a material way? Can it be shown to be useful in a moral or honorable sense? (83–89.) Here he points out that the real debate will occur when material expediency and honor are in conflict, when duty and inclination come to the grapple. "As a speech must be adapted, not alone to the truth, but also to the opinions held by the audience, we must first realize that people are of two kinds, one uneducated and uncultivated who prefer utility to honor, and the other humane and cultivated who place honor above all things" (90). He proceeds to analyze the causes and motives for action and emphasizes the need of precedents in amplifying any case.

This whole treatment by Cicero is concerned with deliberative rhetoric as a function of legislation in the senate, of which he was a member. We would be surprised if it were not. Whereas Quintilian, as we shall see, had his eye on the school rather than the senate. Moreover, like Cicero, he differed from Aristotle, who considered that expediency or the useful was the only topic of deliberation, in assuming that the topics are three.

The same topics of deliberation supply arguments both for actual deliberative oratory and for the school exercise of the suasoria. In discussing the school exercises Quintilian says of the topics of deliberation: "That these three topics do not enter into every subject of suasoria is too evident to need explanation. Many teachers, however, declare that there are more than three topics. But the topics they would add are readily seen to be included under the three. Thus lawfulness, justice, piety, equity, and mercy, with whatever like virtues one may add, are included under honor. On the other hand if the question turns on whether a thing is easy, important, pleasant, free from danger, it is included under the topic of expediency. These subtopics come into play when we meet opposition. 'It is indeed expedient, but it is difficult, unimportant, unpleasant, dangerous.' . . . Often, too, we say that expediency should be disregarded so that we may do what is honorable . . . or again that we should prefer expediency to honor . . . but even in this case we must not admit that this course is dishonorable. . . . Nor is what is expedient to be compared only with what is inexpedient. Two advantages may be compared so that we may choose the greater—or of two disadvantages, that we may choose the less. On the other hand in a suasoria there can never be any discussion if the evidence is all on our side. For, if there is no place for contradiction, what reason can there be for discussion? Thus almost every suasoria is based on nothing but a weighing of one side against another, and we must consider what we would attain and by what means so that we may estimate whether there is greater advantage in what we pursue or greater disadvantage in the means by which we pursue it. Expediency may also depend on a question of time. (It is expedient, but not now); or of place (not here); or of persons (not for us, not against them); or of a mode of proceeding (it is expedient, but not thus); or of degree (it is expedient, but not to this extent)" (III.viii. 26–35).[67]

Thus Quintilian explores the methods of discovering the arguments (*inventio*) which may be used for or against any line of action in school or out. Milton in the *Areopagitica* built his whole argument against censorship of books on the three topics of deliberation. The licensing act, he said, should be repealed because: (1) censorship of books is impossible to enforce (people print them anyhow); (2) it is dishonorable (as a papistical invention); (3) it is inexpedient (as interfering with the search for and discovery of truth). C. S. Lewis, in *The Screwtape Letters,* believes that here and now we should guide our conduct thereby. Screwtape says of God: "The Enemy [of evil] loves platitudes. Of a proposed course of action He wants men to ask very simple questions. 'Is it righteous? Is it prudent? Is it possible?' Instead men ask: 'Is it in accordance with the general movement of our time? Is it progressive or reactionary? Is that the way history is going?' questions which are unanswerable." [68] This discovery of arguments as outlined by Quintilian for schools, as applied by Milton in oratory, and as applied by Lewis to the conduct of private life is essential if the thinker is to have sound counsel for himself or for others.

JUDICIAL. As epideictic rhetoric endeavors to demonstrate virtue or vice in the present and deliberative rhetoric debates the expediency of actions proposed for the future, so judicial rhetoric (*genus judicale*) debates the justice of past actions. It is the forensic rhetoric of the advocate, who attacks an opponent or defends

---

[67] Cf. Aristotle *Rhetoric* 1.3; III.17; *Ad Herennium* III.1–9.
[68] Lewis, *The Screwtape Letters* (London, 1942), p. 129.

his client in the courts of law. As judicial rhetoric was the earliest of the three kinds, it remained the most important in the forum and the schools and occupies the greatest space in ancient text-books. Most of the rhetorical precepts which I have reported earlier in this chapter have been precepts for the practice of judicial rhet-oric. Thus although status may be applied to the investigation of questions which might arise in all kinds of rhetoric, it is especially useful in investigating judicial cases. Likewise the division of a speech into five parts is strictly applicable only to judicial questions. Consequently, since the problems of judicial rhetoric occupy the largest space of this book, they will receive very little space here. I shall endeavor no more than to present briefly Aristotle's phil-osophical and psychological views.

"There are three things we must ascertain," he states in his *Rhetoric,* "first, the nature and number of the incentives to wrong-doing; second, the state of mind of wrongdoers; third, the kinds of persons who are wronged."

Aristotle first considers the incentives or motives which cause people to do wrong to others: "For it is plain that the prosecutor must consider, out of all the aims that can ever induce us to do wrong to our neighbors, how many, and which, affect his ad-versary; while the defendant must consider how many, and which, do not affect him" (1.10). He finds seven causes for action: chance, nature, compulsion, habit, reasoning, anger, or appetite. All of these he analyzes as possible causes for wrongdoing. As appetite is the cause of all actions which appear pleasant, he dis-cusses pleasure and pain as causes of unjust action (1.11).

Having thus given a brief psychology of motivation to help the advocate find probable arguments for or against a person suspected of wrongdoing, he takes up the state of mind of those who do wrong. "They must suppose that the thing can be done and done by them; either that they can do it without being found out, or if they are found out they can escape being punished." These psychological quirks of the criminal mind he discusses in detail, always bearing in mind the usefulness of this knowledge to the advocate.

When Aristotle proceeds to the kind of people to whom wrong is done, he points out that they are those who have something which the wrongdoer wants, either necessities or luxuries. They are those who are trustful, easygoing, sensitive, frightened. "A man may wrong his enemies, because that is pleasant; he may equally wrong his friends, because that is easy" (1.12).

Since Aristotle defines wrongdoing as "injury voluntarily inflicted, contrary to law," he gives careful attention to laws, written ordinances and unwritten, particular law and universal law, the letter of the law and equity, the wording of a contract and the intentions of the contracting parties. These matters are important, because almost any issue that may come before a court is likely to involve a conflict of law and equity or the like. As I shall point out later, the controversiae debated in the schools of rhetoric almost always turn on these conflicts of law and equity, the letter of a contract and its intention, or upon conflicting laws. The student received thorough practice in the application of the principles.

Although these precepts of ancient rhetoric are clearly designed primarily to train boys and young men to win audiences by addressing them orally in public, we must recall that from the earliest times, these precepts also guided those who addressed the public in writing. The epistles of St. Paul and Seneca, whether read aloud to groups or passed from hand to hand in manuscript, derive their structure and style from the same precepts of rhetoric as do the speeches of Demosthenes or Cicero. So do the verse epistles of Horace and the political, moral, and philosophical essays (or "written speeches") of Isocrates and Cicero. Indeed all ancient literature, verse and prose, was ransacked by the professors of grammar and rhetoric to furnish models of rhetorical style for schoolboys; and the precepts of style elaborated by the rhetoricians guided all writers of Greek and Latin, who in their boyhood had received instruction in the schools of grammar and rhetoric. The same dependence on the rhetorical precepts for style pervades Renaissance Latin and vernacular literature, which cannot properly be understood by one unfamiliar with ancient precepts as repeated by humanist rhetoricians and taught in humanist schools.

Hence the value of ancient rhetorical precept to the modern teacher is by no means limited to the teacher of speech or public address. The precepts are equally valuable to all who teach expository and persuasive writing, freshman composition, or communications. The modern teacher should appraise them, weigh them, reject as well as accept. Thus he will recognize that they offer little or no help in classes in playwriting or storywriting.

I hope that this summary treatment of the precepts of ancient rhetoric will show how the school exercises taught the boys to put them in practice. In the schools, of course, the precepts were not exhaustively presented before the boys did the exercises, but were introduced bit by bit in showing how the models chosen for imitation exemplified them.

V. IMITATION

WHEN Robert Louis Stevenson described himself as "playing the sedulous ape" to other writers in order to learn to write, he was using a neat phrase to describe an activity which must be as old as art itself. Artists have always imitated other artists. "Indeed," as Quintilian says, "the whole conduct of life is based on the desire of doing ourselves what we approve in others . . . thus musicians follow the voice of their teachers, painters look for models to the works of preceding painters, and farmers adopt the system approved by experience" (x.ii.2–8).

But he goes on sensibly to point out that imitation is not sufficient in itself. It is only one way of learning. If no one ever invented and experimented, there would be no improvement in the arts, and if artists did not improve on their predecessors we would still be sailing on rafts. But the ancient world was less inclined than we to approve innovations because of their newness or to abandon good things because they are old. The apostle was a good Roman when he said, "Prove all things; hold fast that which is good" (1 Thes. 5.21). In art, imitation is one technic of holding fast that which is good. Another technic, that of precept, has already been explained. Precept tells the learner what to do. Imitation shows him how others have done it. Precept gives rules based on successful past experience. Imitation gives models or examples to follow. Precept says, "Be industrious." Imitation says, "Consider the ant." This chapter will treat of imitation as a means of training young people in improved command of language in thinking, writing, and speaking and as a method of guiding mature literary artists to a flexible mastery of structure and style.

In antiquity the word imitation (*mimesis*) was used by such writers on art as Plato, Aristotle, and Plutarch with a number of different meanings. It might mean, for instance, imitation of men in action, imitation of ideal truth, imitation of appearances, true or false, in the phenomenal world. But imitation as a way of learning to practice an art has nothing to do with these metaphysical notions of the objects of imitation. Specifically, imitation as a guide to speakers and writers, as a rhetorical exercise, is concerned, not with the speaker's or writer's matter, but with his manner of speaking or writing. It is concerned, not with what he says, but with how he says it.[1]

The distinction can be well illustrated by Cicero's use of Aristotle. In a letter Cicero says that he composed his *De oratore* "in the Aristotelian manner" (*Aristotelio more*). Although no Aristotelian dialogs survive, we may accept Cicero's word that he was imitating Aristotle's literary method of writing dialogs. In the next sentence of the same letter Cicero says that he has "expressed in writing" the oratorical theories of Isocrates and Aristotle. This second activity is not imitation at all, but fair use of literary matter in the public domain (*Ad familiares* i.9.23).

In his *De inventione* (II.1-4) Cicero says that he adopts the best from previous writers on rhetoric just as Zeuxis painted his famous Helen by using as models the five most beautiful girls in Crotona. Here again Cicero, in adopting the theories of earlier writers on rhetoric, was making fair use of material in the public domain. Zeuxis was in part imitating the appearances of the girls and in part imitating an ideal of feminine beauty abstracted from observation of these and other beautiful girls. But in so far as Cicero was imitating Zeuxis he was imitating his eclecticism in assem-

[1] The metaphysical notions of imitation are clearly differentiated by Richard McKeon, "Literary Criticism and the Concept of Imitation in Antiquity," *Modern Philology*, XXXIV, No. 1 (August, 1936), 1-35.

bling in one composition material of different origins. Cicero was imitating his artistic methods.

Closely related to imitation as a method of teaching students to speak and write is imitation as a method of teaching them manners and morals. The teacher of literature in antiquity had both ends in view when he read great poetry with boys: to give them literary models to imitate in their speaking and writing and to give them models of morals and manners to imitate in their lives. As Protagoras says in the Platonic dialog which bears his name: "And when the boy has learned his letters . . . they put into his hands the works of great poets which he reads at school; in these are contained many admonitions and many tales and praises and encomia of ancient famous men which he is required to learn by heart, in order that he may imitate or emulate them and desire to be like them" (325–326).

Polybius extended the same view to the reading of history. "History," he says in the preface to his *Universal History,* "is only interesting as an object lesson in political theory and moral conduct" (1.i).

Literary and rhetorical imitation must be carefully distinguished, not only from fair use, or borrowing, but from unfair use, or plagiarism. Today, as in antiquity, imitation and borrowing and plagiarism are not the same. Fair use of other people's writings, then as now, involved acknowledgement. "The secret and unacknowledged appropriation of another's thoughts and words" is plagiarism (*furta*).[2] It was Martial who first used the word *plagiarius* (kidnapper) to denote a literary thief, one "Fidentius" who had claimed certain of Martial's poems as his own (*Epigrams* i.52, 53). As Cicero says in *Brutus,* apostrophizing the ancient poet Ennius, who had generously used the work of his predecessor Naevius, "As for you, if you acknowledge it, you have borrowed (*sumpsisti*) so much from Naevius, or if you deny it, have stolen it (*surripuisti*)" (xix.76). Demetrius, *On Style,* makes a similar

[2] D'Alton, *Roman Literary Theory and Criticism,* p. 428.

distinction: "A touch of poetic diction adds to the elevation of prose. . . . Still some writers imitate the poets quite crudely. Or rather, they do not imitate them, but transfer them to their pages as Herodotus has done. Thucydides acts otherwise. Even if he does borrow something from a poet, he uses it in his own way and so makes it his own property" (II.112–113). Herodotus had taken over whole phrases from Homer. Thucydides had taken the epithet "wave-encompassed" which Homer had used for Crete and had applied it to Sicily, and in a far different context.

The Value of Imitation

That imitating his elders and betters does help a student to improve whatever ability he has was universally believed in antiquity. The earliest surviving written statement [3] is that of Isocrates, who in *Against the Sophists* says that the teacher must not only expound the principles of the art, but "must in himself set such an example of oratory that the students who have taken form under his instruction and are able to pattern after him will, from the outset, show in their speaking a degree of grace and charm which is not found in others" (17–18). Jaeger points out that Isocrates' published speeches were intended as models not only of content but also of form.[4]

In a famous passage of the *De oratore* Cicero tells how young Sulpicius Rufus improved his natural gifts for oratory by imitating Crassus. To overcome his hurried delivery and redundant style Antonius had urged Sulpicius "to consider the forum as his school for improving himself, and to choose whom he pleased for a master; if he would take my advice, Lucius Crassus." Scarce a year elapsed when Antonius again heard Sulpicius speak. "It is incredible what a difference there appeared to me between him as he was then and as he had been a year before; nature herself led

---

[3] Atkins, *Literary Criticism in Antiquity*, I, 128.
[4] Jaeger, *Paideia*, III, 54, 67, 134.

him irresistibly into the magnificent and noble style of Crassus; but he could never have arrived at a satisfactory degree of excellence in it if he had not directed his efforts by study and imitation in the same course in which nature led him, so as intently to contemplate Crassus with his whole mind and faculties" (II.xxi. 88–89).

But the Greek and Roman boy could learn by imitating not only speakers whom he heard but writers whom he read. In *The Way to Write History,* Lucian of Samosata is typical of antiquity; he takes it for granted that the power of expression is learned by exercise and by studious imitation. "My perfect historian must start with two indispensable qualifications: the one is historical insight, the other the faculty of expression. The first is a gift of nature, which can never be learnt; the second should have been acquired by long practice, unremitting toil, and loving study of the classics" (34). But with tasteless imitation, or rather the theft or borrowing of actual words or phrases from Thucydides and Herodotus, Lucian has no patience.

Imitation was also valued by St. Augustine, who believed that the preacher, as well as the legal advocate and the historian, could learn by imitation. He distinguishes between the value of the study of the precepts of rhetoric for the young student and the greater value of models for imitation by older students preparing themselves to preach. "If one has a keen and fervid talent, he will more easily acquire eloquence by reading and hearing the eloquent than by following the precepts of eloquence" (*De doctrina Christiana* IV.iii).

"Longinus," in analyzing those elements which contribute to elevation of style (or sublimity), in poetry as well as prose, asserts the value of imitation as another road to its attainment. "What manner of road is this? Zealous imitation of the great historians and poets of the past. For many are carried away by the inspiration of another . . . from the natural genius of those old writers there flows into the hearts of their admirers as it were an emanation from the mouth of holiness." And he praises Plato's imitations of Homer. "Plato, who has irrigated his style with ten thousand runnels from the great Homeric spring" (XIII.2–3). I shall conclude the passage from "Longinus" with the words of Dryden's spirited translation (and condensation). "We ought not to regard a good imitation as a theft, but as a beautiful idea of him who undertakes to imitate, by forming himself on the invention and the work of another man; for he enters the lists like a new wrestler, to dispute the prize with the former champion. This sort of emulation, says Hesiod, is honorable, when we combat for victory with a hero, and are not without glory even in our overthrow. Those great men, whom we propose to ourselves as patterns for our imitation, serve us as a torch, which is lifted up before us, to enlighten our passage, and often elevate our thoughts, as high as the conceptions we have of our author's genius." [5]

From Isocrates in 390 B.C. to St. Augustine in c. 400 A.D. belief in the value of imitation was undeviating. It is common knowledge that imitation of the classics received even greater emphasis in the Renaissance than it had in the postclassical age. Indeed, the Renaissance almost killed imitation by overemphasis. But when it is intelligently used, as it was used in ancient times, imitation will continue to be a great aid to anyone who sets about learning to practice any art.

Dionysius of Halicarnassus wrote three books on imitation, all now lost save fragments. In a letter which does survive, Dionysius says that the first book was on the nature of imitation, the second on what writers should be imitated, and the third on how to imitate (*Epistula ad Pompeium* III).[6]

[5] From the "Preface to Troilus and Cressida," in *Essays of John Dryden* (edited by W. P. Ker, 2 vols., Oxford, 1900), I, 206.

[6] See also W. Rhys Roberts, Introduction to Dionysius of Halicarnassus, *Three Literary Letters*, pp. 27–30; Bonner, *Literary Treatises of Dionysius of Halicarnassus*, pp. 39–48.

I have now completed my discussion of the nature of imitation and shall proceed to a discussion of the best models for imitation and methods of imitation approved in ancient times.

Whom to Imitate

If one is to learn by imitating, certainly the choice of models is of the greatest importance, and certainly the effort should be made to choose the best. But what are the best? To answer that question the ancient orators and the professors of literature and of rhetoric applied themselves assiduously. Most of what we call literary criticism in Greece and Rome was produced in an endeavor to discover the best models for imitation. This critical effort was not disinterested. It was pedagogically directed toward producing new generations of distinguished speakers and writers.

One of the first questions to arise was: Shall we imitate the ancients or the moderns?—which authors are the better models, the classic or the contemporary? We should not forget that the Greeks and Romans were as addicted to classicism as the English in the age of Anne. For classicism in any age is rooted in tradition and in veneration of the glories of the past. The great literary classics which all boys read in school naturally became models for their own speaking and writing. Thus Seneca the father writing to his sons: "My boys, you do what is necessary and useful when, not satisfied with models of your own day, you wish to know those of an earlier time, first because the more models you study, the more progress you will make in eloquence . . . then you can estimate to what degree oratorical ability diminishes from day to day and how, by I don't know what sort of iniquity of nature, eloquence deteriorates" (*Controversiae* i. Praef. 6).

But long before there was any Seneca or any Roman oratory Isocrates had said: "And it is my opinion that the study of the philosophy which deals with oratory would make a great advance if we should admire and honour, not those who make the first be-

ginnings in their crafts, but those who are the most finished
craftsmen in each, and not those who speak on subjects on which
no one has spoken before, but those who know how to speak as no
one else could" (*Panegyricus* 10).

Of course Isocrates knew that he was a classic in his own age
and had announced that students should take their teacher as a
model. Cicero too, as quoted earlier in this chapter, showed how
Sulpicius had learned eloquence by imitating his older contemporary Crassus. And, of course, if one is endeavoring to improve
his own speech and oral delivery by imitation, he must imitate
living speakers. Thus Cicero in the *De oratore* advises imitating
"not only orators, but even actors, lest by vicious habits we contract any awkwardness or ungracefulness" (i.xxxiv.156). And immediately after his story about Sulpicius, Cicero points out that
the successive schools of ancient Greek oratory were characterized
by imitation of some particularly outstanding older contemporary
or recently flourishing speaker (ii.xxii–xxiii.92–96). Cicero, of
course, was a great speaker and like Isocrates a classic in his own
day, well worthy of imitation and fit to be the leader of a school
of oratory. And he knew it.

Quintilian, as could be expected, saw the advantage of imitating
both the ancients and the moderns. In discussing what is to be
gained from reading the old writers in grammar school he points
out that although they were stronger in genius than in art, there
are many things the boys may gain from imitating them. "Above
all things they will help the boy acquire a wide vocabulary (*copia
verborum*). . . . There will be seen in them, too, a more careful
regard for structure than in most of the moderns. . . . Purity, certainly, and manliness are to be gained from them, since we ourselves have fallen into all the vices of refinement, even in our
manner of speaking" (i.viii.8–9).

In a later book, still speaking of the schooling of boys, he adds:
"What authors ought to be read by beginners? Some have recommended inferior writers, as they thought them easier of compre-

hension; others have advocated the more florid kind of writers as being better adapted to nourish the minds of the young. For my part I would have the best authors commenced at once and read always; but I would choose the clearest in style and most intelligible. . . . Cicero, as it seems to me, is agreeable even to beginners and sufficiently intelligible, and may not only profit but even be loved; and next to Cicero, as Livy advises, such authors as most resemble Cicero."

Quintilian takes up the question of the ancients and the moderns quite fully. His appraisal is so well balanced and so sensible that I shall reproduce it in full despite its length: "There are two points in style on which I think that the greatest caution should be used with boys. One is that no teacher, from being too much an admirer of antiquity, should allow their style to stiffen from the reading of the Gracchi, Cato, and other like authors; for they would thus become uncouth and dry, since they cannot, as yet, understand their force of thought, and, content with adapting their style, which, at the time it was written, was doubtless excellent, but is quite unsuitable to our day, they will appear to themselves to resemble those eminent men. The opposite danger is lest, captivated with the flowers of modern affectation, they should be so seduced by a corrupt pleasure as to love that luscious style which is more agreeable to the minds of boys in proportion as it is puerile. When their taste is formed, however, and out of danger of being corrupted, I should recommend them to read not only the ancients, from whom our present style will receive additional grace, but also the writers of the present day, in whom there is much merit. . . . It will be possible, therefore, to select from the moderns many qualities for imitation, but care must be taken that they be not contaminated with other qualities with which they are mixed. Yet that there have been recently, and are now, many whom we may imitate entirely I would not only allow but affirm. But who they are is not for everybody to decide. There is less

danger of erring in regard to earlier writers. And I would therefore defer the reading of the moderns, lest the student imitate before he is qualified to judge" (ii.v.15–26).

Quintilian, it would seem, would not encourage the modern
college student to form his style on English prose before Dryden,
nor would he encourage any passion to imitate the mannerisms of
his contemporary literary idol. Alexander Pope in his *Essay on
Criticism* was soundly in the tradition of Quintilian when he wrote:

> In words, as fashions, the same rule will hold;
> Alike fantastic, if too new, or old:
> Be not the first by whom the new are tried,
> Nor yet the last to lay the old aside.
>   —Lines 333–336

Besides the war between the ancients and the moderns, which,
I suppose, will never end, there was the war over the question
whether the student should imitate one model or many. In antiquity the quarrel never became so acrimonious as it did in the
Renaissance, when the issue was drawn over the imitation of
Cicero.[7] But the issue of one model or many was raised in antiquity and thoroughly discussed.

Cicero himself lent a great deal of authority to the arguments
in favor of imitating one man—at least for the young student.
Sulpicius was shown successfully imitating Crassus. In the same
passage Cicero continues: "Let this, then, be the first of my precepts, to point out to the student whom he should imitate, and in
such a manner that he may most carefully copy the chief excellences of him whom he takes for his model. Let practice then
follow, by which he may represent in his imitation the exact resemblance of him whom he chose as his pattern; not as I have
known many imitators do, who endeavor to acquire by imitation
what is easy, or what is remarkable, or almost faulty. . . . He

---

[7] Scott, *Controversies over the Imitation of Cicero.*

who shall act as he ought must first of all be very careful in making this choice, and must use the utmost diligence to attain the chief excellences of him whom he has approved."

Cicero supports his contention by a brief summary of the shifting styles in classic Greek oratory: "What, let me ask, do you conceive to be the reason why almost every age has produced a peculiar style of speaking? . . . The most ancient speakers . . . are Pericles and Alcibiades, and in the same age Thucydides, writers clear, pointed, concise, abounding more in thoughts than in words. It could not possibly have happened that they should all have the same character, unless they had proposed to themselves some one model for imitation. Then behold Isocrates arose, the master of all rhetoricians, from whose school none but real heroes proceeded. . . . Those and many others differ in genius, but in their manner bear a strong resemblance both to each other and to their master; and those who applied themselves to law suits (*causae*), as Demosthenes, Hyperides, Aeschines . . . and a multitude of others, although they were dissimilar in abilities one to another, yet were all engaged in imitating the same kind of natural eloquence; and so long as the imitation of their manner lasted, so long did that character and system of eloquence prevail. . . . So there has always been some one whom the majority desired to resemble" (*De oratore* II.90–96).

Whether one or many should be imitated, common sense would indicate that a student cannot possibly imitate more than one model at a time, lest he expire like the fabled chameleon that broke into bits trying to adjust his color to those of a Scotch tartan. The student may, however, in his exercises imitate different models at different times. Certainly the consensus of antiquity was against the continued or slavish imitation of one model. After his schooldays Cicero did not tie himself to imitation of any one man. And Quintilian, in his tenth book, addressing mature speakers who have completed their formal schooling, is firmly against it: "I should not advise anyone to devote himself entirely to any one model so as to imitate him in all respects. Of all the Greek orators Demosthenes is by far the most perfect. Yet others, on some occasions, have spoken better. But he who most deserves to be imitated is not the only one to be imitated. 'What then,' the reader may ask, 'is it not sufficient to speak on every subject as Cicero spoke?' To me, assuredly, it would be sufficient, if I could attain all his excellences. Yet what disadvantage would it be to assume occasionally the energy of Caesar, the asperity of Caelius, the accuracy of Pollio, the judgment of Calvus? For apart from the fact that a wise student should if possible make whatever is excellent in each author his own, it is also to be considered that if, in a matter of such difficulty as imitation, we fix our attention on only one model, scarcely any one portion of his excellence will allow us to become masters of it. Accordingly, since it is almost denied to human ability to copy fully the pattern we have chosen, let us set before our eyes the excellences of several, that different qualities from different writers may fix themselves in our minds and that we may adopt for any occasion the style that is most suitable to it" (x.ii.24-26).

Seneca, writing to his boys, neatly sums up the argument against imitating one model and at the same time points out that imitation alone will not make a great speaker or writer: "Nor is one man to be imitated, no matter how eminent he may be, for the imitation can never equal the model. That's the way things are: the similitude always falls short of the real thing" (*Controversiae* I. Praef. 6).

In seeking models for imitation, ancient or modern, one or many, the ancient critics and teachers and speakers and writers were seeking excellence. The student was constantly urged to imitate the excellences of his model or models and was constantly urged to avoid the faults and mannerisms which ancient as well as modern artists were recognized as having. But what are the chief excellences which the student should imitate in his models?

As I have intimated, the philosophers and the critics were not in complete accord as to what are the excellences of structure and style which the student should strive to attain. Then as now different people admired different qualities in style. "Some like them plain; some like them colored."

The issue was joined in Cicero's day under the banners of Atticism and Asianism. The leading Atticists in Rome were Calvus and Brutus, who advocated an oratorical style that was plain, simple, and lucid, with a minimum of rhetorical ornament, rhythm, and emotional appeal. As models for imitation they set up the Athenian writers Thucydides, Lysias, and Xenophon. They accused their opponents, who employed an ornate style, of Asianism—that is, of having been corrupted by the bad taste and opulence of Asiatic degeneracy. The Atticist movement was an attack on Cicero, whose style was copious, rhythmical, and emotional. Cicero met the attack in two of his most delightful essays on oratory, the *Brutus* and the *Orator*.[8]

The *Brutus* is in the form of a dialog in which Brutus, Pomponius Atticus, and Cicero are represented as interlocutors. The *Orator* is in the form of an epistle addressed to Brutus. Although they are both controversial treatises attacking the Atticism of Brutus, both maintain a charming note of friendship and urbanity. The *Brutus* follows a chronological plan. In the dialog Cicero surveys Greek eloquence and then proceeds to a much fuller account of Roman oratory and Roman orators down to his own day, pointing out for praise the development in oratorical prose of a richer, more brilliant style, characterized by perfection of finish. Here and in the *Orator* he points out that Isocrates and Demosthenes were quite as Athenian as Lysias; and he urges for imitation a rhythmical prose which commands periodic structure and figurative language. At the same time he takes as severe an attitude as the Atticists toward "Asiatic" bombast and meretricious bad taste. Cicero places himself on the middle ground between the

[8] See Hendrickson's and Hubbell's introductions to their translations of *Brutus* and *Orator* in Loeb Classical Library.

extremes of the florid on the one hand and the austere on the other.

Thus in ancient discussions of the best models for imitation we see in operation the skillful application of the most precise methods of literary criticism seeking to discover and to know the best that had been said and written. Today we are likely to assume that the literary critic should stop with analysis and appreciation. He should function, it is thought, in a world of contemplation and understanding, not in a world of action and of practice. But the critics of Greece and Rome thought of themselves first as teachers. They planned that their analyses and appreciation of literature should carry over into imitation and thus into improved literary practice.

As "Longinus," that great figure in ancient literary criticism, puts it: "In every systematic treatise there are two requisites: the author must first define his subject; and secondly, though this is really more important, he must show us by what means of study we may reach the goal ourselves" (i.i).

How to Imitate

The author of the treatise *Ad Herennium* tells us, "Imitation impels us *to employ a studious method* to be similar to someone in speaking" (i.ii.3), the italics are mine. For the ancient teachers were better aware than are most teachers today that the benefits of imitation do not just happen. They must be achieved by the employment not only of one studious method but of several. We shall now consider the methods employed by Greek and Roman teachers who used imitation as one of the means of teaching rhetoric.

The first means was careful analysis of the model, an analysis intended to point out the excellences and the faults of structure and style in the model, with an explanation of the means used by the author of the model in achieving them. The teacher offered his analyses either in textbooks or in treatises or in lectures. Undoubtedly the instruction by lecture far outweighed the instruction by treatise. But a number of treatises survive, and we can in them see how analysis of a model contributed to teaching.

The author of the *Ad Herennium* believed that the writer of textbooks should himself be a model of eloquence. "First of all whatever models a writer on an art exhibits should be his own production. . . . Would it not be ridiculous if a teacher who offers to teach eloquence to others should seek his models from others? That is not the way Chares studied sculpture with Lysippus. Lysippus did not show him a head by Myron, an arm by Praxiteles, a breast by Polycletus. Rather the student saw the master himself make all these parts. The works of others he could study for himself" (iv.vi.9). Hence all of the model sentences which are used as illustrations of the various figures of speech in Book iv were claimed by the teacher who wrote the book. Such self-sufficiency on the part of the author of a textbook on rhetoric was, however, as unusual in antiquity as it is today. Indeed our author adapted many of his models from other writers.

Aristotle, in his *Rhetoric,* advocates and explains the periodic style. In the following passage all the illustrative sentences he offers as models for imitation are quoted from the *Panegyricus* of Isocrates, who had first developed and taught this balanced period:

"The periodic style which is divided into members is of two kinds. It is either simply divided, as in

> I have often wondered at the conveners of national gatherings and the founders of athletic contests

or it is antithetical, where, in each of the two members, one of one pair of opposites is put along with one of another pair, or the same word is used to bracket two opposites, as

> They aided both parties, not only those who stayed behind but those who accompanied them: for the latter they acquired new territory larger than that at home, and to the former they left territory at home that was large enough.

Here the contrasted words are 'staying behind' and 'accompany-ing,' 'enough' and 'larger.' So in the example,

> Both in those who want to get property and to those who desire to enjoy it

where 'enjoyment' is contrasted with 'getting.' Again:

> It often happens in such enterprises that the wise men fail and the fools succeed.
>
> They were awarded the prize of valor immediately, and won the command of the sea not long afterward.
>
> Some of them perished in misery, others were saved in disgrace.
>
> . . . to possess in life or to bequeath at death.

All these passages have the structure described above. Such a form of speech is satisfying, because the significance of contrasted ideas is easily felt, especially when they are thus put side by side. Such, then, is the nature of antithesis" (III.9).

After such appreciative analysis of model sentences the student is well prepared to imitate the model by composing sentences which have the same antithetical pattern. Students in my own classes have found the composition of such sentences as exciting as crossword puzzles. But unless the student is directed to compose some sentences which imitate the structural pattern of the model sentences, the reading of such an analysis as Aristotle's will not carry over into the student's own speaking and writing.

The same technic of analysis and appreciation was applied to poetry by writers on rhetoric and literary criticism. The result aimed at was not so much imitation by other poets as imitation of those methods of composition which might be appropriate to rhe-torical prose. It is ironical that the only two surviving major odes of Sappho owe their survival to two rhetoricians who quoted them with appreciative analysis in their treatises. Dionysius of Hali-carnassus had a literary theory that the arrangement of words in rhythmical groups contributed more to finish and charm of style than the choice of words. Whereupon he quotes Sappho and shows in some detail that in the *Hymn to Aphrodite* there is not a single instance of a word ending with a vowel when the next word begins with one. He points out that the style of Isocrates has the same smoothness in prose. This careful avoidance of hiatus is a stylistic virtue, he thinks, to be imitated by any writer who wishes to avoid harshness (*De compositione verborum* xxiii).

"Longinus" quotes the other ode for a different rhetorical purpose. He is pointing out that elevation of style is furthered by selecting appropriate constituent elements and fusing them into an organic whole. In his comment he says: "Sappho, for instance, never fails to take the emotions incident to the passion of love from the symptoms which accompany it in real life. And wherein does she show her excellence? In the skill with which she selects and combines the most striking and intense of those symptoms:

> I think him God's peer that sits near thee face to face and listens to thy sweet speech
>> and lovely laughter.
> 'Tis this that makes my heart flutter in my breast. If I see thee but for a little, my voice comes no more
>> and my tongue is broken.
> At once a delicate flame runs through my limbs; my eyes are blinded
>> and my ears thunder.
> The sweat pours down: shivers hunt me all over. I am grown paler than grass and very near to death I feel.

"Is it not wonderful how she summons at the same time, soul, body, hearing, tongue, sight, colour, all as though they had wandered off apart from herself? She feels contradictory sensations, freezes, burns, raves, reasons—for one that is at the point of death is clearly beside herself. She wants to display not a single emotion but a whole congress of emotions. Lovers all show such symptoms as these, but what gives supreme merit to her art is, as I said, the skill with which she chooses the most striking and combines them into a single whole" (x.1–3).

How many Greek and Roman orators learned to select and combine emotional symptoms by imitating Sappho's literary methods, as "Longinus" analyzes them, we cannot know. But when "Longinus" became available to readers in the Renaissance, we do know that Ben Jonson learned by imitating her. In *The New Inn* the lovesick lady in the play speaks as follows:

> Thou dost not know my sufferings, what I feel,
> My fires and fears are met; I burn and freeze,
> My liver's one great coal, my heart shrunk up
> With all the fibres, and the mass of blood
> Within me is a standing lake of fire,
> Curled with the cold wind of my gelid sighs,
> That drive a drift of sleet through all my body,
> And shoot a February through all my veins.
> Until I see him I am drunk with thirst,
> And surfeited with hunger of his presence.
> I know not wher I am, or no, or speak,
> Or whether thou dost hear me (v.ii.45–56).[9]

This is not borrowing or translating. It is "Imitation, to be able to convert the substance or Riches of another Poet, to his owne use," as Jonson himself puts it in *Timber* (130).[10]

The quotations from Aristotle and from "Longinus" are offered only as examples of what appears, to greater or less extent, in all surviving Greek and Roman treatises on literary criticism and rhetoric.[11] What I wish to emphasize is that ancient rhetoricians

---

[9] My attention was called to this instance of imitation by Gilbert, *Literary Criticism. Plato to Dryden*, pp. 159, 535–536.

[10] See D. L. Clark, "The Requirements of a Poet," *Modern Philology*, XVI, No. 8 (December, 1918), 413.

[11] See especially Dionysius *Three Literary Letters;* Aristotle and "Longinus"; Cicero, *De oratore, Brutus,* and *Orator;* Quintilian x; and Seneca, *Controversiae* and *Suasoriae*.

analyzed models for imitation and—yes—horrible examples to be shunned.

But however valuable the analysis of models might be in a written treatise, oral analysis in the classroom is infinitely more valuable. The teacher not only analyzes a model; he is a model. As Quintilian brings this truth home:

"Though the teacher may point out to his students, in their course of reading, plenty of examples for their imitation, yet the living voice feeds the mind more nutritiously, and especially the voice of the teacher, whom his pupils, if they are but rightly instructed, both love and respect. How much more readily we imitate those whom we like can scarcely be expressed" (ii.ii.8).

The most delightful lecture on rhetoric reported from antiquity fully lives up to Quintilian's ideal. It analyzed a model speech to point out its bad style and chaotic structure, which the student was urged to avoid. It then offered a better model, composed by the teacher on the same theme, which the student should imitate. The lecture, or conference, took place under a plane tree by the Ilyssus. The student was named Phaedrus; the teacher was Socrates; and the complete management of the class hour is reported by Plato. I shall quote freely from the *Phaedrus,* and I wish my readers to consider this great dialog, for the moment at least, not as a philosophical and poetical prose idyl, but as a model lesson in rhetoric. I wish my readers to analyze and appreciate it as a model of teaching, and I wish them to make an effort to imitate the teaching methods of Socrates at their earliest opportunity.

Phaedrus is represented as having with him the manuscript of a speech by Lysias, which Phaedrus greatly admires. Socrates induces him to read aloud this speech which has as theme: "That a youth should accept a non-lover rather than a lover." When he has finished reading, Phaedrus says, "Now, Socrates, what do you think? Is not the discourse excellent, more especially in the matter of language?"

Socrates avoids a head-on collision with his pupil by ironically

agreeing that the speech was admirable and asserting that he was
ravished by it. But at further urging from Phaedrus he proceeds
to criticism of the language, which is the aspect of the speech
which interests the pupil at the moment:

Soc. Well, but are you and I expected to praise the sentiments of
the author, or only the clearness, and roundness, and finish, and
turnure of the language? As to the first I willingly submit to
your better judgment, for I am not worthy to form an opinion,
having only attended to the rhetorical manner; and I was
doubting whether this could have been defended even by Lysias
himself; I thought, though I speak under correction, that he repeated himself two or three times, either from want of words or
from want of pains; and also, he appeared to me ostentatiously
to exult in showing how well he could say the same thing in two
or three ways.

Phaedr. Nonsense, Socrates, what you call repetition was the especial merit of the speech; for he omitted no topic of which the
subject rightly allowed, and I do not think that anyone could
have spoken better or more exhaustively.

From this extreme praise Socrates dissents. He tentatively suggests that Sappho or Anacreon or possibly a prose writer of the past
might have dealt better with the theme; in fact he himself "might
make another speech as good as that of Lysias, and different."

Phaedr. That is grand. . . . Only promise to make another and
better oration, equal in length and entirely new, on the same
subject; and I will promise to set up a golden image at Delphi,
not only of myself, but of you, and as large as life.

Soc. You are a dear golden ass if you suppose me to mean that
Lysias has altogether missed the mark, and that I can make a
speech from which all his arguments are to be excluded. The
worst of authors will say something which is to the point. Who,
for example, could speak on this thesis of yours without praising
the discretion of the non-lover and blaming the indiscretion of

the lover? These are the commonplaces of the subject which must come in (for what else is there to be said?) and must be allowed and excused; the only merit is in the arrangement of them, for there can be none in the invention; but when you leave the commonplaces, then there may be some originality (235–236).

Phaedrus continues to urge the teacher to produce his model oration, and after Socrates has feigned reluctance, lack of rhetorical training, and inability, he allows himself to be persuaded to speak on the same theme.

In his speech Socrates, unlike Lysias on the same theme, begins with definition and analysis. "Let us first of all agree in defining the nature and power of love . . . let us further enquire whether love brings advantage or disadvantage." He then proceeds to an ironical belittling of the lover and with much more logic and sequence than Lysias brought to bear. But he breaks his speech off in the middle and only summarizes his conclusion: "I will only add that the non-lover has all the advantages in which the lover is accused of being deficient."

Phaedrus is not to be fobbed of the speech promised him. He wants the lesson to go on. So Socrates continues, but he shifts his attack from a criticism of Lysias' *inventio* and *dispositio* to a criticism of the theme itself as being philosophically untrue. Hence, says Socrates, he must purge himself by a recantation. The recantation is a speech urging the fair youth to accept the lover rather than the non-lover. The speech is justly famous for its definition of love as a madness of a noble sort, its analysis of the noble madnesses, including poetry, and the myth of the soul as a pair of winged horses and a charioteer. Phaedrus, as would all readers these thousands of years, admits that it is much finer than the first oration and doubts that Lysias would be willing to make so fine and long a speech on the same theme.

Socrates has now won over the pupil by producing a model oration far superior to that produced by the rival teacher. Phaedrus is now ready to believe what Socrates teaches him. Hence Socrates sums up the main points developed in the lesson. His analysis of the *dispositio* of Lysias' speech shows it to be pretty flabby.

Soc. Will you tell me whether I defined love at the beginning of my speech?

Phaedr. Yes, indeed; that you did and no mistake.

Soc. Then I perceive that the Nymphs of Achelous and Pan the son of Hermes, who inspired me, were far better rhetoricians than Lysias the son of Cephalus. Alas! how inferior to them he is! But perhaps I am mistaken; and Lysias at the commencement of his lover's speech did insist on our supposing love to be something or other which he fancied him to be, and according to this model he fashioned and framed the remainder of his discourse. Suppose we read his beginning over again.

Phaedr. If you please; but you will not find what you want.

Soc. Read, that I may have the exact words.

Phaedr. "You know how matters stand with me, and how, as I conceive, they might be arranged for our common interest; and I maintain I ought not to fail in my suit because I am not your lover, for lovers repent of the kindnesses which they have shown, when their love is over."

Soc. Here he appears to have done just the reverse of what he ought; for he has begun at the end, and is swimming on his back through the flood to the place of starting. His address to the fair youth begins where the lover would have ended. Am I not right, sweet Phaedrus?

Phaedr. Yes, indeed, Socrates; he does begin at the end.

Soc. Then as to the other topics—are they not thrown down anyhow? Is there any principle in them? Why should the next topic follow next in order, or any other topic? I cannot help fancying in my ignorance that he wrote off boldly just what came into his head, but I dare say that you would recognize a rhetorical necessity in the succession of the several parts of the composition?

Phaedr. You have too good an opinion of me if you think that I
have any such insight into his principles of composition.

Soc. At any rate, you will allow that every discourse ought to be a
living creature, having a body of its own and a head and feet;
there should be a middle, beginning, and end, adapted to one
another and to the whole?

Phaedr. Certainly.

Soc. Can this be said of the discourse of Lysias? See whether you
can find any more connection in his words than in the epitaph
which is said by some to have been inscribed on the grave of
Midas the Phrygian.

Phaedr. What is remarkable in the epitaph?

Soc. It is as follows:—

> I am a maiden of bronze and lie on the tomb of Midas;
> So long as water flows and tall trees grow,
> So long here on this spot by his sad tomb abiding,
> I shall declare to passers-by that Midas sleeps below.

Now in this rhyme whether a line comes first or comes last,
as you will perceive, makes no difference.

Phaedr. You are making fun of that oration of ours.

Soc. Well, I will say no more about your friend's speech lest I
should give offence to you: although I think that it might
furnish many other examples of what a man ought rather to
avoid. But I will proceed to the other speech, which, as I think,
is also suggestive to students of rhetoric (263–264).

And the dialog continues with further evidence that, logically
and philosophically conceived, rhetoric is inferior to philosophy
but that logical and philosophical rhetoric is superior to the popular rhetoric of Lysias. It concludes with a passage of praise for
Isocrates as a philosophical rhetorician. The reader at this point
should turn to Plato and reread the whole *Phaedrus*.

An appreciative analysis of this lesson in rhetoric, as a model
for teachers, would be inadequate if it did not highlight the
amazing tact of the teacher, who, from start to finish, is concerned

with weaning his pupil from admiration of a faulty model and urging him to admire and emulate a superior model of oratory. Socrates is frequently ironic, but never sarcastic. He points out flaws in the rhetoric and in the philosophy of Lysias, but does not attack his person. He uses all his powers to win Phaedrus to awareness of sound rhetoric and to imitation of a worthy model. He leads his pupil; he does not drive him. And he is careful not to give offense. Socrates is a good model for a teacher to imitate, just as, to Quintilian, the Socratic dialogs were a good model for the lawyer to imitate if he wished to learn to question witnesses (v.vii.28).

Less charming than Plato's account of Socrates as a teacher of Phaedrus, but better adapted to the conditions of class instruction of a number of students, are Quintilian's recommendations for handling the prelection as groundwork for imitation. He believed that such prelection should be part of secondary education under the grammaticus rather than a part of advanced instruction under the rhetor. But about the method he is quite firm:

"The teacher, after calling for silence, should appoint one pupil to read—and it will be best if they are selected by turn that they may thus accustom themselves to clear pronunciation. Then, after explaining the controversy (*causa*) with which the oration is concerned—so that the students will have a clearer understanding of what is to be said—the teacher should leave nothing unnoticed which is important to be remarked as to the thought (*inventio*) or the style (*elocutio*). He should point out what method is adopted in the *exordium* for conciliating the judge; what clearness, brevity, and apparent sincerity is displayed in the statement of facts (*narratio*); what design there is in certain passages, and what well-concealed artifice—for that is the only true art in pleading which cannot be perceived except by a skillful pleader. The teacher should then point out what good judgment appears in the division of the matter into heads, how subtle and frequent are the points of argument, with what force the speaker excites, with what charm he soothes; what severity is shown in his invectives, what urbanity in his jests; how he commands the feelings, forces a way into the understanding, and makes the opinions of the judges coincide with what he asserts. In regard to the style he should point out what words are appropriate, eloquent, or impressive, when amplification deserves praise, and when there is virtue in its opposite; what phrases are happily metaphorical, what figures of speech are used, where the word order is smooth and polished yet manly and vigorous.

"Nor is it without advantage that speeches corrupt and faulty in style, yet such as many, from depravity of taste, would admire, should be read before the boys and that it should be pointed out how many expressions in them are inappropriate, obscure, high-flown, low, mean, affected, or effeminate; expressions which are not only praised by the majority, but, what is worse, praised for the very reasons they are vicious. For straightforward language, naturally expressed, seems to some of us to have nothing of genius; but whatever departs in any way from normal speech, we admire as something exquisite. . . .

"Nor should the teacher merely point out these things. He should frequently ask questions and test the judgment of his students. Thus carelessness will not come upon them while they listen, nor will the instruction fail to enter their ears. And at the same time they will be led to find out and understand for themselves, which is the aim of this exercise. For what object have we in teaching them but that they may not always require to be taught?

"I will venture to say that this exercise, if practiced diligently, will contribute more to the improvement of the students than all the textbooks of rhetoric, valuable as these doubtless are. . . . For in learning almost anything precepts are of less value than experience.

"Shall a teacher declaim that he may be a model for his students, and will not Cicero and Demosthenes, if read and thus analyzed, profit them more?" (II.v.6–16.)

The value of the analytical and appreciative lecture or prelection as a preparation for the students' exercises in imitation is attested by its long life. In his *Metalogicus* (c.1159) John of Salisbury gives a full account of its successful use by that great teacher, Bernard of Chartres, who, says John, "would spur some by exhortation, others by punishment, to imitate what they had heard." [12]

The original purpose of the prelection is still implicit in the *explication des textes* practiced in the schools of France.[13] Some American teachers use the prelection most effectively. Much greater use of it could profitably be made.

Exercises in Imitation

The Greek and Roman teacher, having decided that imitation was an exceedingly valuable exercise in teaching the young to speak and write, having chosen the best models for imitation, having elaborately pointed out in the model the excellences to imitate and the faults to avoid, turned the exercise over to the student. The student must now imitate, and that he did. As Quintilian pointed out, if the student admired his model—either his teacher or a favorite author—he would want to imitate him, and if he wanted to imitate, he would do so in the practice speaking and writing which was part of his regular school routine. These imitative exercises were, of course, discussed pro and con by the author's classmates and the teacher then as they are today.

But in addition there are a number of exercises and activities, still used today, which the ancients rightly considered as exercises in imitation. These imitative exercises are paraphrase, translation, and learning by heart. These exercises have the added ad-

---

[12] Baldwin, *Medieval Rhetoric and Poetic*, pp. 160–164.
[13] Brown, *How the French Boy Learns to Write*, p. 154.

vantage of being useful not only in the classroom but later, when the speaker or writer wishes to continue his efforts at self-cultivation.

The simplest exercise in imitation consists in learning the model by heart. Memorizing good literature in order to create work resembling it, however, is not to be confused with the cultivation of memory (*memoria*) as one of the five parts of rhetoric. Quintilian will be sufficient witness to memorizing as an aid to imitation: "As to learning by heart I would recommend for that purpose select passages from orations, or histories, or any other sort of writings deserving of such attention. . . . The boys will thus accustom themselves to the best writings, and they will always have in their memory something which they may imitate and will unconsciously reproduce that model of style which has been impressed upon their minds. They will have at command, moreover, an abundance of the best words, phrases, and figures, not sought for the occasion, but offering themselves spontaneously from a treasure house, as it were, within them" (ii.vii.2–4).

The value of translation as an imitative exercise was recognized by all Romans. The Greeks, of course, had no one to translate from, hence did not use translation as an exercise in imitation. But Roman literary culture was in large measure derived from Greek culture, much as North European culture is in turn derived from Roman and secondarily from Greek and Hebrew culture. Translation from the language of a high culture into the language of a low culture is necessary for elevation and enrichment of the lower. Cicero was quick to recognize that both the Latin language and Roman eloquence could be improved by imitation, through translation, of Greek literature. In the *De oratore* he has Crassus say: "Afterward I thought proper (and continued the practice when I was older) to translate the orations of the best Greek orators. By following this practice I gained this advantage, that while I rendered into Latin what I had read in Greek, I not only used the best words, and yet such as were of common occurrence, but also formed some words by imitation, which would be new to our countrymen, taking care, however, that they were appropriate" (1.155).

Quintilian echoes Cicero and adds more details to his praise of translation: "Our old orators thought it an excellent exercise to translate from Greek into Latin. Lucius Crassus, in Cicero's *De oratore*, says he often practiced it. And Cicero himself, speaking in his own person, recommends it again and again, and has even published translations of Plato and Xenophon which he had done as exercises. It was also approved by Messala; and there are extant several translations of speeches made by him. He even rivaled the speech of Hyperides for Phryne in delicacy, a quality most difficult of attainment by a Roman. The object of such exercise is evident; for the Greek authors excel in copiousness of matter, and have introduced a vast deal of art into their eloquence. In translating them we may use the very best words since all that we use will be our own. As to figures of speech, which are the greatest ornament of oratory, we may be under the necessity of thinking out a great number and variety of them because the Roman tongue differs greatly from that of the Greeks" (x.v.2–3).

Although Pliny the Younger, in his letter to Fuscus, is advising an older man on the conduct of his private studies, he is undoubtedly drawing on his experience as a former student in the famous school of Quintilian when he writes: "You ask me what method of study I think you should use in that retirement in the country which you have so long enjoyed. It is particularly useful, and many recommend it, to translate either from Greek into Latin or from Latin into Greek. From the practice of this exercise you will acquire a propriety and brilliance of vocabulary, a wealth of figures (*copia figurarum*), a vigor of statement. Moreover from the imitation of the best writers you will learn their faculty of rhetorical invention (*similia inveniendi facultas*). At the same time what a reader might overlook cannot escape a translator. Thus you will gain both understanding and judgment from translation" (*Epist.* vii.9).

Overdepartmentalization has done much to rob the modern teacher of this valuable tool (translation) for improving the student's command of his own language. Foreign languages are often taught by foreigners less familiar with English than with their own tongues. By the direct method they often help the student to an idiomatic command of the foreign language, but they know less of pure and idiomatic English, and hence they cannot help the student to the artistic mastery of his own language by means of the imitative exercise of translation. The Roman professor of rhetoric was expert in the Greek language and in Greek rhetoric. His students had been trained by the grammaticus in Greek language and literature; hence he could use translation as an exercise in rhetoric and did so. Likewise in France, a generation ago, the same master taught both Latin and French and used translation from Latin as a powerful agent for improving the student's command of French style.[14] My friend, Father Francis P. Donnelly, of Fordham University, has lamented to me that the same system, so long maintained in the Jesuit *ratio studiorum,* of having the same teacher for Latin and English, is being abandoned for departmentalization.[15] Since we teachers of speaking and writing in English are prevented from using translation for its chief educational purpose—the illumination of the study of the students' own language—we should at least use our influence in the attempt to have foreign language departments staffed by teachers who command the English language and who use translation as an exercise in speaking and writing better English.

But we are not prevented from using the related exercise of

[14] *Ibid.,* p. 160.
[15] See also Donnelly, *Principles of Jesuit Education in Practice,* Chapters I, XVII, and XXI.

paraphrase; we can have students take the writings of authors of English and turn them into different form, say from verse to prose, or from English to "basic English," as is sometimes done today. Cicero practiced this exercise in his youth but abandoned it in favor of translation for reasons which Quintilian subsequently refuted. Crassus, in *De oratore,* voices Cicero's objections: "In my daily exercises as a youth, I practiced chiefly that exercise which I knew Caius Carbo, my old adversary, was accustomed to practice. This was to set myself some poetry of the greatest distinction or read over as much of a speech as I could retain in my memory. Then I would declaim on the subject matter of what I had been reading, so far as possible using other words. But later I perceived a fault in this exercise: that Ennius, if I exercised myself on his verses, or Gracchus, if I set myself one of his speeches, had already used such words as were most appropriate to the subject and were the most elegant and altogether the best. Thus if I used the same words, I gained nothing; if I used others, it was even prejudicial to me, as I habituated myself to use words that were less appropriate" (1.154).

Quintilian, however, has no doubt at all that paraphrase is a beneficial exercise. In fact he says: "About the utility of turning poetry into prose I believe no one has any doubt." It would seem that he was less fearful of carrying poetical expressions into prose and that he felt that words appropriate to prose were not necessarily worse words than those appropriate to poetry: "For the eloquence of poetry may help to elevate prose style; and there is nothing to prevent our turning the boldness of expression, allowed by poetic license, into the exactness of expression appropriate to prose. To the poet's thoughts we may even add oratorical vigor, fill in omissions, prune redundancy. For I would not have our paraphrase a mere interpretation, but an effort to vie with and rival our originals in the expression of the same thoughts.

"I therefore differ from those who disapprove of paraphrasing Latin orations on the pretext that, as the best expressions have already been used, whatever we express differently must of necessity be expressed worse. For we should not despair of the possibility of finding something better said than it has been said before. Nor has nature made eloquence so meagre and poor that we cannot speak eloquently except in one way. Even granted that our expression is neither better than the original nor equal to it, it can certainly come near it. Do we not ourselves at times speak twice or oftener, sometimes a succession of sentences, on the same subject? Are we to suppose that though we compete with ourselves, we may not compete with others? If a thought could be expressed well in only one way, it would be right to suppose the road closed to us by our predecessors. But in fact there are innumerable ways of expressing a thought and many roads leading to the same goal. There is something to be praised in conciseness as well as copiousness, in metaphorical as well as literal, in direct as well as figurative expression" (x.v.4–8).[16]

I am sure I do not know whether Cicero would be convinced by Quintilian's defense of paraphrase. We, at least, can recognize that Quintilian taught the exercise of paraphrase as a freer and more creative act than it seems to have appeared to Cicero. Quintilian expected his students, in effect, to write a new theme on the same subject, saying the same thing that his author had said, but changing the tone of the style as well as the words. The paraphrase might be longer or shorter than the original, more or less metaphorical, more or less figured, and of course modernized, since the original was always chosen from the early writers. To use a metaphor from music, the student was set to write variations on a theme composed by a master.

Indeed, Quintilian's statements on paraphrase resemble what other ancient writers considered a different and more advanced imitative exercise. Pliny, in the letter to Fuscus which I have already quoted, speaks of it as emulation: "When you have read

[16] Benjamin Franklin, in his *Autobiography,* tells how he taught himself to write by imitating Addison through paraphrase.

and studied an author until you comprehend him, it might be
well to write something on the same matter and argument in
emulation, comparing and carefully weighing your presentation
with your model's to discover where you or he may be superior"
(*Epist.* vii.9).

Similar advice is given by Dio Chrysostom in his discourse on
training for public speaking addressed to some real or imagined
man of affairs, who was to prepare himself to speak by careful
reading of the best authors, including Menander, Euripides,
Homer, Thucydides, Demosthenes, and especially Xenophon.
Then he was to dictate or write imitative exercises based on his
reading: "When you write, I do not think it best to write these
made-up school exercises; yet if you must write, take one of the
speeches that you enjoy reading, preferably one of Xenophon's,
and either oppose what he said, or advance the same arguments
in a different way" (*Discourse* xviii.18–19).

Such practice writing interests and benefits a student much
more than the constrained paraphrase—almost a construe—which
some teachers assign, not to promote power in expression, but
only to see if the student has understood his author. A glance at
Dryden's *Fables* shows that creative translation and paraphrase
can produce original works of art. Compare Dryden's paraphrase
with Chaucer's original *Nun's Priest's Tale*. Or compare his translation of Ovid's tale of Baucis and Philemon with the original or
with a literal translation of Ovid's Latin.[17] Students who have
nothing to say will gain both something to say and improved ability to say it through exercises in translation and paraphrase if
they are taught creatively as Quintilian urged.

I wish to reiterate that modern teachers would make their
teaching more effective if they made fuller use of the exercises
of imitation. As practiced by the ancients, imitation did not stifle
originality. It did not starve but rather nourished the students'

[17] For early loose or creative views of translation see Amos, *Early Theories
of Translation.*

own talents. We are often told, and rightly, that we cannot surpass our models by imitating them. But how many students in school or college ever get within speaking distance of the models we might offer them? For the self-willed genius no schooling is well fitted. He must invent his own educational system as he proceeds with his own self-education. But most great artists have attended the schools and have imitated great artists of the past, at least until they developed their own unique and original manner.

VI. THE ELEMENTARY
EXERCISES

THE GRECO-ROMAN GRAMMAR SCHOOL, as I have already briefly
noted, offered instruction not only in what we recognize as grammar and literature, but also in the writing and speaking of elementary exercises in rhetoric. But before I discuss these elementary
exercises, progymnasmata, in the composition of prose themes, I
wish to consider briefly the question, Did the grammaticus teach
verse writing in his school as the Renaissance schoolmaster undoubtedly did in his grammar school? We have full evidence that
the grammaticus taught prosody and taught the boys to read
poetry with correct observance of quantity and pause. But there
is only indirect evidence that he set the boys exercises in verse
writing as part of their study of poetry. That he did set them such
exercises is at least exceedingly probable, as Jullien has shown.[1]
For one thing, some early verse of distinguished Roman poets was
produced when they were still schoolboys. Virgil composed the
Culex when he was sixteen.[2] Ovid boasts of his own precocity
(*Tristia* iv.x.57). Lucan at fourteen or fifteen had already written
a poem (Statius *Silvae* ii.7, 54, 73). Horace says it was in his early
youth that he was dissuaded in a dream from his ambition to be a
poet in Greek (*Satire* i.x.31). What is more probable than that he

---

[1] Jullien, *Les Professeurs de littérature dans l'ancienne Rome*, pp. 326–331.
[2] *Ibid.*, p. 327.

had been introduced to exercises in writing Greek verse in school before he had thought of writing Greek poetry?

"The skillful management of language, especially the language of poetry," as Jullien says, "is never the free gift of genius, or any superiority of spirit, or a sudden acquisition. It is the fruit of time and culture. Vocations for poetry could not declare themselves so early or so brilliantly if they had not been prepared for with much care in the grammar school."

Even imperial poets, if we believe Suetonius, must be trained in verse writing and were so trained. When Nero was a boy, under the tutorship of Seneca, he studied all the liberal arts, but as his mother turned him from philosophy, and Seneca kept him from the study of the early orators, he turned to the study of poetry. "He composed verses eagerly and without labor," says Suetonius, "and did not, as some think, publish the verses of others as his own. There have come into my hands writing tablets and paper books with some well-known verses of his written in his own hand . . . composed just as one does when thinking and creating, as many words were erased, crossed out, and written in above" (*Nero* lii).

An amusing bit of evidence for the persistence of Latin verse writing by schoolboys during the Middle Ages is contained in Tale CLXIII of the *Gesta Romanorum,* in which Celestinus, son of Alexander, is given over to a philosopher to be well instructed. The preceptor sets the boy a theme to be turned into correct verses. The boy vainly endeavors to execute his task and is so troubled that he listens readily to the devil, who meets him and speaks thus: "Young man, I am the devil in human form, and the best poet that ever lived: care nothing about your master, and promise to serve me faithfully, and I will compose such delectable verses for you that they shall excel those of your pedagogue himself." The boy agreed, and the devil produced the verses, which I shall not transcribe. But the teacher recognized them as too good for the boy to have written, as teachers have both before and since, and said, "My child, have you stolen your verses or made them?" "I made them, sir," lied the boy. "My dear boy," urged the master, "tell me if anyone made these verses for you. . . . Unless you tell me the truth, I will flog you till the blood run." [3] So the boy confessed and renounced the devil and was absolved.

The elementary exercises in writing and speaking prose themes must have been an equal torment to schoolboys from remote antiquity. They were first referred to as progymnasmata in the anonymous *Rhetorica ad Alexandrum* (20), a treatise of the fourth century B.C. I have already quoted Cicero to the effect that one of the exercises, the thesis, had been taught by Aristotle in his own school (*Orator* xiv.46). According to Suetonius, many of the elementary exercises were used in the Roman schools from the first century B.C. Quintilian describes them briefly but with approval in the first century A.D. (I.ix; II.iv.) But the earliest surviving textbook written to guide schoolboys in the composition of progymnasmata is that of Theon, who dates from the second century. We may add to this for consideration the later Greek textbooks by Hermogenes and Aphthonius.

"The schoolmaster, Theon of Alexandria, called Aelius, wrote a textbook on progymnasmata," according to Suidas. "He also wrote commentaries on Xenophon, Isocrates, and Demosthenes as well as treatises on rhetorical argument, oratorical structure, and many more." [4] Also of the second century, but later than Theon, was Hermogenes of Tarsus, who, in addition to his *Progymnasmata,* left rhetorical treatises on *status, inventio,* and the laws of style, derived from Demosthenes and Plato as models.[5] The *Progymnasmata* of Hermogenes was translated into Latin by the grammaticus Priscian of Caesarea, who was teaching Latin in

[3] Wynnard Hooper's revision of Swan's translation of the *Gesta* (London, 1877), p. 311.
[4] Wulfius' Latin version of *Suidas* (Basel, 1581), p. 435.
[5] Kroll, *Rhetorik,* Sect. 40.

Constantinople around 515 A.D. This Latin version, *Prisciani Grammatici Caesariensis de praeexercitamentis rhetoricae ex Hermogene liber,* was very popular in postclassical times, the Middle Ages, and the Renaissance.

The most recent Greek schoolmaster to write a *Progymnasmata* was Aphthonius, who was teaching at Antioch at the end of the fourth and the beginning of the fifth century. Aphthonius follows Hermogenes very closely, omitting no exercise and adding only to the extent of dividing one exercise into two. His strongest bid for popularity was that he added a brief model theme to each pattern of his formulary. Saintsbury called it "one of the most craftsmanlike cram-books that ever deserved the encomium of the epithet and the discredit of the noun." [6] Aphthonius' teacher, the sophist Libanius, left a collection of model themes to guide the young in the composition of elementary exercises, of suasoriae and of controversiae.

All these textbooks were available to schoolmasters and schoolboys in the sixteenth and seventeenth centuries both in Greek and in many Latin translations. I shall mention briefly only a few of these Renaissance versions which I have examined. Camerarius published the Greek text of Theon with a Latin translation and model themes in Latin from the Greek of Libanius. Hermogenes, in Priscian's Latin, was available in many editions of Priscian's grammar and in such collections as the Aldine *De rhetori* (1523) and the *Antiqui rhetores Latini* (1599). Far and away the most popular in the Renaissance was Aphthonius, in a Latin version put together by Reinhard Lorich in 1542 from previous translations by Rudolph Agricola and Joannes Maria Cataneo, adorned with his own elaborate scholia and additional model themes and appropriate quotations from Quintilian and from Priscian's Hermogenes. Camerarius did an independent translation from the Greek (Leipzig, 1567), with additional models from such Greek authors as Aristotle, Xenophon, and Plutarch, but Lorich's

[6] Saintsbury, *A History of Criticism*, I, 92.

Latin Aphthonius, in a revised and somewhat enlarged edition of 1546, held its place in the schools.[7]

One thing, common to all the *Progymnasmata,* accounts for their success and hence for their continued use at least through the seventeenth century. They all give patterns for the boys to follow. They present a graded series of exercises in writing and speaking themes which proceed from the easy to the more difficult; they build each exercise on what the boys have learned from previous exercises; they repeat something from the previous exercise, yet each exercise adds something new. The teachers who taught the classes and wrote the textbooks never take anything for granted except a teacher with a group of boys assembled for the purpose of learning to compose themes.

In Hermogenes [8] there are in all twelve exercises which introduce the boys to the rudiments, at least, of all three kinds of rhetoric. Deliberative rhetoric is represented by fable, tale, chreia, proverb, thesis, legislation; judicial rhetoric by confirmation and refutation, and commonplace; epideictic rhetoric by encomium, impersonation, comparison, and description.

The first exercises in oral and written composition assigned to small boys in grammar school were reproductions of narratives. The boys would retell or paraphrase fables, stories, or episodes from the epic and dramatic poets and from the historians they were reading in school. These exercises gave the boys practice in putting words together correctly and aided them in an understanding of literature. When the boys grew up, they would be able to draw on their knowledge of old stories for illustrations and allusions in their mature speeches. As Quintilian says: "Stories told by the poets should, I think, be treated by boys, not with a

[7] In "The Rise and Fall of Progymnasmata," *Speech Monographs,* XIX (November, 1952), 259–263, and in *John Milton at St. Paul's School,* pp. 230–249, I treat the Latin Aphthonius as it was adapted to the conditions of sixteenth- and seventeenth-century grammar-school practice in Europe.

[8] The translations of Hermogenes are adapted and condensed from the translation published by Baldwin in *Medieval Rhetoric and Poetic,* pp. 23–38, by permission of Baldwin's literary executor.

view to eloquence, but for the purpose of increasing their knowledge" (1.ix).

FABLE. The first exercise is the retelling of fables from Aesop.
Quintilian says: "Let the boys relate orally the fables of Aesop,
which follow next after the nurse's stories, in plain language . . .
and afterwards to express the same simplicity in writing" (1.ix).

Hermogenes not only recommends fables as the first assignment in composition, but suggests different ways of carrying out
the assignment and points out some of the values to be derived:
"Fable is the approved thing to set before the young, because it
can lead their minds into better measures. . . . All alike are called
Aesopic, because Aesop used fables for his dialogs.

"The description of a fable is traditionally something like this.
It may, they say, be fictitious, but thoroughly practical for some
contingency of actual life. Moreover it should be plausible . . .
by our assigning to the characters actions that befit them. For
example, if the contention be about beauty, let this be posed as
a peacock; if someone is to be represented as wise, there let us
pose a fox; if imitators of the actions of men, monkeys.

"Fables are sometimes to be expanded, sometimes to be told
concisely, now by telling in bare narrative, and now by feigning
the words of the given characters. For example. 'The monkeys
in council deliberated on the necessity of settling in houses. When
they made up their minds to this end and were about to set to
work, an old monkey restrained them, saying that they would
more easily be captured if they were caught within enclosures.'
Thus if you wish to be concise; but if you wish to expand, proceed in this way. 'The monkeys in council deliberated on the
founding of a city; and one coming forward made a speech to
the effect that they too must have a city. "For, see," said he, "how
fortunate in this regard are men. Not only does each of them
have a house, but all going up together to public meeting or
theater delight their souls with all manner of things to see and

hear." ' Go on thus, dwelling on the incidents and saying that the decree was formally passed; and devise a speech for the old monkey. So much for this."

He adds that the appropriate style for the narration of fables should be not periodic and elaborate, but simple and easy. He remarks also that orators frequently use fables as a form of argument.

The model theme which Aphthonius gives for the fable shows how simple this first exercise was expected to be: "It was the middle of the summer and the tree-crickets were chirping away in tuneful song, but it was the lot of the ants to work and gather the harvest, so that they might thence be able to supply themselves during the winter. When winter came, the ants subsisted on these stores; their lot was one of enjoyment brought to fulfillment, but joy ended in want for the tree-crickets. So it is that youthful folly which has not been prone to work fares ill in its old age." [9]

TALES. The next elementary exercise in composition involved the reproduction of stories from the poets and historians which the boys were reading under the guidance of the teacher of grammar. The *Ad Herennium* (I.viii), Cicero *De inventione* (I.xix), Quintilian (II.iv), and Hermogenes classify these narrative exercises into four kinds.

The first of these narratives were fabulous fictions which the boys retold from the epic and dramatic poets. These stories, says Quintilian, are "remote, not merely from truth, but from the appearance of truth." They would include such mythological subjects as Ovid used in his *Metamorphoses,* which, indeed, may well be considered as school exercises elevated to great literature.

The second narrative exercise was the retelling of plausible (what we would call realistic) fictions. These, suggest Cicero and

[9] Ray Nadeau, "The Progymnasmata of Aphthonius in Translation," *Speech Monographs* XIX (November, 1952), 265.

Quintilian, may be drawn from the comic poets. Quintilian considers these narratives based on the poets as appropriate exercises to be assigned by the teacher of grammar. The remaining elementary exercises should be practiced under the supervision of the teacher of rhetoric.

The third narrative exercise was the retelling of stories from the historians. The *Ad Herennium* and Cicero specify that these stories should deal with incidents "remote from our memory," —legendary subjects susceptible to imaginative treatment. They were not to be long historical narratives, but brief and pointed episodes.

The fourth narrative exercise dealt with persons rather than happenings. As Cicero describes this exercise: "That sort of narration which deals with persons is of such a sort that in it not only the facts themselves, but also the conversations of the persons concerned and their very minds can be thoroughly seen."

As an example Cicero gives a speech from the *Adelphi* of Terence. The girl tells how the father reproached her for leading his boy into excesses and quotes his words. Such an exercise gave the boys practice in composing speeches appropriate to fictitious and historical characters.

Hermogenes traverses much of the same ground and adds suggestions as to how the tale was used as an exercise:

"A tale, they say, is the setting forth of something that has happened or of something as if it had happened. . . .

"The forms of the tale are said to be four: the mythical; the fictitious, which is also called the dramatic, as those of the tragic poets; the historical; and the political or personal. But for the present we consider the last.

"The modes of the tale are five: direct declarative, indirect declarative, interrogative, enumerative, comparative. Direct declarative is as follows: 'Medea was the daughter of Æetes. She betrayed the Golden Fleece'—and it is called direct because the whole discourse, or the greater part, keeps the nominative case.

Indirect declarative is as follows: 'The story runs that Medea, daughter of Æetes, was enamored of Jason,' and so on—and it is called indirect because it uses the other cases. The interrogative is this mode: 'What terrible thing did not Medea do? Was she not enamored of Jason?' and so on. The enumerative mode is as follows: 'Medea, daughter of Æetes, was enamored of Jason, betrayed the Golden Fleece, slew her brother Absyrtus,' and so on. The comparative is as follows: 'Medea, daughter of Æetes, instead of ruling her spirit, was enamored; instead of guarding the Golden Fleece, betrayed it; instead of saving her brother Absyrtus, slew him.' The direct mode is suited to stories, as being clearer; the indirect, rather to trials; the interrogative to cross-questioning; the enumerative, to perorations, as rousing emotion."

Thus we see that the exercise was calculated not to teach narrative movement, but to give the student practice in using grammatical constructions and rhetorical sentence patterns.

Quintilian seems to have the same idea that these early exercises in retelling stories are directed primarily at drilling for correctness: "I should wish narrations to be composed with the utmost possible care; for it is of service to boys at an early age, when their speech is but just commenced, to repeat what they have heard in order to improve their faculty of speaking. Let them accordingly be made, and with very good reason, to go over their story again, and to pursue it from the middle, either backwards or forwards; but let this be done only while they are still at the knees of their teacher, and, as they can do nothing else, are beginning to connect words and things, that they may thus strengthen their memory. So, when they shall have attained the command of pure and correct language . . . there will be a proper time for acquiring facility of speech. But in the meantime it will be sufficient if a boy with all his care, and with the utmost application of which that age is capable, can write something tolerable. To this practice let him accustom himself and make it natural to him. He only will succeed in attaining the eminence at which we aim, or the point next below it, who shall learn to speak correctly before he learns to speak rapidly."

Aphthonius points out that the narrative themes should make clear: who performed the action, what was done, the time when, the place where, how it was done, the cause. The stories, he adds, should possess the virtues of clarity, brevity, probability, and propriety of word use. They were in effect imitative exercises in paraphrase.

CHREIA. The next two exercises, chreia and proverb, have much in common. Both are elementary exercises in the amplification of a theme or topic. The boys were given a statement of something said or done and shown how to enlarge on it; to dilate; to expatiate, by iteration, comparison, contrast, illustration, example, and the like. Essentially chreia and proverb are exercises in what is sometimes called the methods of developing the topic sentence of a paragraph.

A chreia is a brief exposition of what a person said or did, for the purpose of edification. Some chreiae are of words, as, in the example given by Hermogenes, "Plato said that the Muses dwell in the souls of the fit." Some are of deeds only, and I cite Quintilian's example, "Crates, having met with an ignorant boy, beat his tutor" (1.ix.5). For an example of a mixed chreia of both words and deeds Hermogenes gives: "Diogenes, seeing an ill-bred boy, struck his tutor, saying, 'Why did you teach him thus?'"

The theme or chreia proper was the moral essay the boys would write, memorize, and speak on such a theme. According to Aphthonius the schoolboy was to develop the theme of the chreia as follows: begin with praise of the sayer or doer; then give an exposition or paraphrase of the chreia; tell why it was said or done; introduce a contrast; then a comparison; add an example; support with confirmatory testimony; conclude with a brief epilog.

Says Hermogenes, "Now let us come to the actual working out.

Let this be as follows: first, brief encomium of the sayer or doer; then paraphrase of the chreia itself; then proof or explanation. For example, Isocrates said, 'The root of education is bitter, but its fruit sweet.'

"*Encomium:* 'Isocrates was wise'—and you will slightly develop this topic.

"*Paraphrase:* 'Said,' etc.—and you will not leave this bare, but develop the significance.

"*Proof direct:* 'The greatest affairs are usually established through toil, and, once established, bring happiness.'

"*By contrast:* 'Those affairs which succeed by chance require no toil and their conclusion brings no happiness; quite the contrary things that demand our zeal.'

"*By illustration:* 'As farmers who toil ought to reap the fruit, so with speeches.'

"*By example:* 'Demosthenes, who shut himself up in his room and labored much, finally reaped his fruit, crowns and public proclamations.'

"*By authority:* 'Hesiod says, "Before virtue the gods have put sweat"; and another poet says, "The gods sell all good things for labor." '

"*Epilog:* Last you will put an exhortation to follow what was said or done."

Quintilian is inclined to classify another exercise as a chreia, one developing a theme by cause and effect: "My teachers were accustomed to prepare us for conjectural causes by a kind of exercise far from useless, and very pleasant to us, in which they desired us to investigate and show why Venus among the Lacedaemonians was represented armed; why Cupid was thought to be a boy, and winged, and armed with arrows and a torch, and questions of a similar nature, in which we endeavored to ascertain the intention, or object about which there is so often a question in controversiae. This may be regarded as a sort of chreia" (II.iv.26).

To make one of these a chreia of deeds, he would phrase the theme, "The Lacedaemonians represented Venus armed," and develop it according to the regular formula, adding a section of conjecture as to the cause.

PROVERB. As an exercise in writing and speaking the proverb (in Greek *gnome*, in Latin *sententia*) does not lead the student forward to the mastery of a different problem from that presented by the chreia. It furnishes additional practice in doing what is essentially the same thing. Ancient schoolmasters knew the pedagogical value of what we might call incremental repetition. But let me quote from Hermogenes: "A proverb is a summary saying, in a statement of general application, dissuading from something or persuading toward something, or showing what is the nature of each: dissuading, 'a counselor should not sleep all night'; persuading, 'he who flees poverty must cast himself upon the monster-haunted deep and down steep crags.' Or it does neither of these, but makes a declaration concerning the nature of the thing: 'Faring well undeservedly is for the unintelligent the beginning of thinking ill.' . . .

"The working out is similar to that of the chreia; for it proceeds by brief encomium of him who made the saying; direct exposition; proof; contrast; enthymeme; illustration; example; authority. Let the proverb be, for example, 'A counselor should not sleep all night.' You will briefly praise the speaker. Then you will go on to paraphrase of the proverb, as 'It befits not a man proved in counsels to sleep through the whole night'; proof, 'Always through pondering is one a leader, but sleep takes away counsel'; contrast, 'As a private citizen differs from a king, so sleep from wakefulness'; 'How, then, might it be taken? If there is nothing startling in a private citizen's sleeping all night, plainly it befits a king to ponder wakefully'; illustration, 'As helmsmen are incessantly wakeful for the common safety, so should chieftains be'; example, 'Hector, not sleeping at night, but pondering, sent Dolon to the ships to reconnoiter.' The last topic is one from authority. Let the conclusion be hortatory."

This formula is quoted, in Priscian's version, in the Latin Aphthonius that was used as a textbook by Milton in grammar school. As I have shown elsewhere, the future poet imitated it closely in his "Prolusion on Early Rising." [10]

The *Ad Herennium* exemplifies proverb as one aspect of expolitio, a figure of speech. Expolitio is iteration, a dwelling on one idea with variations in wording. I shall quote in full, because the illustration gives a better idea of rhetorical dilation even than Hermogenes: "When we speak on a theme we may utilize a number of methods of amplification; for when we have announced the theme simply, we may adduce a reason, then iterate either with or without reasons, then bring in a contrast, then bring in a comparison and an example, then draw a conclusion. Consequently an expolitio, which is composed of a number of figures of speech and figures of thought may be thus luxuriantly adorned:

"Thus the following theme is developed in seven parts so that you may see how easily a simple theme may be expatiated upon with the help of the precepts of rhetoric: [theme] 'In the defense of the republic the wise man shuns no peril.' [reason] 'For often one who does not wish to perish for the republic must perish with the republic. And since all agreeable things are received from the fatherland, nothing disagreeable suffered for the fatherland should be deemed grievous.' [iteration] 'Consequently whoever flee that peril which must be undergone for the republic act foolishly, for they cannot escape the evil, and they show themselves to be ingrates to the state. But those who in their own peril dread the peril of the fatherland, those are thought to be wise men, for they render that honor which they owe to the republic and prefer to perish for the many than to perish with the many.'

[10] D. L. Clark, *John Milton at St. Paul's School*, p. 235.

[contrast] 'For it is exceedingly unjust to render to nature when she compels and not give to your country when she requests that life which you accepted from nature but conserved with the help of your country; and, when you can die for your country with the greatest virtue and honor, to prefer to live in dishonor and cowardice; and, when you are willing to face peril for friends and parents, and other relatives, to be unwilling to enter the battle for the republic which includes all these names and besides the sacred name of fatherland.' [comparison] 'And just as he is to be condemned who on a voyage prefers his own safety to that of his ship, so is he to be reprehended who, in the battles of his fatherland, provides for his own rather than for the common safety. For from the wreck of a ship many may escape in safety; from the shipwreck of the fatherland no one can swim safe to shore.' [example] 'It seems to me that Decius understood this well. He is said to have sacrificed himself and to save his legions to have thrown himself into the midst of the enemy. He relinquished his life, but did not lose it. For a trifling price he won a sure reward, for a small one he won the greatest. He gave his life; he won his fatherland. He relinquished his mortality; he gained glory, which, handed down from antiquity with the greatest praise, increases daily more and more.' [conclusion] 'Wherefore if it is proper to confront peril for the republic, as is demonstrated by reason and proved by example, they must be considered wise men who avoid no peril for the safety of the fatherland.'

"Expolitio, therefore, is of these sorts, concerning which we are induced to speak at length, not only because when we plead a cause it strengthens and adorns our speech, but much more because by means of it we gain practice in copiousness of style" (IV.56–58).

REFUTATION AND CONFIRMATION. The chreia and the proverb were exercises primarily in expository method. The exercise of refutation and confirmation was the earliest and most elementary assignment in argument. The subject matter was the same as that of the stories and tales which the boys had previously retold. Quintilian suggests that this exercise might follow directly after the retelling of the tales: "To narrations is added, not without advantage, the task of refuting and confirming them. This may be done, not only in regard to fabulous subjects, and such as are related in poetry, but with regard even to records in our own annals; as if it be inquired whether it is credible that a crow settled upon the head of Valerius when he was fighting, to annoy the face and eyes of his Gallic enemy with his beak and wings, there will be ample matter for discussion on both sides of the question; as there will also be concerning the serpent, of which Scipio is said to have been born, as well as the wolf of Romulus and the Egeria of Numa. As to the histories of the Greeks, there is generally license in them similar to that of the poets. Questions are often wont to arise, too, concerning the time or place at which a thing is said to have been done; sometimes even about a person; as Livy, for instance, is frequently in doubt, and other historians differ one from another" (II.iv.18–19).

Quintilian gives several examples of the sort of story the boys might refute or confirm, but he mentions only one heading, that of credibility. Hermogenes, however, names six headings under which the stories might be considered—the same headings or topics which are useful in refuting or confirming any allegation:

"Destructive analysis is the overturning of the thing cited; constructive analysis, on the contrary, is confirmation. . . .

"Destructive analysis proceeds by alleging that the thing is obscure, incredible, impossible, inconsistent or, as it is also called, contrary, unfitting, inexpedient: obscure, as 'in the case of Narcissus the time is obscure'; incredible, as 'it is incredible that Arion in the midst of his ills was willing to sing'; impossible, 'it is impossible that Arion was saved on a dolphin'; inconsistent or contrary, 'quite opposite to preserving popular government is wishing to destroy it'; unfitting, 'it was unfitting for Apollo, being a god,

to love a mortal woman'; inexpedient, when we say that it is of
no use to hear this.

"Confirmation proceeds by the opposites of these."

Aphthonius, who makes separate exercises of confirmation and
refutation, gives two amusing model themes for and against the
credibility of the story of Apollo and Daphne. First he points out
that the story is incredible because if Daphne was the daughter
of the river god Ladon and of the Earth, she would have been
drowned if she had been brought up by her father and would
have been invisible if brought up by her mother underground.
He then produces a model theme in support of the credibility of
the story.

COMMONPLACE. The exercise in refutation and confirmation gave
the boys practice in supporting the truth or falsity of an allegation of fact. Such skill as the boys developed might in later life
be put to use in courts of law, when questions would arise as to
whether or not certain things had or had not taken place. The
commonplace, on the other hand, assumed the facts to be established and gave practice in coloring them, in throwing a favorable
—or especially an unfavorable—light upon them. In the school
exercise, as Quintilian shows, the plea was against the vice itself,
not against any particular person who had practiced it: "Commonplaces—I speak of those in which, without specifying persons,
it is usual to declaim against vices themselves, as against adultery,
gambling, licentiousness—are of the very nature of speeches at
trials, and, if you add the name of an accused party, are real accusations. These, however, are usually altered from their treatment
as general subjects to something specific, as when the subject
of a declamation is a blind adulterer, a poor gamester, a licentious
old man. Sometimes also they have their use for defense; for we
occasionally speak in favor of luxury or licentiousness" (II.iv.22).

The last statement may need a word of explanation. The lawyer
for the defense, if he could not actually praise his client's vices,

would have the duty at least of trying to palliate them, as Cicero does in his oration for Caelius.

Some speakers wrote out and memorized commonplaces to have them ready to insert as ornamental digressions in extemporaneous speeches, but Quintilian disapproved the practice (II.iv.27–32).

Quintilian's treatment of commonplace is merely a definition and a suggestion. Hermogenes, on the other hand, is even more thoroughgoing than usual in indicating the headings under which the commonplace should be developed and then fully illustrating his headings by developing the commonplace of temple robbing:

"The so-called commonplace is the amplification of a thing admitted, of demonstrations already made. For in this we are no longer investigating whether so-and-so was a robber of temples, but how we shall amplify the demonstrated fact. It is called commonplace because it is applicable to every temple robber.

"The procedure must be as follows: analysis of the contrary, the deed itself, comparison, proverb, defamatory surmise of the past life [of the accused] from the present, repudiation of pity by the so-called final considerations and by a sketch of the deed itself. . . .

"Before proceeding to the deed itself, discuss its contrary. 'Our laws have provided for the worship of the gods, have reared altars and adorned them with votive offerings, have honored the gods with sacrifices, festal assemblies, processions.' Then the application to the indictment. 'Naturally, for the favor of the gods preserves cities; and without this they must be destroyed.' Now proceed to the case in hand. 'These things being so, what has this man dared?' and tell what he has done, not as explaining it, but as heightening. 'He has defiled the whole city, both its public interests and its private; and we must fear lest our crops fail; we must fear lest we be worsted by our enemies,' etc. Next go on to comparison. 'He is more dangerous than murderers; for the difference is the object of attack. They have presumed against human life; he has outraged the gods.' And you will bring into the denunciation the lesser, since they are destructive. 'Is it not shocking to punish the thief and not the temple robber?' You may draw defamation of the rest of his life from his present crime. 'Beginning with small offenses, he went on to this one last, so that you have before you in the same person a thief, a housebreaker, and an adulterer.' You may cite the proverb in accordance with which he came to this pass, 'Unwilling to work in the fields, he wished to get money by such means.' Use also the repudiation of pity by the so-called final considerations of equity, justice, expediency, possibility, and propriety, and by description of the crime. 'Look not on him as he weeps now, but on him as he despises the gods, as he approaches the shrine, as he forces the door, as he lays hands on the votive offerings.' And conclude upon exhortation. . . . So much for the present; the ampler method you will know later."

Aphthonius says that practice in commonplace prepares the student to rouse the feelings of the audience in the peroration of an actual speech. He gives the following formula for the *inventio* and *dispositio* of a commonplace: "Begin with the contrary, analyzing it, not to inform, for the facts are assumed, but to incite and exasperate the auditors. Then introduce a comparison to heighten as much as possible the point you are making. After that introduce a proverb, upbraiding and calumniating the doer of the deed. Then a digression, introducing a defamatory conjecture as to the past life of the accused; then a repudiation of pity. Conclude the exercise with the final considerations of legality, justice, expediency, possibility, decency, and the consequences of the action." His model theme is a commonplace against a despot.

ENCOMIUM. Encomium, like commonplace, was an exercise in epideictic oratory. Commonplace taught the student to enlarge on praise of virtue and dispraise of vice. The exercise of encomium taught him how to praise a person or thing for being virtuous and to dispraise a person or thing for being vicious. Aphthonius made separate exercises of encomium and vituperation, but most rhetoricians included both in one exercise, pointing out that both are based on the same topics or the same places of invention and that the same persons and things may be dispraised instead of being praised.

Quintilian suggests that exercises in encomium might well follow the refutation and confirmation of stories: "The pupil will then proceed by degrees to higher efforts, to praise illustrious characters and censure the immoral—an exercise of manifest advantage, for the mind is thus employed about a multiplicity and variety of matters. The understanding is formed by the contemplation of good and evil. Hence is acquired, too, an extensive knowledge of things in general, and the pupil is soon furnished with examples, which are of great weight in every kind of cause and which he will use as occasion requires" (1.ii.20).

It is clear that the characters which the boy is to praise and dispraise will come from his reading of poetry and history. Hence Quintilian's suggestion that the exercise come early, while the boys are still reading literature in the grammar school. Aphthonius gives a model theme in praise of Thucydides and one in dispraise of Philip of Macedon. When these boys became men they would have many opportunities to deliver philippics against contemporary evil men and encomia of the virtuous dead.

On no exercise did the writers of progymnasmata lavish more detailed and elaborate directions. To illustrate the subtle refinement and systematic overanalysis of Greek rhetoric Marrou can find no better example than Theon's treatment of the topics of encomium in thirty-six divisions and subdivisions, which he has reduced to tabular form.[11]

Let us turn to Hermogenes for his definitions and divisions, equally detailed and elaborate, on the nature and procedure of encomium:

"Encomium is the setting forth of the good qualities that be-

[11] Marrou, *Histoire de l'éducation dans l'antiquité*, p. 274.

long to someone in general or in particular: in general, as encomium of man; in particular, as encomium of Socrates. We make encomia also of things, such as justice; and of animals without reason, such as the horse; and even of plants, mountains, and rivers. . . . Encomium differs from praise in that the latter may be brief, as 'Socrates was wise,' whereas encomium is developed at some length. Observe, too, that censure is classified with encomia by euphemism or because both are developed by the same topics. . . .

"Topics for encomia of a man are his race, as Greek; his city, as Athens; his family, as Alcmaeonidae. You will say what marvelous things befell at his birth, as dreams or signs or the like. Next his nurture, as, in the case of Achilles, that he was reared on lions' marrow and by Chiron. Then training, how he was trained and educated. Not only so, but the nature of the soul and body will be set forth, and of each under these heads: for the body—beauty, stature, agility, might; for the soul—justice, self-control, wisdom, manliness. Next his pursuits, what sort of life he led—that of philosopher, orator, or soldier, and most properly his deeds, for deeds come under the head of pursuits. For example, if he chose the life of a soldier, what did he achieve in this? Then external resources, such as kin, friends, possessions, household, fortune, etc. Then time, how long he lived, much or little, for either gives rise to encomia. A long-lived man you will praise on this score; a short-lived, on the score of his not sharing those diseases which come from age. Then, too, from the manner of his end, as that he died fighting for his fatherland, and, if there were anything extraordinary under that head, as in the case of Callimachus, that even in death he stood. You will draw praise also from the one who slew him, as that Achilles died at the hands of the god Apollo. You will describe also what was done after his end, whether funeral games were ordained in his honor, as in the case of Patroclus; whether there was an oracle concerning his bones, as in the case of Orestes; whether his children were famous, as Neoptolemus. But the greatest opportunity in encomia is through comparisons, which you will draw as the occasion may suggest."

Hermogenes continues to give, in briefer form, the formulas for encomia of animals, things, plants, and cities. The boys undoubtedly spoke and wrote encomia of all varieties, thus gaining through repetition practice in dilating on the topics of praise.

Aphthonius gives the following formula: "Begin with an *exordium*. Then subjoin what stock the person is, divided as follows: of what people, of what country, of what ancestors, of what parents. Then explain his education under these heads: talents, arts, laws. Then introduce the chief of all the topics of praise, his deeds, which you will show to be the results of his excellences of mind, as fortitude or prudence; his excellences of body, as beauty, speed, vigor; his excellences of fortune, as his high position, his power, wealth, friends. Then bring in a comparison in which your praise may be heightened to the utmost. Finally conclude with an epilog urging your hearers to emulate him."

The use of parentage in encomium is wittily illustrated by Aristotle's story of Simonides and the mule race: "Simonides, when the victor in the mule race offered him only a poor fee, refused to compose an ode, pretending to be shocked at the idea of composing it on 'semi-asses,' but on receipt of a proper fee wrote the ode beginning: 'Hail! daughters of storm-footed mares,' although they were equally the daughters of the asses" (*Rhetoric* III.2).

Milton's *L'Allegro* and *Il Penseroso* begin with exercises in encomium and vituperation. The former assigns a defamatory ancestry to Melancholy; the latter, an encomiastic one.

It is clear from these exercises in commonplace and encomium, which included dispraise as well as praise, that little attention, if any, was paid to the facts or alleged facts adduced in support of the topics. A "defamatory conjecture" was as good as historical fact if it would sharpen the point of invective. The tradition of vituperation is clear and explicit in the invective of Hilary of Poitiers against Constantius. "His divisions," says Haarhoff, "correspond perfectly to those of the schools. He spares no form of contumely, even at the expense of historical fact." [12] Milton exhibits the same indifference to fact in his vituperation of Salmasius and Morus.[13]

COMPARISON. Both Quintilian and Hermogenes take up comparison immediately after encomium, and both recognize that logically it is not really a new exercise, but a slight modification of previous exercises. As I have said, this combination in composition exercises of new problems with repetition of old ones is part of the pedagogical system of the graded course.

After making his brief remarks on encomium Quintilian continues: "Next succeeds exercise in comparison, which of two characters is the better or the worse, which, though it is managed in a similar way, yet both doubles the topics, and treats not only the nature, but the degrees of virtues and of vices. But on the management of praise and the contrary, as it is the third part of rhetoric [the epideictic], I shall give directions in the proper place" (II.iv.21).

Quintilian does give the directions in Book III, Chapter vii, where in his discussion of epideictic oratory he covers, only more fully, the ground which Hermogenes covers in his discussion of the elementary exercise of encomium. Thus it would seem that the school exercise differed from mature examples of epideictic oratory only in being shorter and simpler.

Because comparison proceeds under the same headings or topics as encomium and commonplace, Hermogenes' treatment is sum-

[12] Haarhoff, *Schools of Gaul,* p. 164. Hilary's invective is in Migne x.577.
[13] D. L. Clark, *John Milton at St. Paul's School,* p. 242.

mary: "Comparison has been included under commonplace as a means of our amplifying misdeeds, and also under encomium as a means of amplifying good deeds, and finally has been included as having the same force in censure. But since some of no small reputation have made it an exercise by itself, we must speak of it briefly. It proceeds, then, by the encomiastic topics; for we compare men as to their city, race, nurture, pursuits, affairs, external relations, and the manner of death and what follows. . . .

"Now sometimes we draw our comparisons by equality, showing the things which we compare as equal either in all respects or in several; sometimes we put the one ahead, praising also the other to which we prefer it; sometimes we blame the one utterly and praise the other, as in a comparison of justice and wealth. There is even comparison with the better, where the task is to show the less equal to the greater, as in a comparison of Heracles with Odysseus. But such comparison demands a powerful orator and a vivid style; and the working out always needs vivacity because of the need of making transitions swift."

So we see in his conclusion Hermogenes shifting away from the school exercise to the professional encomium. I find my own mind making a similar shift. Sometime in his school career Plutarch must have practiced the elementary exercise of comparison. Would it not have shown him the fundamental technic which he uses in the *Parallel Lives?*

IMPERSONATION. The exercise of impersonation, most usually termed prosopopoeia, required the pupil to compose an imaginary monolog which might appropriately be spoken or written by a historical, legendary, or fictitious person under given circumstances. Hermogenes subdivides the exercise into three varieties: "Ethopoeia is an imitation of the character of a person assigned —what words Andromache might say to Hector. The exercise is called prosopopoeia when we put the person into the scene, as in Aristides the sea is imagined to be addressing the Athenians.

The difference is plain; for in the one case we invent words for a person really there, and in the other we invent also a person who is not there. They call it eidolopoeia when we suit words to the dead, as Aristides in the speech against Plato, for he suited words to the companions of Themistocles."

Aphthonius follows this outline very closely, "It is an imitation and expression of a person assigned." He gives the same subdivisions: ethopoeia, when the pupil composes lines for a known person to speak, as what Hercules might have said to Eurysthenes; eidolopoeia, when he composes lines for the dead to speak; and prosopopoeia, when both persons and lines are feigned. Aphthonius gives as his model theme the lines Niobe might speak over the bodies of her dead children.

This exercise was valuable to the boys insofar as it introduced them to the principles of "ethical" proof (*ethos*) in rhetoric: that the speech should be appropriate to the character of the speaker, the character of the audience, and the speech situation. Hermogenes makes this clear in his warning: "Always keep the distinctive traits proper to the assigned persons and occasions, for the speech of youth is not that of age, nor the speech of joy that of grief. Some impersonations are of the habit of mind, others of the emotion of the situation, and others a combination of the two. An example of the habit of mind would be what a farmer might say on seeing a ship for the first time. Of the emotion, what Andromache might say to Hector. An example of the combined, in which habit of mind and emotion meet, what Achilles might say to Patroclus—emotion at the slaughter of Patroclus, habit of mind in his plan for the war." His suggested plan for the composition of impersonations is to begin with the usually difficult situation of the present in which the persons find themselves, then revert to the past, which may be contrasted with the present as being much happier, and finally forecast the future impressively. "Let the figures and the diction conform to the persons assigned."

Hermogenes' doctrine of decorum, or appropriateness to the emotion and habit of mind of the persons, suggests epic and drama as much as rhetoric. As the future public speaker was nourished by the poets in the grammar school, so we see poetical theory and practice nourished by the elementary exercises in rhetoric. That such a relationship does exist between poetry and prosopopoeia Quintilian fully recognizes: "Prosopopoeia [as an exercise] greatly improves the powers of those who would be poets or historians" (III.viii.49). And he adds, "Nor am I ignorant that poetical and historical prosopopoeiae are sometimes given in the schools by way of exercise, as the pleading of Priam to Achilles, or the address of Sylla to the people on laying down the dictatorship."

The *Heroides* of Ovid, who had been trained in the school exercise, are excellent examples of what words Dido might say to Aeneas or what Medea might say to Jason.

DESCRIPTION. The exercise in description, which the Greeks called ecphrasis, was designed to train boys in vivid presentation of details. It taught them to describe graphically and to display particulars to the eyes of the mind. Indeed Quintilian, Theon, Hermogenes, and Aphthonius all use the image, "bringing before the eyes what is to be shown." Quintilian discusses the value and nature of these word pictures under the name of *enargeia,* a figure. "Let us number *enargeia* among the ornaments of style, because distinctness, or, as some call it, representation, is something more than mere perspicuity; for while perspicuity merely lets itself be seen, *enargeia* forces itself on the notice. It is a great merit to set forth the objects of which we speak in lively colors, so that they may as it were be seen. . . . In this quality of style, as in all others, Cicero displays the highest excellence. Is any one so incapable of conceiving images of objects, that, when he reads the description in the oration against Verres, 'The praetor of the Roman people, with sandals, with a purple cloak after the

Greek fashion, and a tunic reaching to his feet, stood upon the shore, leaning on a courtesan,' he does not seem to behold the very aspect and dress of the man, and even to imagine for himself many particulars that are not expressed?" (vɪɪɪ.iii.61–65.)

Description as an exercise for schoolboys is explained clearly by Hermogenes: "An ecphrasis is an account in detail, visible, as they say, bringing before one's eyes what is to be shown. Ecphrases are of persons, actions, times, places, seasons, and many other things: of persons—Homer's "crooked was he and halt of one foot"; of actions—a description of a battle by land or sea; of times—of peace or of war; of places—of harbors, seashores, cities; of seasons—of spring or summer, or of a festal occasion. And ecphrasis may combine these, as in Thucydides the battle by night; for night is a time and battle is an action.

"Ecphrasis of actions will proceed from what went before, from what happened at the time, and from what followed. Thus if we make an ecphrasis on war, first we shall tell what happened before the war, the levy, the expenditures, the fears; then the engagements, the slaughter, the deaths; then the monument of victory; then the paeans of the victors and, of the others, the tears, the slavery. Ecphrases of places, seasons, or persons will draw also from narrative and from the beautiful, the useful, or their contraries. The virtues of the ecphrasis are clearness and visibility; for the style must through hearing operate to bring about seeing. But it is no less important that the expression correspond to the thing. If the thing be fresh, let the style be too; if it be dry, let the style be similar.

"Note that some precisians do not make ecphrasis a [separate] exercise on the ground that it has been anticipated both in fable and in tale, in commonplace and in encomium; for in these too, they say, we expatiate descriptively on places, rivers, deeds, and persons."

Aphthonius follows Hermogenes very closely, even to Thucydides' combined description of a battle which took place at night.

For his model theme Aphthonius describes in detail the Acropolis of Alexandria, comparing it and contrasting it with the Acropolis of Athens, and going into great detail over the halls, porticos, temples, and library.

Quintilian's discussion shows how the elementary exercise in description could prepare the boys to make their mature public addresses vivid and hence more persuasive. The exercise could and did, however, encourage descriptive dilation for its own sake, not as a means to persuasion. In the hands of the sophists of the second and third century the ecphrasis became a literary form that delighted audiences with epideictic word-painting. Philostratus specialized in depicting paintings and sculpture in words. Famous ecphrases imbedded in literature include the storm in the first book of the *Aeneid,* the house of fame in Ovid's *Metamorphoses,* and Cleopatra's barge in Plutarch. In the hands of less skillful authors the ecphrasis became a tinsel showpiece, the "purple patch," ridiculed by Horace in *To the Pisos* (14–19). Lucian in *How to Write History* warns against the misuse or overuse of ecphrasis: "Restraint in description of mountains, walls, rivers, and the like, is very important; you must not give the impression that you are making a tasteless display of word-painting and expatiating independently while history takes care of itself" (26, 57).

THESIS. I have already discussed the thesis or general question (*quaestio infinita*). It was a familiar oratorical and literary form, which had been taught as an exercise in rhetoric by Aristotle. Quintilian discusses the thesis between the commonplace and the chreia; he probably considered it a grammar-school exercise. In his discussion he shows how the exercise, whether in grammar school or school of rhetoric, prepares the student for more advanced exercises and for adult public address: "Theses, which are drawn from the comparison of things, as whether a country life or city life is more desirable, and whether the merit of a lawyer or a soldier is the greater, are attractive and copious subjects for exercises in speaking, and contribute greatly to improvement in both deliberative and judicial oratory. The latter of the two subjects just mentioned is handled with great copiousness by Cicero in his pleading for Murena. Such theses as the following, whether a man ought to marry, and whether political offices should be sought, belong almost wholly to deliberative oratory, for, if persons be but added, they will be suasoriae" (II.iv.24–25).

Theon, Hermogenes, and Aphthonius place the thesis as the next to last exercise. It is more advanced and more difficult than the preceding. It is the first of the argumentative exercises. The previous exercises in narration, exposition, and description all introduced the stock topics or commonplaces used in support of an allegation, but the conclusion of each is foregone. But on the contrary, in a thesis much may be said on both sides. I offer the evidence of Hermogenes: "The limits of the thesis are traditionally that the thesis is a discussion of a matter considered apart from every particular circumstance. For the thesis usually occupies the field of general debate, not referring to any assigned person, but simply taking a typical course of exposition, as of any person whatsoever, by consideration of such things only as are inherent in the subject matter. Thus when we analyze the advisability of marriage, we speak not with reference to such and such a person, as Pericles or Alcibiades, nor to one in such and such circumstances, time of life, or fortune; but subtracting all these, we consider simply the subject in itself, making our analysis of what is inherent in that, whether this should be done by anybody whatsoever because such and such are the results for those who do so. . . .

"Some theses are political, some not. Political are such as fall within common considerations, the advisability of studying oratory, etc.; unpolitical are such as are peculiar to a certain field of knowledge and proper to those versed in it, whether the heavens are spherical, whether there are many worlds, whether the sun is a fire.

"The thesis differs from the commonplace in that the commonplace is the amplification of a subject matter admitted, whereas the thesis is an inquiry into a matter still in doubt. Some theses are simple, others relative, others twofold: if we discuss the advisability of marriage, simple; if the advisability of marriage for a king, relative; if we discuss whether it is better to contend in games than to farm, twofold, for we must dissuade from the one and persuade to the other.

"Theses are determined by the so-called final topics—justice, expediency, possibility, propriety; e.g., that it is just to marry and make to life the contribution of life itself; that it is expedient, as bringing many consolations; that it is possible by analogy; that it is fitting, as showing a disposition not savage. Thus for your constructive argument; your destructive will be from the opposites. You will refute also whatever theses may be found on the other side. At the end, exhortations on the common moral habits of mankind."

Aphthonius goes a little farther. A thesis, he says, "is an investigation of a question in an oration. It may be political or speculative. Political, as 'Should one take a wife? Go on a journey? Build walls?' Speculative, as 'Are the heavens spherical? Are there many worlds?'" He, like Quintilian, shows how a thesis, "Should one fortify a city?" becomes a suasoria (in Greek *hypothesis*), if names are added, "Should the Lacedaemonians fortify Sparta against the Persian invasion?"

He also recognized the advanced nature of the exercise by pointing out that a thesis should have the same *dispositio* as an oration. The thesis should begin with an *exordium*, may add a statement of facts, proceed to confirmation and refutation, and conclude with an epilog. His list of sources for arguments differs slightly from that of Hermogenes. "The arguments," he says, "are drawn from the final topics of justice, legality, expediency, and possibility." His model theme supports the thesis that a man should take a wife.

The thesis has had a long life as a school exercise. Among Milton's Prolusions, Latin theses composed and delivered when he was a student at Cambridge, is one, "Whether day is better than night," and another, "Whether knowledge is better than ignorance." High school students still compose theses on whether country life or city life is to be preferred. The thesis is also susceptible to poetical and epistolary treatment. The first seventeen of Shakespeare's sonnets are theses in favor of a man marrying. St. Paul deals with the same thesis, with less unqualified support, in 1 Corinthians.

LEGISLATION. The final elementary exercise gave the boys practice in speaking for or against a law. There is no surviving evidence that the boys were to introduce new laws for consideration in a real or imagined legislative body. They were to speak for or against old laws, whether still in force or already repealed, or for or against the fictitious laws which were involved in the themes of the controversiae debated in the schools of declamation. Thus Aphthonius gives as his model theme an attack on the ancient Roman law, no longer in force in his own time, which gave an injured husband the right to kill the adulterers if he took his wife and her lover together in the act of adultery. Lorich, in his edition of the Latin Aphthonius for sixteenth-century school boys, gives a model theme in favor of the Lex Oppia, which restrained the extravagance of women's dress. The law was passed in 215 B.C. and repealed despite Cato's opposition in 195. The speeches for and against the law are given by Livy in Book XXXIV.

The boys were taught to defend a law with arguments drawn from such topics as justice, legality, expediency, and possibility, according to Aphthonius. Is the law just? Is it in conflict with other laws? Is it expedient? Is enforcement possible? Later, in the schools of rhetoric and later still in the law court, the student would make use of this training in attacking laws adverse to the interests of his real or imagined client or in defending laws favorable to his case.

Quintilian devotes considerable space to this exercise: "The praise or censure of laws requires more mature powers, such as may almost suffice for the very highest efforts. Whether this exercise partakes more of the nature of deliberative or of controversial oratory is a point that varies according to the custom and right of particular nations. . . . In either case, however, few arguments, and those almost certain, are advanced; for there are but three kinds of laws, relating to sacred, public, or private rights. . . .

"Points about which questions usually arise are common to all laws; for a doubt may be started, either concerning the rights of him who proposes the law, or concerning the validity of the proposal itself. . . . But such considerations do not enter into these early exercises, which are without any allusion to persons, times, or particular causes. Other points, whether treated in real or in fictitious discussions, are much the same; for the fault of any law must be either in words or in matter. As to words, it is questioned whether they be sufficiently expressive; or whether there is any ambiguity in them. As to matter, whether the law is consistent with itself; whether it ought to have reference to past time, or to individuals. But the most common inquiry is, whether it be proper or expedient.

"Nor am I ignorant that of this inquiry many divisions are made by most professors. But I, under the term proper, include consistency with justice, piety, religion, and other similar virtues. The consideration of justice, however, is usually discussed with reference to more than one point; for a question may either be raised about the subject of the law, as whether it be deserving of punishment or reward, or about the measure of reward or punishment, to which an objection may be taken as well for being too great or too little. Expediency, also, is sometimes determined by the nature of the measure, sometimes by the circumstances of the time. As to some laws, it becomes a question whether they can be enforced. Nor ought students to be ignorant that laws are sometimes censured wholly, sometimes partly, as examples of both are afforded us in highly celebrated orations" (ii.iv.33).

Hermogenes is very brief, perhaps because he is in some doubt whether this should be taught as an elementary exercise: "Some include in their exercises the discussion of a law. And since in practice lawmaking and the categories falling within it constitute a separate study, they make this distinction. In practice there is a particular circumstance; in an exercise there is not. For example, if 'in dearth of necessities it is proposed that governmental positions be put on sale,' you have an occasion in the dearth. In an exercise there is none, but simply a proposal to put governmental positions on sale, without occasion or other circumstance.

"It is determined as evident, just, legal, possible, expedient, proper. Evident, as in Demosthenes 'but that this is just is simple and evident for all to know or learn'; legal, as when we say 'it is contrary to the ancient laws'; just, as when we say 'it is contrary to nature and morals'; possible, as when we say 'nor can it be done'; proper, as when we say 'it hurts our reputation.' "

Summing up his discussion of all the elementary exercises Quintilian concludes: "On such subjects did the ancients, for the most part, exercise the faculty of eloquence, borrowing their mode of argument, however, from the logicians" (ii.iv.41).

CONCLUSION. There are several very interesting things for the modern teacher to note in these ancient Greco-Roman elementary exercises in speaking and writing. For one thing, the earliest of them, those practiced while the boys were still studying in the grammar school, were closely related to the study of literature. The boys paraphrased and retold stories which they were reading. They were trained to utilize proverbs and sententious sayings from the poets as amplifying material in developing themes. They were trained to make similar use of episodes from history and from biography. In exercises in prosopopoeia they were trained to compose speeches which historical or famous fictitious characters might have appropriately addressed to one another under known circumstances. From their reading they praised characters for their virtues and condemned them for their vices. Such a correlation could have been possible only when the boys had the same teacher for literature and for their elementary exercises in the composition of oral and written themes.

Another interesting thing to notice is the preoccupation with religion, morals, and right conduct. With the Greeks and Romans, Homer and the other early poets took the place the Bible has with us. Consequently the teacher of grammar, with whom the boys read these poets, took on something of the function of the Sunday school teacher as well as those of the teacher of grammar, literature, and composition. Of course pagan morals were taught. There was nothing about faith, hope, and charity; but there was frank and thorough inculcation of the cardinal pagan virtues of fortitude, justice, prudence, and temperance. And good citizenship was taught, not as a vague ideal, but as a moral and religious duty. The boys were trained for their place as members of the ruling class.

Another characteristic of these elementary exercises will strike the modern teacher—the tendency to deal with the general rather than with the particular. From the earliest exercises in fable and tale, where the emphasis was on the general moral idea illustrated rather than on the story for its own sake, this tendency to generalize persists through the chreia, the commonplace, and the thesis. The typical themes were: whether any man ought to marry, that any temple robber or any adulterer ought to be punished, how any old man or any braggart soldier would speak, what descriptive details are typical of any war or the capture of any city. This tendency to deal with the general and the universal is, of course, characteristic, not only of the classics, but of the classicists of later ages.

In the elementary exercises in rhetoric the tendency to deal with general considerations of the possible, the true, the just, the fitting, or the expedient had its value. The exercises equipped the boys with a ready command of the arguments and other amplifying material that could be adduced in support of the commoner major premises, and might easily persuade audiences of their truth. In more advanced exercises in declamation, the boys would have to deal with fictitious particular cases, and in their mature careers as orators they would have to deal with actual cases. As Cicero's practice convincingly shows us, one of the most effective oratorical procedures is to show that the case under consideration comes as a minor premise under one of these large generalizations or major premises. In school the boy learned how to plead for the conviction of all temple robbers. As an orator, he had only to prove that John Doe had robbed a temple and proceed with the commonplace.

It is furthermore evident that the ancient teacher did not ignore the question, "What shall I say?" The elementary exercises not only set definite assignments but prescribe how they are to be developed and amplified. The aim of the exercises was not to develop the personality or originality of the boys, but to instill in them the habit of discovering everything that might be said for or against a general proposition. In exercise after exercise the boys were directed to an exploration of the topics or commonplaces where one looks for arguments. Is it possible? Is it credible? Is it in character? Is it just? Is it moral? Is it fitting? Is it expedient? Moreover, the boys were shown where to look for answers to these questions. They were to adduce historical parallels, apposite sayings from the poets and philosophers, descriptive details, comparisons, contrasts, causes and results, simple enthymemes. Teaching was generally focused on *inventio,* that part of rhetoric which deals with the discovery of arguments appropriate to the theme under discussion. The modern teacher of speech and writing could do more of this than he does. The ancient elementary exercises afforded training in the rudiments, not only of *inventio,* but of *dispositio* as well, stressing the order of what we would call the paragraphs within the whole composition. The very first exercises called for the following of a sequence already established by the poet whose story the boys were retelling. Chreia and proverb, the first exercises in exposition, called for definite, though frankly conventional, sequence. The boy was conducted by leading strings in his first halting steps in speaking and writing, was coached in how to go from the opening praise of sayer or doer to the final admonition to go and do likewise.

Also in commonplace and in encomium the boys were given valuable, though wooden, formulas for sequence. Skillful writers and speakers today could follow these wooden and conventional formulas and get credit for orderly and persuasive planning of their discourse. In fact, many of them do. But the reader will observe that prescriptions for sequence are given only in the earliest of the elementary exercises. The Roman boy was not kept in leading strings.

But the Greco-Roman system of secondary education, as exemplified in the elementary exercises, was not without fault. For one thing the assignments were drawn from the literature of antiquity, not from the facts of the students' own time. Proverbs, examples, and contrasts were drawn too exclusively from the early poets and from early and legendary history. If the student spoke for or against a law, it was a fictitious or hypothetical law, not a law that might be of contemporary interest or might be affecting their own lives. They might debate the relative merits of country or city life, but not the relative merits of republican or imperial government. They might consider critically the myths of Apollo and Daphne or of Arion, but they might not question the eagle that, rising from the funeral pyre of Augustus, proclaimed his divinity. My last two examples absolve the schools from at least some of the fault. The absolutism of the imperial Roman system precluded free discussion of contemporary social and political problems. From the time of Quintilian on, schoolmasters were paid by the state and they had a natural preference for keeping alive and drawing their salaries. When Sidonius Apollinaris, fifth-century senator and bishop, was advised to write a history, he declined. "To tell lies," he wrote in one of his letters, "is disgraceful; to tell the truth, dangerous" (iv.22.5).

Sidonius as a Christian had more feeling about the truth than had the usual Greek or Roman pagan. Therefore it is not surprising that the elementary exercises harp on expediency and not on truth as a main heading in persuasion. The aim of the rhetorical exercises was not in general to make truth prevail, but to make one side of a debatable question seem as plausible as possible and then turn around and make the other side of the question seem just as plausible. In the speech against the temple robber the fifth heading was "defamatory surmise of the past life of the accused from the present." The student was not asked to find out whether a given temple robber had actually been a thief, a burglar, an adulterer. He was merely directed to surmise that a temple robber would have a shady past, and then to dilate on the conjecture.

VII. DECLAMATION

"I LIKE that exercise," said Crassus, "which you are accustomed to practice, to lay down a case similar to those which are debated in the forum and to speak on it as nearly as possible as if it were a real case."

The exercise which Crassus thus describes and approves in the *De oratore* (1.149) of Cicero was later called declamation. From the time of Crassus to the break-up of the Roman Empire declamation was taught in the schools of rhetoric after the boys had completed the elementary exercises of the progymnasmata. In Greece declamation had been taught in one form or another since the fourth century B.C.[1]

Declamation as a school exercise was of two kinds: the suasoria and the controversia. The suasoria was an exercise in deliberative oratory. It set out to persuade a person or a group of people to do something or not to do it. For the most part the suasoria used historical or quasi-historical material. The student was to persuade Alexander to invade India or to persuade Agamemnon not to sacrifice Iphigenia. The controversia, on the other hand, was a school exercise in the judicial oratory of the law courts. The student spoke on fictitious legal cases, prosecuting or defending a fictitious or historical person in a civil or a criminal process. In the Roman schools the controversia was always considered

---

[1] Quintilian II.iv.41. Philostratus, *Lives of the Sophists* 1.5. W. Hofrichter sums up the evidence on the early history of declamation in his Breslau dissertation, *Studien zur Entwickelungsgeschichte der Deklamation.*

as more advanced, more difficult, and more important than the suasoria.

There was no advanced school exercise in the oratory of praise and blame, dealing with vice and virtue in the present. Cicero considered it more literary than practical, although a good wet nurse for the young orator (*Orator* 37–42). Hence it is not surprising to find it taught, as encomium, as one of the elementary exercises of the progymnasmata. Moreover, on occasion, a speaker has plenty of opportunity in deliberative and judicial oratory to praise virtue and condemn evil, to praise good men and to condemn evil men. Consequently in developing the themes of suasoria and controversia in school the boys had continuing practice in epideictic oratory.

To the usefulness of declamation and its place in the school system Quintilian testifies: "When the pupil has been well instructed and sufficiently practiced in the elementary exercises, the time will have arrived to enter on suasory and judicial themes for speaking. But before I go further, I must say a few words on the art of declamation, which, of all the exercises, is at once the most recently discovered and much the most useful. For it comprehends all the elementary exercises and presents a close resemblance to reality. It has accordingly been so much adopted that it has been thought by many sufficient of itself to develop eloquence, since no excellence in oratory can be specified which is not found in this rhetorical exercise" (ii.x.1–2).

Highly as he thought of declamation as an exercise well fitted to prepare boys for actual pleadings in the forum, he nevertheless recognized the dangers of abuse if the exercise became an end in itself and if the themes were drawn from situations too remote from real life. These abuses he recognized in his own day: "The practice, however, has so degenerated through the fault of the teachers, that the license and ignorance of declaimers has been among the chief causes that have corrupted eloquence. But of that which is good by nature we may surely make a good use.

Let, therefore, the themes themselves be as like as possible to truth; and let declamations to the utmost extent practicable imitate those pleadings for which they were introduced as preparatory exercises. . . .

"Those, assuredly, who think that the whole exercise of declaiming is altogether different from forensic pleading, do not see even the reason for which the exercise was instituted. For if it does not prepare for the forum, it is merely like theatrical display or insane raving" (ii.x.3–8).

As we shall see upon closer study of declamation, the exercise did become increasingly remote from reality, using fantastic and unreal themes, and in the hands of many teachers and declaimers it did, as Quintilian feared, become an art of theatrical display. As we consider the conditions of school instruction, we can readily understand how it came about that the school exercise of declamation finally became a literary form to be practiced and applauded as a fine art and contributed a declamatory color to all literature produced under the Empire.[2]

To begin with, the teacher was expected to be a model of speaking for his students to imitate. He was expected constantly to show the students how. When he assigned fictitious themes for their declamations, he pointed out lines of argument which could be followed in supporting each side. After the boys had written and declaimed their practice exercises and after the exercises had been criticized by teacher and class, the teacher declaimed on the same theme, sometimes on one side, sometimes on the other, sometimes on both sides (ii.iv–vi; x.ii.39). Parents and relatives were allowed to visit the class. When the teacher himself was to declaim, he was likely to have a good many visitors. Hence his task became, not only to teach rhetoric to the boys, but also to practice rhetoric with sufficient brilliance to

[2] See Duff, *A Literary History of Rome in the Silver Age;* Summers, *The Silver Age of Latin Literature* (1920); Wright, *Later Greek Literature;* W. A. Edward, Introduction to his edition of *Suasoriae of Seneca* (1928), pp. xv–xx.

impress the parents paying the tuition. As his reputation increased he had more visitors. He set aside special days for public declamation; on those occasions he expatiated on the themes of the school exercises before large and cultivated audiences. Finally he would go on lecture tours to exhibit his rhetorical virtuosity in declaiming for pay to enthusiastic audiences in the great provincial cities of Africa, Europe, and Asia. But he seems rarely to have given up teaching. If he no longer taught a class of boys, he at least gave private instruction to wealthy patrons. I shall avoid so far as possible a consideration of declamation as an art form practiced by famous rhetors except for the light thrown on the activities of the school where suasoria and controversia were taught as school exercises in rhetoric.

But the perverseness and the ostentation of teachers were not the only evil influences at work to make exercises in declamation under the Empire more and more unreal and remote from actual pleadings, deliberative and judicial, in the forum. Another influence was the Empire itself. Under the dictatorship of the principate freedom of discussion in the school and in the forum ceased. It was not safe to discuss live issues. The more remote from reality or fictitious a theme was, the safer it was. Rhetoric is a living force only under some form of democratic or republican government. It dies or is emasculated under tyrannies, absolutisms, or dictatorships.[3]

For instance, the author of the *Ad Herennium* could and did use themes for declamation drawn from the most hotly contested issues of his own age, the bloody contest between the democratic party, led by Marius, and the aristocratic party, led by Sulla, who won in 82 B.C. and set out to extirpate the democrats, slaughtering them by the thousands. When issues are settled by armed force,

---

[3] Harry Caplan quotes fully from writers of the first century who discuss the decay of oratory and concludes, "We learn that some of these clearly realized that eloquence flourishes best on soil dedicated to free institutions."—"The Decay of Eloquence at Rome in the First Century," *Studies in Speech and Drama in Honor of Alexander M. Drummond*, pp. 295–325.

not by political means, issues are not freely discussed in school or out.[4]

How declamation was taught in the schools under the Empire may be learned from various contemporary sources. Quintilian again and again explains his own methods, criticizes the methods of others, and makes recommendations for improved procedures. Seneca records his experiences as boy and man, as student, as auditor in the declamation schools, and as auditor at public exhibitions of declamation by famous teachers.[5] Lucian of Samosata and Petronius (*Satyricon* 2) paint satirical pictures of professors and their declamation schools. Tacitus points out how much better the old-fashioned method of teaching was than that of the up-to-date schools of declamation (*Dialogus* 35).

Four declamations of Lucian survive among his literary epistles and dialogs; these are readily accessible to the modern reader in the Fowler translation.[6] Not available in English are three collections of model declamations in Latin prepared for use in the schools. The major declamations of Quintilian, almost certainly not by him, tell us much. They comprise nineteen model controversiae. An English translation by John Warr was published for use in English schools in 1686.[7] The minor declamations of Quintilian, which may at least possibly be based on his lecture notes, set the theme and announce the laws for 145 controversiae, analyze the issues, and give notes for treatment.[8] The declama-

---

[4] *Ad Herennium* iii.2; iv.68; i.21, 24, 25. Gwynn (*Roman Education*, pp. 59–69) associates the *Ad Herennium* with Plotius Gallus and the democrats.

[5] See Seneca, *Controversiae et Suasoriae* (ed. with translation into French by H. Bornecque, Paris, 1932) and *Suasoriae* (ed. with translation into English by W. A. Edward, Cambridge, 1928).

[6] *The Works of Lucian of Samosata*, translated by H. W. Fowler and F. G. Fowler. See especially II, 173, and III, 218. Lucian's authorship of these declamations is questioned by C. R. Thompson.

[7] *The Declamations of Quintilian, Being an Exercitation or Praxis upon His XII Books, concerning the Institution of the Orator* (London, printed by F. R. for John Taylor, 1686).

[8] Ritter, *Die Quintilianischen Deklamationen;* Gwynn, *Roman Education from Cicero to Quintilian*, pp. 204–218.

tions of Calpurnius Flaccus are almost identical in manner and in treatment with the minor declamations of Quintilian, and in Renaissance editions they are frequently bound with both the major and the minor declamations.

A great deal more information about the teaching of declamation and its teachers can be gleaned from the collective biographies in *Lives of the Sophists* by Philostratus and the Lives of the Rhetoricians by Suetonius.[9]

Suasoria

A suasoria, as we have seen, is an academic exercise in deliberative oratory. Actual deliberative oratory urges a person or an assembly to take action in the future. In his *Panegyricus* Isocrates counsels the Greeks to union against the Persians. Demosthenes, in his Philippics, counsels the Greeks to resist the Macedonian ruler. Aristeides, a professor of rhetoric in the second century, composed a deliberative oration which persuaded Emperor Marcus Aurelius to rebuild Smyrna after it had been destroyed by an earthquake (Philostratus, *Lives of the Sophists* 582). In a deliberative oration, the *Areopagitica,* John Milton counseled the English Parliament to repeal a law requiring the licensing of books prior to publication.

Whenever anyone deliberates about anything, he asks himself certain questions. What shall I do this afternoon, tomorrow, or next year? What shall I advise my sister, my employer, my Congressman to do in the future? What action do I advise for my state or national government? In an effort to help the thinker and speaker find answers to these questions, ancient rhetoric suggested that he would find all of the reasons, pro and con, if

[9] Useful secondary sources, in addition to those already cited, include Arnim, *Leben und Werke des Dio von Prusa;* Bornecque, *Les Déclamations et les déclamateurs d'après Sénèque le père;* Summers, "Declamations under the Empire"; Bonner, *Roman Declamation in the Late Republic and Early Empire;* and M. L. Clarke, *Rhetoric at Rome.*

he would ask three specific questions about the issue being deliberated. Is it possible? Is it expedient? Is it honorable?

Students in school or college do not usually have enough knowledge or experience to give actual counsel. For this and for other good reasons the school exercises in deliberative oratory in Greece and Rome were based on themes from legend and history—themes familiar to the boys from their reading and from the lectures of the professor of literature (the grammaticus). If a boy, in his suasoria, was to counsel Alexander, Caesar, Cicero, or Agamemnon, he would have to imagine himself one of their contemporaries and then compose such a speech as a contemporary might deliver. Hence the exercise of suasoria, as it was practiced in the schools, required that the student compose prosopopoeiae. These are speeches in which the student supplies the words which someone else, real or fictitious, might in agreement with the laws of necessity and probability have composed and delivered under a given set of circumstances. Whenever a character in a play or novel is represented as making a speech the result is prosopopoeia. The speeches Shakespeare wrote for Brutus and for Antony to deliver in *Julius Caesar* are justly famous prosopopoeiae. So are the speeches Milton composed for the fiends to deliver in the parliamentary session in Pandemonium, *Paradise Lost,* Book II. As we shall see later in this chapter most controversiae as well as all suasoriae were composed as prosopopoeiae in the declamation schools.

The seven suasoriae reported by Seneca were all to be spoken as prosopopoeiae. In the first the speaker must imagine himself to be one of Alexander's war counsel, or his mother, urging him not to attempt to cross the ocean, or else to be Alexander insisting that he is going to do it. In the second the speaker must imagine himself to be one of the Spartans at Thermopylae urging his fellow soldiers to stand and fight the Persians or else urging them to retreat. In the third the speaker is to speak in the person of Agamemnon telling the augur Calchas why he does not intend to sacrifice his daughter Iphigenia. In the fourth he speaks as a counselor urging Alexander to pay no attention to the warnings of the astrologer but to enter Babylon forthwith. The speaker in the fifth is to imagine himself a member of the Athenian assembly debating issues of war and peace in the Persian war. In the sixth and the seventh he imagines himself a friend of Cicero counseling him to plead for Antony's mercy, to escape to Brutus, to burn his writings, or to die nobly.

The same is true of the two suasoriae of Lucian, *Phalaris I* and *Phalaris II*. Both speeches endeavor to persuade the priests of Delphi to accept a votive offering of a sculptured bull from the Sicilian tyrant Phalaris. In the first the emissaries speak in the person of Phalaris. In the second the speaker is a priest of Delphi. What gives point to the debate is the tradition that Phalaris had a nasty habit of roasting his enemies alive in a hollow bronze bull.

Although only seven themes are quoted in what survives of Seneca's *Suasoriae,* mentions here and there in classical literature enable me to list additional themes. Quintilian mentions these: "Cato deliberates whether he should take a wife" (III.v.13). "Numa deliberates whether to accept the kingship when the Romans offer it" (VII.i.16). Juvenal as a schoolboy "counselled Sulla to retire from public life and sleep his fill" (*Satire* 1.16), and Persius, remembering his schooldays, says: "I used often, I remember, as a boy to smear my eyes with oil if I did not want to speak the noble words of the dying Cato—a speech which would be much applauded by my idiot of a master, and that to which my father, sweating with delight, would have to listen with his invited friends" (*Satire* III.45). The *Ad Herennium* gives three from Roman history: "The senate deliberates whether to allow Scipio to accept office as consul before he has attained the legal age." "The senate deliberates, during the Social War, whether or not to extend citizenship to the Allies." "The soldiers cut off by the Carthaginians deliberate what to do" (III.2, 8).

The largest number of themes for suasoriae are those recorded by Philostratus in his *Lives of the Sophists*. Naturally enough the Greek rhetoricians preferred themes from Greek history. Indeed, they practiced suasoriae in their schools much more than did the legalistic-minded Romans, who in their schools devoted much greater attention to controversiae.

The following themes are accompanied, in parentheses, by the paragraph numbers in the text of Philostratus: "The Lacedaemonians debate whether they should fortify themselves by building a wall" (514). "The Lacedaemonians debate whether or not to receive the men who had returned from Sphacteria without their weapons" (528). "Isocrates tries to wean the Athenians from their empire of the sea" (584). "That the trophies erected by the Greeks [after the Peloponnesian war] should be taken down" (538). "That the Athenians should return to their demes after the battle of Aegospotami" (538). "Demosthenes advises the Athenians to flee in their triremes at the approach of Philip" (543). "The wounded in Sicily implore the Athenians who are retreating thence to put them to death with their own hands" (574). "Pericles urges that the Athenians should keep up the war even after the oracle declared Apollo would be an ally of the Lacedaemonians" (575). "Artabazus endeavors to dissuade Xerxes from making a second expedition against Greece" (575). "Callias tries to dissuade the Athenians from burning the dead" (602). "The citizens of Catania debate whether they shall migrate after an eruption of Aetna" [in 425 B.C.] (620). "Demades argues against revolting from Alexander while he is in India" (620). "The speaker endeavors to recall the Scythians to their early nomadic life, since they are losing their health in the cities" (572, 620).[10]

No one of these themes from Greek history deals with a historical occurrence later than the invasion of India by Alexander in

[10] R. Kohl catalogs the themes of declamation drawn from Greek and Roman history in his *De scholasticarum declamationum argumentis ex historia petitis*.

327 B.C. Philostratus records that these themes were chosen for suasoriae delivered by Greek rhetoricians in the first and second centuries of our era. These rhetoricians, then, were having their pupils practice deliberative oratory on events which occurred four and five hundred years before their own day, much as modern teachers of literature ask their pupils to discuss the characters and motives of Othello, Hamlet, or the Wife of Bath as they are represented in the works of Shakespeare and Chaucer.

The dramatic art required by prosopopoeiae is recognized by Lucian in his comparison with the art of the pantomimic dancer: "The pantomime is above all things an actor: that is his first aim, in the pursuit of which he resembles an orator, and especially the composer of declamations, whose success, as the pantomime knows, depends like his own upon versimilitude, upon the adaptation of language to character; prince or tyrannicide, pauper or farmer, each must be shown with the peculiarities that belong to him" (*Of Pantomime* 65).

In these dramatic impersonations required by school exercises in suasoria the boys were taught that if they would move the feelings of others, they must be moved themselves. To learn this art they must learn to cultivate imagination. Quintilian says: "In the schools it would be proper for the learners to feel moved with the subjects on which they speak and imagine that they are real, especially as we discuss matters in school more frequently as parties concerned than as advocates. We assume the character of an orphan, of a person that has been shipwrecked, or one who is in danger of losing his life. To what purpose is it to assume their characters if we do not adopt their feelings?" (vi.ii.36.)

The use and value of prosopopoeiae in school declamations is explained fully and at length by Quintilian in an important passage: "Prosopopoeiae seem to me to be of the greatest difficulty, for they add to the other tasks of suasoriae the difficulty of impersonating character. For in speaking on the same subject Caesar, Cicero, and Cato must be represented as speaking differently.

But the exercise is most useful, either because it is a twofold task, or because it benefits future poets and historians; to orators, of course, it is indispensable. For there are many speeches composed by Greek and Latin orators for others to deliver, wherein what was said had to be adapted to the condition and character of the speaker. Did Cicero think in the same way or assume the same character when he wrote for Pompey as when he wrote for Ampius and the others? Did he not, rather, bearing in mind the fortune, rank, and actions of each, express the character of all to whom he gave words, so that, though they spoke better than they could by nature, they yet appeared to speak in their own persons? A speech is not less faulty which is unsuited to the speaker than that which is unsuited to the subject to which it ought to be adapted. Lysias, accordingly, is seen to deserve great praise for preserving so exact an air of truth in the speeches he wrote for the uneducated. Hence especially should declaimers bear in mind what befits each character; for they speak in very few controversiae as advocates, but for the most part impersonate sons, fathers, rich men, old men, morose or good-natured persons, misers, superstitious people, cowards, or mockers; so that actors in comedy have scarcely more parts to master on the stage than they have in their declamations. All of these impersonations may be regarded as prosopopoeiae, which I have classified under suasoriae, from which they differ only in the personation of characters" (III.viii.49–54).

The school exercises of suasoriae required the student to adapt the speech not only to the imagined speaker, but also to the subject and to the audience. As Quintilian says in analyzing the problem of deliberative oratory: "In persuasion or dissuasion there are three points to be borne in mind: what is the subject of deliberation? Who deliberate? Who would sway their deliberations?" (III.viii.15.) The successful speaker bears these points in mind so that he may be sure that what he says will be appropriate to his subject, to his audience, and to himself. Some of Seneca's wittiest satire in his *Suasoriae* is leveled at the bad taste and extravagance of some declaimers who neglected the basic need for appropriateness (1.4; II.12, 17, 21).

The suasoria, as an academic exercise, was carefully designed to keep the pupil's attention fixed on this threefold problem of adaptation. The themes were so stated that the subject of deliberation was clear to any boy who had received the conventional schooling in ancient history and classical literature. The use of prosopopoeiae made the boys inevitably aware that in impersonating a historical or legendary person they must try to speak in character and endeavor to make their speech appropriate to what was common knowledge of the imagined speaker's character. The statement of the theme of a suasoria put special emphasis on just who made up the audience for the speech, and the teacher emphasized that the student's speech must be adapted to that audience. The boys were to imagine that they were speaking to a well-known historical or legendary personage whose character traits had been vividly portrayed by the historians and the poets or to groups of people who were reputed to have certain marked characteristics, such as the Spartans, the Scythians, or the Roman Senate. It is the lack of an audience, real or imagined, that is responsible for a great deal of the pointlessness in the practice speaking and writing in our own schools and colleges today. In this respect, at least, the Roman and Greek boy was better educated than our youths today.

Just how the ancient professor of rhetoric helped his students to adapt their suasoriae to the characters of their imagined audiences is, like so many points of school procedure, made most explicit by Quintilian: "The feelings of our audience are various and the audience itself is of two classes, for those who seek our counsel are either single individuals or many, and in each class there are differences. Thus if the audience is made up of many, it makes a great difference if it is a senate or a people, Romans or townspeople, Greeks or barbarians. If the audience is a single person, it

makes a difference whether in our suasoria we urge Cato or Marius
to run for office, or advise Scipio or Fabius on the conduct of the
war. Likewise we must take into account the sex, rank, and age of
our audience. But their moral character will make the chief difference. To recommend honorable conduct to honorable men is
very easy. But if we attempt to persuade bad men to right conduct,
we must take care not to reproach them for their evil lives. The
minds of such an audience are to be influenced, not by discoursing
on virtue, for which they have no regard, but by praise, by allusion
to popular opinion, and if such vanities do not move them, by
emphasizing what they may gain by following your advice, or
perhaps more effectively, by showing how much is to be dreaded
if they do not. Aside from the fact that the minds of unprincipled
men are most easily moved by fear, I am not sure whether the fear
of evil has not naturally more influence than hope of good, for
they find it easier to understand what is evil than what is good"
(III.viii.37–40).

At this point Quintilian seems worried that some readers will
think that he recommends teaching boys dishonorable means of
persuasion. This he denies, and since the moral issues are not
peculiar to suasoria alone, he refers his readers to Book XII, where,
in Chapter i, he makes clear his doctrine that the orator must be a
good man and that oratory must be used for good purposes. But
he still believes that school exercises should teach the boys to deal
adequately with evil men and, since he believes that the end justifies the means, to use even shady methods to accomplish honorable
ends. So he continues:

"In the meantime let us consider that these moral questions do
belong in the exercises of the schools, for the nature of evil must be
known that we may better defend the good.

"For the present let me say that if a speaker sets out to persuade
a good man to dishonorable conduct, let him not urge it because it
is dishonorable, as some declaimers do who urge Sextus Pompey
to engage in piracy just because it is evil and cruel. Even in

addressing bad men we should put what is evil in a good light. For no man is so evil as to wish to seem so. Thus Sallust makes Catiline speak as if he were driven to criminal acts not by wickedness but by indignation. . . .

"How much more is this pretension to honor to be maintained in persuading those who have a real regard for their good name. Accordingly if, in a suasoria, we counsel Cicero to implore the mercy of Antony or even to burn the *Philippics* (supposing such to be the condition on which Antony offers him his life), we shall not advance his love of life as an argument (for if this has any influence on his mind, it will maintain that influence even if we are silent); we shall exhort him to preserve himself for the service of his country. He will need such a reason that he may not be ashamed of his supplication to Antony" (iii.viii.43–47).

Seneca reports in his *Suasoriae* (vi, vii) two versions of this popular theme on a supposititious episode in the life of Cicero. He also tells a story of a thoughtless schoolboy who was cleverly caught up by his professor, Arellius Fuscus, for failing to adapt a suasoria to the character he was imagined as addressing. Seneca (iv.4) tells the story as follows:

"Fuscus delivered a declamation about the woman who had three times given birth to a dead child and then said she had dreamed she must bring forth in a grove. When Fuscus was declaiming on the side of the grandfather who refused to recognize the child [which was alleged to have been born in the grove] he handled the stock argument against dreams. Then after declaring that whoever represented the gods as attending upon women in childbirth wronged their majesty, he quoted amid great applause the following lines of Virgil:

Is that forsooth a task for gods above?
Are such the cares that irk their calm repose?

A certain pupil (to spare his feelings I shall not name him) was delivering this suasoria about Alexander [this is the fourth in Seneca's collection, urging Alexander to pay no attention to the warnings of the astrologer but to enter Babylon forthwith] in the presence of Fuscus and thought to quote the same line with equally good effect. Then says Fuscus to him, 'If you had said this in the presence of Alexander, you would have learned that in Virgil there is also this line:

He buried his sword as far as the hilt.'"

Seneca did not need remind his readers that Alexander was notorious as a very arrogant and irascible man who fancied himself as a son of the god.

American schools and colleges are blessed as the schools of imperial Rome were not. Our students and teachers can practice deliberation on live and actual issues of contemporary politics, and they will continue to enjoy these blessings without fear of assassination or concentration camp so long as the issues of contemporary politics are settled by discussion and vote instead of by armed force or by threats of force. The *Ad Herennium* shows that Roman professors of rhetoric preferred to have their students practice deliberation on living and contemporary issues, instead of fictitious and remote ones, when it was safe and possible to do so.

Nevertheless I hope that this chapter has shown that there are benefits to be derived from school deliberations of historical themes. Why should not an American boy or girl find vitality in American history if historical themes like these were assigned? "Washington urges his troops at Valley Forge to renewed courage." "Benedict Arnold deliberates whether to betray West Point to the British." "Lincoln deliberates whether or not to free the slaves." "Wilson urges the people to vote for the League of Nations." Our students would thus learn a great deal that they now do not know about adaptation of a speech to speaker and to audience as well as a great deal about American history.

Whatever advantages modern American schools have over ancient schools of rhetoric in respect to vitality of themes for discussion, modern textbooks on rhetoric and modern teaching technic are far behind the Greeks and Romans in discovering the reasons which may be adduced for or against any possible line of conduct. Few American students, young or old, have been trained in the topics of deliberation to ask, "Is it possible? Is it expedient? Is it honorable?" Yet the use of these questions is as simple as it is efficacious. Once he has been taught the topics of deliberation the modern student knows just what to do with them and goes about doing it.

Controversia

Actual judicial oratory, as Aristotle points out in the *Rhetoric,* "either attacks or defends somebody. . . . The party in a case at law is concerned with the past; one man accuses the other, and the other defends himself, with reference to things already done. . . . Parties in a law case aim at establishing the justice or injustice of some action and they bring in all other points as subsidiary and relative to this one. . . . Thus the litigant will sometimes not deny that a thing has happened or that he has done harm. But that he is guilty of injustice he will never admit" (1.3).

It is well to remember that judicial oratory is not restricted to what is said in court before a judge or a jury. The speaker, or writer, may, as it were, plead before the bar of public opinion. Hence, some of the most famous examples of judicial oratory in the past have never been heard in a court of law. Although Isocrates' *On the Antidosis* goes through the pretense that it was delivered in court, it was intended to circulate among readers to defend the writer's reputation from the attacks of detractors, as were the *Defensio pro se* of Milton and the *Apologia* of John Henry Newman. One of the most famous of all, the *Apology of Socrates,* was not only not delivered in court but was not written by Socrates. It is a prosopopoeia written by Plato and was no different from a controversia written and delivered by a schoolboy on the same subject. No different, that is, in kind: no schoolboy has as yet equaled its literary quality.

The philosophical basis of accusation and defense in matters of justice and injustice is carefully outlined by Aristotle. " 'Law' is either special or general. By special law I mean the written law which regulates the life of a particular community, by general law, all those unwritten principles which are supposed to be acknowledged everywhere. . . . The second kind makes up for the defects of a community's written code of law. This is what people call equity; people regard it as just; it is, in fact, the sort of justice which goes beyond the written law.

"Equity bids us be merciful to the weakness of human nature; to think less about the laws than about the man who framed them, and less about what he said than about what he meant; not to consider the actions of the accused so much as his intentions, nor this or that detail so much as the whole story; to ask not what a man is now but what he has always or usually been. . . . If the written law tells against our case, clearly we must appeal to the universal law and insist on greater equity and justice. . . . This is the bearing of the lines of Sophocles' *Antigone,* where Antigone pleads that in burying her brother she had broken Creon's law, but not the unwritten law. . . . Or perhaps we point out that the law in question contradicts some other highly esteemed law or even contradicts itself. . . . If, however, the written law supports our case, we urge the judges not to give a verdict contrary to law" (1.10–15).

Even this drastic condensation of Aristotle's important discussion points out an essential of every case which students could argue profitably in ancient schools or can now argue in the moot courts conducted in most law schools in America. Whether a case be actual or fictitious, it must have two sides if it is to be argued. The students must argue on both sides, one after the other. Hence it is that the cases which may be most instructively argued in school are those cases which present a conflict between law and equity, between the letter of the law and the intention of the law, between contradictions in the law itself, between the relative claims of one higher law and another, between greater and less injustices.

Aristotle's use of a quotation from a tragedy of Sophocles as an illustration of the conflict between the written law and the unwritten law shows how useful fictitious cases quoted from the poets or invented for the occasion may be to the teacher of rhetoric. The controversiae in the schools of Greece and Rome came to be based almost exclusively on fictitious themes. Some of these themes were wildly improbable, romantic, fantastic. Some dealt with shocking crimes of adultery, rape, incest, mayhem, and homosexuality—the same crimes which fill our newspapers and furnish plots for our novels.

But as formulated as themes for controversiae these fictitious or hypothetical cases were designed to promote a great deal of intellectual activity on the part of the students. So long as a theme did indeed force the student to think through an intricate lawyer's puzzle, the teachers seemed not to care even if the theme involved the acceptance of impossibilities, perversions of history, and nonexistent laws.

My first example is one of the earliest recorded in Roman rhetoric. It appears in Cicero's *De inventione:* "From contrary laws a controversy arises when two or more laws appear to be at variance with one another. In this manner: There is a law, 'That he who has slain a tyrant shall receive the reward of men who conquer at Olympia, and shall also ask whatever he pleases of the magistrate, and the magistrate shall grant it to him.' There is also another law, 'When a tyrant is slain, the magistrate shall also put to death his five nearest relations.' Alexander, who was the tyrant of Pherae, a city in Thessaly, was slain by his own wife, whose name was Thebe, at night, when he was in bed with her. She as her reward demands the liberty of her son whom she had by the tyrant. Some say that according to the law the son ought to be put to death. The case is brought to trial" (II.49).

In fact Alexander, tyrant of Pherae, was murdered by his brothers, not by his wife, and he had no son.[11] Moreover neither law cited was ever valid in Rome. But the hypothetical situation does afford a satisfactory classroom illustration of a conflict of laws and, moreover, affords opportunity for appeals to the feelings both for and against Thebe.

My next illustration, from Seneca, presents a theme involving a conflict between law and equity, a favorite conflict in the schools. Tradition captions it

THE DAUGHTER OF THE PIRATE CHIEF

"A young man captured by pirates writes his father for ransom. He is not ransomed. The daughter of the pirate chief urges him to swear that he will marry her if he escapes. He swears. Leaving her father, she follows the young man, who, upon his return to his home, takes her to wife. A well-to-do orphan appears on the scene. The father orders his son to divorce the daughter of the pirate chief and marry the orphan. When the son refuses to obey, the father disowns him" (*Controversiae* i.vi.6).

The case is imagined as coming before a court when the son brings action for reinstatement. By actual Roman law a son was required to obey the father during the father's lifetime (*patria potestas*). Only under school law could a parent disown a child for disobedience—a useful law for the school, for otherwise many an interesting dispute could not have been imagined as getting into court. Hence, in this controversia, the father had the law on his side. But the son had the higher law on his side. If he obeyed his father he would violate his sacred oath, given to his wife, whom, it seems, he loved. This romantic theme seems to bear the seal of Hollywood. It did in fact furnish the plot for the fifth tale of the *Gesta Romanorum* and in turn for Scudéry's *Ibrahim; ou l'illustre Bassa*. In the *Gesta* the father pardons the son.

In another absurdly ingenious theme both sides have support

[11] Hofrichter, *Studien zur Entwickelungsgeschichte der Deklamation*, p. 27.

from the same law. But where is the equity, if any? Seneca presents the case, which may bear the title

THE RAVISHER OF TWO

"Law: The victim of rape may choose to have her ravisher put to death or to marry her without dowry. A certain man raped two girls the same night. One girl chose to have him killed. The other girl chose to marry him" (*Controversiae* I.v.5).

Here the young man finds the moral law as well as the legal demand of one of the girls against him. The legal demand of the other girl for his life and hand in marriage is supported by the disinclination of a tolerant society to inflict death on the ravisher whose victim wishes to marry him. This popular theme also appears in Calpurnius Flaccus (49) and furnishes the plot for the fourth tale of the *Gesta Romanorum,* in which the judge decides in favor of the girl who chose marriage.

More and different legal points are raised in the following theme, which seems to owe something, at least, to the tragic dilemma of Orestes, compelled by moral law to kill the murderer of his father, who happened to be his mother. The theme is stated under the title

THE BRAVE VETERAN WITHOUT HANDS

"Law: Whosoever takes a couple in adultery and kills them both then and there may not be prosecuted.

"A brave soldier lost his hands in the wars. He surprised a man in adultery with his wife, by whom he had an adolescent son. He ordered his son to kill the criminals. The young man refused to kill them. The adulterer escaped. The man disowned his son" (*Controversiae* I.4).

The first law was an old one of the Roman republic. The young man was, of course, bound by law to obey his father and bound by the higher law not to kill his mother. On the other hand, the wife was taken in adultery, and the husband had the legal right to kill her along with her paramour. But did the law give him a right to delegate this power when he was unable in his maimed condition to exercise it in person? An ingenious speaker could make out a good case for either side of this controversy, and we may be sure that in Roman declamation schools many an ingenious speaker did.

According to the studies of Bornecque, out of 74 controversiae only 20 turn on actual Roman law in force at the time of Seneca.[12] But the subsequent studies of S. F. Bonner indicate that very few of the laws are clearly fictitious, although some were probably obsolete in the time of Seneca, and some may have been little more than customs, and a few imaginary.[13]

To many of the critics of Roman declamation the use of fictitious laws is a most serious fault, contributing unreality to what should have been preparation for the sternest reality of legal argument in the forum. But Quintilian, at least, had no strong objection to the use of imaginary laws in school controversiae: "In the exercises of the schools some laws are laid down merely to connect a series of circumstances in a case, thus: 'Let a father, who recognizes a son that he has exposed, take him back on paying for his subsistence. Let it be lawful for a father to disinherit a son who is disobedient to his admonitions. A father who has taken back a son that he had exposed requires him to marry a rich relation; the son wishes to marry the daughter of the poor person who had brought him up. The law regarding children exposed is a subject for moving the feelings; but the decision depends on the law concerning disinheritance" (VII.i.14-15).

Certainly one of the most vital and useful types of controversia was that which dealt with reality. Such would be the controversiae which dealt with actual legal cases that had come up for trial in the past. Thus Socrates had been tried and condemned, and Plato when he wrote the *Apology* knew what Socrates had said or might have said in his own defense. Likewise Quintilian reports, "Brutus wrote a declamation in defense of Milo as an ex-

[12] Bornecque, *Les Déclamations et les déclamateurs d'après Sénèque le père,* p. 73.
[13] Bonner, *Roman Declamation,* pp. 48-131.

ercise, although Celsus erroneously thinks he delivered it" (x.i.23). Usually a historical controversia was composed as an answer to some famous speech which had already been published. But Quintilian prefers the method of Brutus: "Let the student set down cases in writing, either the same that he has heard pleaded, or others, provided that they be on real facts and let him handle both sides of the question. . . . And let him exercise himself with arms that will decide real contests as we observed Brutus did in composing a speech for Milo. This is a much better exercise than writing replies to old speeches, as Cestius did to Cicero's speech in behalf of Milo, though he could not have a sufficient knowledge of the other side from reading only the defense" (x.v.20).

Quintilian for like reasons would have approved the moot-court procedure at Yale. In a letter of March 29, 1943, Dean A. G. Gulliver of the School of Law, Yale University, described this moot-court procedure to me as follows: "It differs from the system in force in most of the law schools in . . . that the cases are argued from the records on appeal (i.e., the transcript of the testimony and other evidence) of a case that has actually been tried in the courts. We believe this to be more satisfactory than arguments from purely hypothetical statements of facts. It increases the interest of the students in the work and it also gives them valuable training in presenting the interpretation of the testimony most favorable to their client. As you no doubt appreciate, the presentation of the 'facts' is frequently just as important in legal arguments as the presentation of propositions of law."

In its adherence to actuality this moot-court procedure gives splendid exercises to the law student. Perhaps it is in all respects superior to the method generally used in other law schools, where the exercises in legal argument are based, like the usual ancient controversia, on fictitious or hypothetical cases. But a well-planned fictitious case, in which much may be said on both sides, can also, as history shows, give the student sound training in "presenting the interpretation of the testimony most favorable to his client."

The procedure of examining the status of any case, actual or fictitious, which furnished a foundation for all sound judicial oratory
in antiquity, was taught effectively in the Greek and Roman
declamation schools in controversiae based on fictitious and hypothetical themes. If the student is to conjecture as plausibly as possible concerning the "facts" not established and to interpret the
"facts" as favorably as possible for his client, he must, like the
actual advocate, determine the issue in doubt. To determine this
issue, or status, he must ask the familiar three questions:

(1) Does the issue hinge on a question of fact? (*an sit*) Did it
happen? Did A kill B?

(2) Or, the facts being admitted, is it a question of definition?
(*quid sit*) Is the killing, for instance, to be defined as murder or
as manslaughter?

(3) Or does the issue hinge on the interpretation of the nature
of the act? (*quale sit*) Was it good or bad?

How the Roman teacher trained his students to apply status to
the issues of fictitious themes of controversiae will now appear.

DID HE DO IT? (AN SIT)

Most cases which are tried in court turn on questions of fact.
Did Ruth Snyder kill her husband? Did Bruno Hauptmann kid-
nap the Lindbergh baby? Did Ernest Booth rob the bank? Likewise in our popular mysteries we find a dead body in a locked
room with a Malay kris buried in the heart. Who did it? (Or in
classic American, Who dun it?) Among the ancient themes for
controversiae only a few turn on, Who did it? (*an sit; status
facta; status conjecturalis*). But among these are several of the
most interesting. An early controversia, reported by Seneca, might
be called

THE CASE OF THE INFANT WITNESS

"After the death of his wife, by whom he had a son, a certain
man took a second wife. In his house he had a handsome butler.
Because there were frequent quarrels between stepmother and

stepson, he ordered the young man to live elsewhere. The young man rented the adjacent house. There was a rumor of adultery between the butler and the second wife. The father was found killed in the bedroom, his wife was wounded, the party wall was broken through. It pleased the nearest relatives to ask the five-year-old child, who slept in the same room, if he recognized the murderer. He pointed an accusing finger at the butler. The son brought an accusation of murder against the butler; the butler accused him of parricide" (*Controversiae* vii.5).

The following issues were raised by the rhetoricians from whose treatment Seneca quotes: Can the court trust so small a child as a witness? Is it probable that a son would kill his father and only wound his stepmother? Is it probable that the stepmother was the butler's mistress? His accomplice? Did the son have motive and opportunity? Did the butler? Is it probable that the son would break down the party wall between the houses to gain access to the bedroom? Or was that evidence manufactured? The issue, however, rests finally on the question, Can the court accept the testimony of the five-year-old witness? The defense of the butler must lie only in impugning the witness and resting his case on the probabilities, which are none too good, in his favor.

Aristotle in his *Rhetoric* seems to have said all that need be said on using the evidence of witnesses. This school case, as well as others I shall adduce, seems to have been planned to exercise students in the application of the theoretical principles which the philosophers and teachers of rhetoric urge. Aristotle's statement follows: "In dealing with the evidence of witnesses, the following are useful arguments. If you have no witnesses on your side, you will argue that the judges must decide from what is probable; that the probabilities cannot be bribed to mislead the court; and that probabilities are never convicted of perjury. If you have witnesses and the other man has not, you will argue that probabilities cannot be put on trial, and that we could do without the evidence of witnesses altogether if we need do no more than balance the pleas advanced on either side" (1.15).

The testimony of witnesses, circumstantial evidence, and a weighing of probabilities all enter into a murder mystery which appears as the second of the major declamations of Quintilian. The case hinges on the *status conjecturalis*. The question is, Who did it? [14] The plot is related to that of "The Infant Witness" in that it turns on the triangle of father, son, and stepmother. But it is much more interesting, much more difficult of solution. It is:

THE CASE OF THE BLIND MAN AT THE DOOR

"A young man carries his father out of their burning house. When he goes back for his mother, he cannot find her but loses his eyesight in the search. The father marries a second wife. She comes to her husband one day and says that the young man is planning to poison him, that the young man has the poison in his breast, and that he has promised her half the estate if she will administer the poison to her husband. The father goes to the blind son and asks him if this is true. The son denies it. The father searches him and finds poison in his breast. He asks his son for whom he has prepared it. The son keeps silent. The father leaves him and, changing his will, makes his second wife his heir. The same night there is a commotion in the house. The household rushes to the master's bedroom and find him killed and the wife seemingly asleep by the side of the body and the blind son standing at the door of his own room, his bloody sword under his pillow. The blind son and the stepmother accuse one another of the murder."

The circumstantial case against the son is very strong. The evidence shows that the father had found poison on his person. His bloody sword was found under his pillow. He was awake at the door of his room when the household found the body. Moreover,

---

[14] Other declamations of Quintilian which turn on *status conjecturalis* are I, V, XVIII, XIX.

the stepmother testified that he had plotted to poison his father. The father had believed her evidence to the extent of making his second wife, not his son, his heir. This disinheritance might give the son a motive for the murder.

But the model declamation, which is given in full in the declamations of Quintilian, is for the blind son. Because of his infirmity the blind young man is imagined as not pleading his own cause, but as being represented by an advocate. The model speech rests the defense entirely on probabilities since there is no testimony of witnesses favorable to the young man. The defense follows these lines: The young man could not have stabbed his father because of his blindness. That the stepmother accuses him is evidence of her own guilt. The mass of circumstantial evidence piled up against the blind son suggests a frame-up. If he had committed the murder he would have been more circumspect. He loved his father, else he would not have saved him first from the burning house. It was easy for the stepmother to deceive the aged father and to plant the poison on the person of the blind son. That the young man had no ready answer when his father asked what the poison was for pleads his surprise and innocence. The father's murder did not benefit the son. That the stepmother could sleep through the hubbub which roused the household is improbable. The bloody sword under the pillow is not sufficient evidence that the son had used the sword against his father. The affection of a son for his father, based on kinship, is stronger than that of a wife for a husband, based as it is on sex. The woman was strong enough to stab her husband in his sleep. She had opportunity (in bed with the victim) and motive (to inherit before the old man could change the will again). If the son needed an accomplice for poisoning his father, his stepmother would be the least probable person for him to approach. That he did so is unlikely. That he offered her one half the estate to help him by administering the poison is unsupported. If the father had really believed that his son had planned to poison him, he would have charged him with parricide or disowned him, not merely have changed his will. Finally the advocate implores the judges to pity the impoverished, outcast, friendless, unfortunate young man.

Even a youth who was not planning to take up the practice of law as a career could gain a great deal from arguing on both sides of such controversiae. He would at least learn to take the first steps toward wisdom; he would learn not to believe a thing just because someone says it is so. When we know something to be an indisputable fact, we do not argue whether it is or is not a fact (*an sit*). But if we do not know, we can only conjecture. These controversiae of the declamation schools helped to train the youth to form his conjectures according to the laws of necessity and probability. The rhetorical exercises were thus based on Isocrates' philosophy of rhetoric, that the business of rhetoric was not with truth, but with opinion.

WHAT DID HE DO? WHAT WAS DONE? (QUID SIT)

The controversiae in which the critical issue turned on the status of fact are in the minority. In by far the most of them the facts are supposed to be admitted by both sides; they are established in the themes. The principal issue will be found in the status of definition or in the status of quality. The following controversia turns on the status of definition. It is a very early one. Suetonius, who recounts it in his *On Rhetoricians* (1), says it dates from the time of Crassus, when Cicero was a boy, and adds:

"The old controversiae were based either on history, as sometimes they are today, or on something that had happened recently in real life. Accordingly they were usually presented with even the names of the localities included. At any rate that is true of the published collections.

"Some young men from the city went to Ostia in the summer season, and arriving at the shore, found some fishermen drawing in their nets. They made a bargain to give a certain sum for the haul (*bolus*). The money was paid, and they waited for some time until the nets were drawn ashore. When they were at last drawn out, no fish were in them, but a closed basket of gold. Then the purchasers said the haul belonged to them, the fishermen said it was theirs." [15]

In this early controversia the facts are all granted. There is no dispute as to what happened. The dispute turns on the status of definition. The speaker for the fishermen would define "haul" as fish only, asserting that this was the intention of the contract. The speaker for the young men would define "haul" as everything in the net. The speakers debate the issue in the realm of intentions, probabilities, and interpretations just as real advocates would and must do in disputes involving actual contracts and wills.

The status of definition likewise enters as the issue in one of Lucian's surviving controversiae, the *Tyrannicide*. Of this we have both the theme and the text of the declamation. The theme is stated as follows: "A man forces his way into the stronghold of a tyrant, with the intention of killing him. Not finding the tyrant himself, he kills his [i.e., the tyrant's] son and leaves his sword sticking in his body. The tyrant, coming and finding his son dead, slays himself with the same sword. The assailant now claims that the killing of the son entitles him to the reward of tyrannicide" (Fowler translation II, 173).

The law, a school law appearing in a number of controversiae, is "Who kills a tyrant shall receive a reward." In Lucian's declamation it is supposed that the reward has been refused and the slayer of the son has brought suit to secure it. The status is that of definition. What is tyrannicide? The state claims the man should have killed the tyrant with his own hands. The plaintiff insists, "The law looks only at the end; of the means it says nothing." He asserts he brought about the death of the tyrant. Is tyrannicide to be defined as (1) "to slay a tyrant with one's own hand" or (2) "to bring about the death of a tyrant, directly or indirectly"? The

[15] Suetonius wrote between 106 and 113 A.D. Crassus died in 91 B.C. The published collections of moot-court cases from which Suetonius drew his case are unfortunately lost.

speaker dilates on the evils of tyranny and the benefits of democracy, but *the* status is that of definition. It was a popular declamation in the Renaissance. Both Erasmus and Thomas More translated it into Latin and wrote Latin declamations against the claimant.[16]

In the following dispute about a contract the case turns on definitions of "violence" and "force." Did the father sign the contract of his own free will or was he constrained by violence? The case is one of those reported by Seneca (IX.3) and can be called

THE CASE OF THE MAN WHO RECLAIMED
ONE OF TWO EXPOSED CHILDREN

"Law: Things done under pressure of force and fear are not legally binding. Contracts made according to law are valid. Whoever acknowledges as his a child he has exposed may reclaim the child upon paying the costs of the child's upbringing. A certain man took two boys who had been exposed and brought them up. When the natural father looked for them, this man promised to show him where they were if he might keep one of them. They made a contract on these terms. The man returned the two sons to the father and reclaimed one of them." [17]

The father, it is understood, refused to return one of the boys, insisting on keeping both. The foster father brought suit to recover one of the boys, insisting that the contract had been signed by the natural father of his own free will and hence was legally binding. The natural father asserted that the contract was invalid as being signed under constraint of violence.

Porcius Latro, speaking for the foster father, set out to show that the cause of the father's signing of the contract could not be defined as "violence." This is Seneca's summary of Latro's argument: "In this case was there violence or constraint? There was no violence. By violence the law means force of arms, imprisonment, and the greatest danger. Nothing of the sort was applied to him. But he

[16] Thompson, *The Translations of Lucian by Erasmus and St. Thomas More,* pp. 29–44.
[17] *Gesta Romanorum* 116 uses this theme.

says, 'Violence and constraint were applied when willy-nilly I had to yield. I was constrained, for I could not have one son unless I promised the other.' I answer, In the first place it is not violence when one has to endure one thing in order to accomplish another, but an agreement. For instance I cannot have a house unless I buy it; there is no other house for sale; the seller sees his opportunity and takes advantage of it. You cannot nullify your purchase; otherwise chicanery would have no bounds. But the other repeats, 'I was constrained.' You were constrained? At the beginning and now also you could have avoided [making such a contract]. You could have found the boys in another way; you could have hoped for other traces. But you were not able to find them in another way. Therefore this way seemed better to you. . . . Finally, did the foster father use violence? 'You,' says the father, 'used violence against me when you would not tell me where the boys were unless I signed the contract.' No, I retort, it is not employing violence to promise something under certain conditions. If there was any violence, it was employed by you against yourself when you brought yourself to expose your two boys."

The last retort of Porcius Latro's shows how appeals to the feelings would be used against the father. Since the boys were assumed to be twins exposed at the same time, appeals to the feelings were used on the other side against separating them. The rhetoricians made clear to the students, however, that the real issue was, "Was the contract made according to law? Did the father sign the contract under the constraint of force and fear (*vim metumque*)?"

Definition is also the status on which turns an accusation of homicide which Quintilian says he used in his own school: "That definition may be better known to my young men (for I shall always think of the young men in my school as mine) I shall use as an example a fictitious controversia. Some youths, who were in the habit of associating together, agreed to dine on the seashore.

One of them being absent from the dinner, the others erected a sort of tomb to him, and inscribed his name upon it. . . . His father, returning from a voyage across the sea, landed on that part of the coast, and, on reading his son's name, hanged himself. The young men were alleged to be the cause of the father's death. The definition of the accuser will be, 'He that commits any act that leads to the death of another is the cause of the other's death.' The definition of the accused will be, 'He who knowingly commits any act by which the death of another must necessarily be caused,' etc. But setting aside definition, it is enough for the accuser to say, 'You were the cause of the man's death, for it was through your act that he died, since if you had not acted as you did, he would now be alive.' To this the advocate of the accused will reply, 'He by whose act the death of a person has been caused, is not necessarily to be condemned for it, else what would become of accusers, witnesses, and judges in capital cases? Nor is there always guilt in the person from whom the cause proceeded; for instance, if a person invites someone to dinner, and he dies of a surfeit committed at it, would he be guilty of his death? Nor was the act of the young men the sole cause of death, but also the credulity of the old man, and his weakness in enduring affliction; for if he had had more fortitude or wisdom, he would still be living. Nor did the young men act with any bad intention, and he might have judged, either from the place of the supposed tomb, or from the marks of haste in its construction, that it was no real sepulcher. What ground is there for condemning them, for everything which constitutes homicide is lacking except the contributory act?' " (iii.iii. 30–34).

Some of the most complicated and interesting themes debated in the declamation schools demanded a great deal of acumen and subtle wit to determine the issue. In some the quality of the admitted actions was of the vilest, but could the doer under the given law be convicted of the crime he was accused of? Such themes were good foolkillers for unwary youths who rushed into a defense or accusation following the sound impulses of their hearts but not using their heads. Thus in Seneca's *Controversiae* we have

THE CASE OF THE MUTILATED BEGGARS

"Law: An action can be brought for injury done the state (lese majesty). A certain man mutilated exposed children and thus mutilated forced them to beg and demanded the profits from them. He is accused of doing injury to the state" (x.4).

Seneca records that the prosecution used appeals to outraged feelings against the "certain man," but the best professors preferred to speak for the defense. They admitted the man was evil but asserted that he was not legally guilty of the crime alleged—injury done the state.

A similar and very famous case involved Flaminius, who was accused of injury done the state, on the charge that he had caused a condemned criminal to be executed at a banquet on the request of a harlot who said she had never seen a man decapitated. Cicero (*De senectute* 12) and Seneca (*Controversiae* ix.2) both give this version. Livy says that Flaminius did it to please a pet boy and that the man decapitated was not a condemned criminal but a free Gaul. Plutarch says it was for a pet boy, but that the victim was a condemned criminal.

The question hinges on whether it was legal to execute the criminal in this place or under these circumstances. If it was illegal, can the crime properly be defined as injury done the state? If the execution was legal, no matter how morally vile Flaminius might be, he could not be convicted on the charge brought.

Another lese majesty case is attached to the name of Parrhasius, the famous painter. Seneca (*Controversiae* x.5) gives the theme as follows and outlines an ingenious defense by Gallio:

"Parrhasius, an Athenian painter, when Philip sold Olynthian captives, bought one of them, an old man. He brought him to Athens. He tortured him, and using him as a model, painted a Prometheus. The Olynthian died under the torture. Parrhasius placed the picture as an offering in the temple of Minerva. He was accused of causing injury to the state.

"Most of the declaimers in treating this controversia divided it not like a controversia but like an accusation, following the plan usually followed by those who speak in an accusation in the forum. In the school, because one does not speak twice, one ought to speak not only for his own side but should rebut as well. The division for the accusation was that Parrhasius had tortured a man, that he had tortured an Olynthian, that he had imitated the punishments inflicted by the gods, that he had placed the picture in the temple of Minerva. If Parrhasius was not going to reply, that division would have been good enough. But nothing is worse than to declaim a controversia in which nothing can be said on the other side. Gallio, for Parrhasius, used a division not unlike that which Latro used in the controversia about the man who mutilated the exposed children, shortening it somewhat. Here is the division. Has the state been injured? What has it lost? Nothing, he said. I shall not yet debate the legal aspects of the controversia. Olynthus lost an old man. 'But you have granted to Olynthians that they be treated on the same footing as Athenians.' Let us consider him as an Athenian. You wouldn't bring an action of injury to the state against me if I killed an Athenian senator, but an accusation of murder. 'Yes, but the good name of Athens has been injured. We have always had a reputation for pity.' The good name of a city has never been injured by the fault of a single man. The good name of Athens is too well established to be overturned in this fashion. 'You have,' they say, 'injured the state because you have placed the picture in the temple.' One injures the state when one takes something from a temple, not when he gives something; when he destroys a temple, not when he adorns it. 'Then a fault was also committed by the priests who accepted the picture.' But why shouldn't they accept the picture? The adulteries of the gods are represented in pictures. Pictures showing Hercules killing his children are placed in the temples. And again can one accuse a person of

injury to the state for doing what he has a right to do? Find a law
according to which he has not a right to do what he did. 'But,' you
say, 'he ought not to have done it.' Views on matters of this sort
are undefined. Nothing of this sort is punished; only that is
punished which is against the law. It is quite sufficient that this
artist, inexperienced in affairs, is innocent in the eyes of the law." [18]

Practice with such themes taught the students that moral indignation is not sufficient to win a case. The prosecution must
prosecute for the right crime if it is to secure a conviction. Or are
laws to be set aside to vent our rage against an evil person?

WAS THE ACTION RIGHT OR WRONG? (QUALE SIT)

The status of quality usually enters a dispute when the facts are
admitted and the definition of the action is agreed upon. Or it may
be introduced to adorn and support a case as a second line of defense; thus, Cicero asserted that Milo had not murdered Clodius,
but that even if he had, it was a good thing for the country. One
of the most agreeable actual cases pleaded by Cicero on the status
of quality is his speech for Archias the poet. Archias, a Greek, had
become a Roman citizen. Enemies of his patron thought to make
political capital out of bringing suit to invalidate his citizenship
by claiming that he had obtained it fraudulently. Cicero said that
of course he was a citizen; he had become a citizen in a legal
manner and had always conducted himself as a citizen. But even if
his claim to citizenship were invalid, he ought to be made a citizen
because he was a good man and a good poet. Most of the speech
is an encomium of poetry. One readily realizes that when a speaker
in a judicial case rests his argument on evidence that the deed and
the doer are either good or bad, he is in effect practicing epideictic
oratory. Whatever the status of a case in the courts of law or of a
theme in a school controversia any speaker would naturally take
every opportunity to eulogize the man he is supporting and vilify
the opponents. But in some cases, as in Cicero's *Pro Archia,* the
whole case is made to turn on the status of quality.

[18] Pierre Louÿs has a story on this theme, *L'Homme de pourpre.*

Seneca in his *Controversiae* (ix.5) reports an interesting theme for a school controversia, which turns in part on the status of definition and to a greater extent on the status of quality:

"Law: Action can be brought for violence. After taking a second wife, a certain man lost two sons by his previous marriage. From the symptoms it was doubtful whether they died of indigestion or of poison. The third son was kidnaped by his maternal grandfather, who had not been admitted to see the other two boys when they were sick. When the father sent out the public crier to seek the boy, the grandfather said that he had him. He was accused of violence."

Votienus Montanus, in his treatment of the theme, carefully pointed out that the grandfather's act could not properly be defined as violence. But he, like all the professors of rhetoric whose treatments are recorded by Seneca, made the issue the moral right of the grandfather to take the boy into his home. Under the circumstances the father's home seemed an unsafe place for the boys.

One of the most famous as well as one of the most charming of the Roman controversiae bears the traditional title *The Poor Man's Bees*. It is the thirteenth of the major declamations of Quintilian. The theme is this: "The law allows an action for injuries suffered wrongfully (*injuria*). A poor man and a rich man were neighbors in the country; their gardens joined. The rich man had flowers in his garden; the poor man, bees. The rich man complained that his flowers were injured by the poor man's bees. He demanded that the bees be removed. When the poor man failed to remove them, the rich man sprinkled poison on his flowers. The poor man's bees all died of the poison. He brings action against the rich man for injuries suffered wrongfully."

This controversia turns entirely on the status of quality. The facts are admitted by both sides. The rich man did poison the poor man's bees. The poor man did suffer damage. But was the damage suffered wrongfully? The whole speech, a prosopopoeia spoken as by the poor man, has no other end than to dilate on the essential wrongness of the rich man and his bee poisoning and the

essential rightness of the poor man and his bees. I subjoin a summary outline of the poor man's plea.

Exordium. It may seem strange that I, a poor man, should have
the daring to sue a rich and powerful enemy, but now my bees are
killed, I have nothing to live for. This may seem an insignificant
case, but to me, a poor man, the bees were all I had.

Narratio. The rich man has built up a large estate by buying up
small holdings. Only my small holding remains, completely sur-
rounded by his estate. [This is colored by a long ecphrasis on the
little farm and the simple and pure pleasures of a frugal country
life. This is followed by a prosopopoeia dramatically presenting
the rich man in the act of arrogantly ordering the bees removed.
Then an ecphrasis, to arouse sympathy, on how the bees suffered
and died as a result of the poison.]

Confirmatio. It is illegal for anyone to possess poison. Possession of poison is evidence of malicious intent. He might as well
have poisoned a man as the bees. Enemies are easier to find than
poison. A poor man is at a disadvantage when a rich man attacks
him. If I got more bees, he might poison them.

Status. He admits the fact that he poisoned my bees (*an sit*).
The question in his plea is, Was damage done (*quid sit*)? and if
so, Was it done wrongfully (*quale sit*)?

Refutatio.

(1) He claims it was not a damage because bees are wild.
(2) He claims it was not done wrongfully, because
    (a) he did it on his own land;
    (b) the bees had damaged his flowers;
    (c) he used only a little poison;
    (d) the bees came of their own accord.
(1′) But it was a damage, because
    (a) it is a damage to lose what it is an advantage to keep;
    (b) the bees were not wild but a homebred swarm;
    (c) all domestic animals were once wild and slaves were
        once free;

(d) the bees were my property and my main source of income.

(2′) Moreover the damage was done wrongfully, because

    (a) if he killed a man on his own land, he would be guilty of murder; hence by killing my bees on his own land he is guilty of wrongful damage.

    (b) If my bees did damage to the flowers in his garden, he should have sued me for damages instead of taking the law into his own hands. If the loss of a few flowers be such a damage to a rich man, how much greater the loss of all my bees to me. [Here follows an ecphrasis on how little damage bees do to flowers and how quickly flowers fade.] He is ungrateful because I used to give him honey every year. [Further dilation on the rich man's wealth and power and the poor man's poverty and weakness.]

    (c) [The small amount of poison is not mentioned in the refutation.]

    (d) That the bees came to the poison of their own accord is no defense, because a man might walk into an ambush of his own accord. What was the rich man's intention? That he destroy my bees. What was the result? That he did destroy them. I suffer a personal loss as well as a property loss because I was fond of my bees.

Peroratio

[An encomium of bees]

(1) Bees do not take offense when we take their honey.

(2) Other domestic animals have to be trained and controlled, but bees work without our bidding.

(3) Other animals injure crops, but not bees.

(4) Men find poison; bees, honey.

(5) Men indulge in sexual lust; but bees engender without sexual pleasure, that enemy of virtue.

(6) A new swarm of bees does not fight for a place in the hive, but goes forth to be hived by man.

(7) Men have to learn mechanical arts, but bees are natural-born mechanics.

(8) A bee hive is a model of civil polity, for
   (a) the life of bees is ordered;
   (b) they save against the future;
   (c) they work for the common good;
   (d) they are industrious;
   (e) they are loyal.

(9) Their combs are works of art.

(10) Their honey is useful as
   (a) medicine;
   (b) food.

Hence, one who would poison bees is unnaturally cruel. The irony is that the man who put poison on his flowers to poison my bees killed his own flowers with the poison.

Margaret Roper, the brilliant daughter of Thomas More, "in imitation or rather emulation of Quintilian, wrote an answer to this speech, in which she defended the rich man," according to Stapleton, More's early biographer, who adds: "Because to defend him is the more difficult, Margaret's art and eloquence should be seen to be the more excellent." [19]

Criticism of Declamation

In my account of declamation as a school exercise in rhetoric I have chosen to seek out what seemed good, useful, and true, what might prove of value to modern teachers in modern schools. In this I differ from Boissier, Bornecque, Summers, Caplan, and Baldwin, who, following the lead of ancient satirists, emphasize

[19] Stapleton, "D. Thomae Mori Angliae quondam cancellarii vita," in *Tres Thomae*, Chapter 11.

the absurdity, shallowness, perverseness, and general silliness of declamations under the Empire. A generation ago I myself sneered at "the utter unreality and hollowness of such rhetoric." [20]

My own change of view from one of ridicule to one of at least qualified approval has been the result of more reading, teaching, and thinking. Could a school exercise that Cicero, Brutus, Cato, Seneca, and Quintilian approved be completely wrongheaded? Could a school system which trained such saints as Basil, Augustine, and Jerome to think, to speak, and to write be entirely ineffective? If it had been wholly foolish could it have maintained itself, as it did, to the end of the Empire, or could it have been praised and revived in the Renaissance by such humanists as Erasmus and Thomas More?

It seems to me that the answer to the rhetorical questions is, "No! A thousand times no!" I trust that my present chapter on declamation has demonstrated some, at least, of the virtues of the exercise when it was taught by sensible and experienced teachers. But since, as Aristotle says, all good things can be abused save virtue herself, even the best friends of declamation must admit it was abused and perverted in some schools and by some teachers. Valuable when used as a preparation for speaking and writing in the forum and the senate, it became educationally footless when cultivated as an end in itself or by teachers unaware of the world outside the school.

We enjoy our own jests at the expense of absent-minded professors. The professor may be a man of high moral character and high professional scholarship in his own field, but the jests usually turn on his unworldliness. Men of the world speak of him as long-haired, starry-eyed, and impractical. The same accusations of impracticality underlie many of the ancient jests at the expense of the professors of rhetoric. Very few surviving Roman jests seem funny to modern readers; but the following seem—to me, at least —both funny and revelatory of the impracticality and unworld-

[20] D. L. Clark, *Rhetoric and Poetry in the Renaissance*, p. 39.

liness, if not the silliness, of some of the professors who taught and spoke declamations in Greece and Rome.

My first jest is at the expense of a famous professor, Albucius Silus, who once pleaded a case in the courts. Intending to amplify his peroration by the use of a figure he said, "Swear, but I will prescribe the oath. Swear by the ashes of your father, which lie unburied. Swear by the memory of your father!" The attorney on the other side, Lucius Arruntius, a practical man, arose. "My client is going to swear," he said. "But I made no proposal," shouted Albucius; "I only employed a figure." The court sustained Arruntius, whose client swore (perjuring himself no doubt), and Albucius retired in shame to the more comfortable shades of his school, where figures were appreciated. "For," says Seneca, who tells the story in his *Controversiae* (Proem vii. 6–7), "he was a man of the highest probity, who knew neither how to inflict injury nor how to endure it."

Some of the silliness in controversiae arose from willful misinterpretation of the theme. Seneca points out (*Controversiae* ix.6) how the following theme was misinterpreted:

"A certain man after the death of his wife, by whom he had a son, took a second wife, by whom he had a daughter. The son died. The father accused the second wife of poisoning him. She was convicted. When she was put to the torture, she confessed that her daughter was an accomplice. The girl was indicted. The father defended her.

"Votienus Montanus neatly derided the absurdities of the professors in this controversia when they declaimed as if, because she was called a girl, she must be an infant; not comprehending that if she had been an infant, there could have been no indictment. Thus we have to assume, he said, that she was of such an age as to make the crime credible. What Cestius said is inadmissible, when he represented the mother as saying to the girl, 'Give brother some poison,' and the daughter as answering, 'Mama, what is poison?' . . .

"Cestius offered in defense, 'If he said this to make fun of me, he is a clever fellow. I know now that it was absurd of me to say that, but I say lots of things not because they please me, but because they please the audience.' " [21] Dryden defends the absurdities of his heroic plays in much the same words. But the defense is more appropriate to the theater than to the school.

Another cause of absurdity was the school habit of making full and careful notes or even memorizing a plea and then following through with no adaptation to changing conditions in the court. The following anecdotes are from Quintilian.

In order to arouse the feelings of the judge, Quintilian is not at all averse to having his client embrace the knees of the judge or bring into court a weeping child or wife. But mishaps may occur. While the advocate is dilating on his client's unhappiness, the client may be laughing. When one little boy was brought in to court in tears to arouse sympathy for his father, the advocate unwisely asked why he was crying. "Because," the boy sobbed, "my tutor pulled my ears."

"Yet all such mishaps are easily remedied by those who can alter the fashion of their speech. But those who cannot vary from what they have composed are either struck dumb at such occurrences or say what is not true. Hence occur such impertinences as these: 'He is raising his supplicating hands towards your knees,' or 'He is locked, unhappy man, in the embraces of his children,' or 'See, he recalls my attention,' etc., though the client is doing no single thing of all that his advocate attributes to him. These absurdities come from the schools, in which we give play to our imagination freely and with impunity, because whatever we wish is supposed to be done. But reality does not allow of such suppositions, and Cassius Severus made a most happy retort to a young orator who said, 'Why do you look so sternly on me, Severus?' 'I did not, I assure you,' replied Cassius, 'but you had written those words, I suppose, in your notes, and so here is a look for you.'

[21] Cf. Petronius 3.

Whereupon he threw on him as terrible a glance as he could possibly assume" (vi.i.37–43).

Although, as we have seen, Quintilian was one of the stanchest adherents of declamation as a school exercise, praising it and using it in his own school, he again and again voices his warnings against its perversion and misuse.

"The declamations, in which we exercise ourselves, as military men with foils, for the battles of the forum, have for some time past departed from the true resemblance of pleading, and, being composed merely to please, are destitute of vigor, there being the same evil practice among declaimers, assuredly, as that which slave dealers adopt when they try to add to the beauty of young fellows by depriving them of their virility. For as slave dealers regard strength and muscles . . . as at variance with grace, and soften down as being harsh whatever would be strong if it were allowed its full growth, so we cover the manly form of eloquence, and the ability of speaking closely and forcibly, with a certain delicate texture of language, and, if our words are but smooth and elegant, think of little consequence what vigor they have. . . .

"Such effeminate eloquence, therefore . . . I shall never consider as worthy of the name of eloquence. . . .

"Let the youth whom I am instructing, therefore, devote himself, as much as he can, to the imitation of truth, and, as he is to engage in frequent contests in the forum, let him aspire to victory in the schools and learn to strike at the vital parts of his adversary and to protect his own. Let the teacher exact such manly exercise above all things and bestow the highest commendation on it when it is displayed. For though youths are enticed by praise to what is faulty, they nevertheless rejoice at being praised for what is good. At present there is this evil among teachers, that they pass over necessary points in silence, and the useful is not numbered among the requisites of eloquence" (v.xii.17–23).

"It is the custom of most speakers, when the order of facts is set forth, to make a digression to some pleasing and attractive commonplace, so as to secure as much favorable attention as possible from the audience. This practice had its rise in the declamatory ostentation of the schools and passed from thence to the forum, after causes began to be pleaded, not to benefit the parties going to law, but to enable the advocates to make a display" (iv.iii.2–3).

Quintilian takes another jibe at ostentatious display of virtuosity by the witty use of an old story:

"There is a frivolous exercise of skill, such as that of the man who sent peas shot from a distance in succession, and without missing, through a needle. Alexander, after witnessing his dexterity, is said to have presented him with a bushel of peas, which was, indeed, a most suitable reward for his performance. To him I compare those who spend their time in great study and labor, in the composition of declamations which they strive to make as unlike as possible to anything that happens in real life" (ii.xx.3–4).

"Some even in the forum neglect [objections] as matters troublesome and disagreeable, and, content, for the most part, with what they have premeditated, speak as if they had no opponent—an error which is still more common in the schools, in which not only are objections disregarded, but the declamations themselves are in general so framed that nothing can be said on the opposite side" (v.xiii.36).

Seneca records one interesting objection to declamation, either as an art form to be practiced by grown men or as a school exercise as preparation for the forum: "Votienus Montanus never declaimed either out of ostentation or even as an exercise. When I asked his reason, he said, "Which do you want, a good reason, or my real reason? My good reason is lest I seem to pride myself; my real reason is that I do not want to get into bad habits. Whoever prepares a declamation writes not to win but to please. He seeks after all allurements. Because arguments are tiresome and are least capable of adornment, he will leave them out. He is content to charm his audience with sententious epigrams and with dilation. He seeks approbation for himself, not for his cause. This fault follows the declaimers to the forum, for they neglect the necessary to strive for the showy. They can even imagine that their adversaries are as foolish as they wish. They reply to their adversaries what they will and when they will. Besides, there is nothing which visits any punishment upon their mistakes. Their folly costs them nothing. Consequently when they go into the forum they can scarcely shake off the dangerous torpor which had grown on them when they were in the security [of the schools]. Moreover [in the schools] they are upheld by frequent applause and their memory is habituated to fixed intervals of quiet. When they come into the forum and every gesture is not received with applause, they weaken or go to pieces. Add to this that [in the schools] no interruption disturbs the mind. No one laughs. No one deliberately contradicts. All faces are familiar. In the forum, if there were nothing else, the forum itself disturbs them. Whether this story commonly told is true or not you are in a better position to know than I. One day when Porcius Latro, that matchless model of declamatory virtues, was pleading for his kinsman Porcius Rusticus in Spain, he became so confused that he began with a solecism, nor, missing a roof and walls, could he go on until he had the trial transferred from the forum to the basilica. In the exercises of the schools the wits are nurtured so softly that they do not know how to endure the clamor, the silence, the laughter, even the sky [of the forum]. But an exercise is not useful unless it resembles the work for which it is a preparation. Moreover, in general, it is more severe than the actual combat. Gladiators train with heavier weapons than they fight with, and the trainer holds out against these arms longer than does an adversary. Athletes exercise against two or three opponents at a time in order to resist a single one more easily. Runners, when they are to be judged for their speed over a short course, run the distance often in training which they will run only once in the race. By design the labor which is undergone when we practice is made heavier so that it will be lighter when we contend. In the declamations of the schools it is exactly the opposite. Everything is easier and freer. In the forum they are given a side [to advocate], in the school they choose one; there they must conciliate the judge, here they command him; there amidst the loud uproar of the crowd the mind must be exerted and the voice carried to the ears of the judge, here every eye is on the eye of the speaker. Just as when one comes from a shady and obscure place into the clear light, he is blinded by the glare, so those who come from the schools to the forum are perturbed by everything new and unaccustomed. Nor will they reach their strength as orators until, having been subjected to much ridicule, they have hardened the boyish spirit which was softened by the pastimes of the schools" (*Suasoriae et Controversiae* IX. Praefatio).

Philostratus, in *Lives of the Sophists,* makes a valuable distinction between sophist and legal pleader and is much more indulgent than Quintilian or Votienus Montanus. Speaking of Heracleides, he says: "When he had been turned out of the chair of rhetoric at Athens in consequence of a conspiracy against him got up by the followers of Apollonius of Naucratis, he betook himself to Smyrna. . . .

"They say that in the presence of the Emperor Severus he broke down in an extempore speech, because he was abashed by the court and the imperial bodyguard. Now if this misfortune were to happen to a forensic orator [*agoraios*], he might well be criticized; for forensic orators as a tribe are audacious and self-confident; but a sophist spends the greater part of his day in teaching mere boys, and how should he resist being easily flustered? For an extempore speaker is disconcerted by a single hearer whose features have a supercilious expression, or by tardy applause, or by not being clapped in the way to which he is accustomed; but if in addition he is aware that malice is lying in wait for him, as on that occasion Heracleides was subtly conscious of the malice of Antipater, his ideas will not come so readily, his words will not flow so easily, for suspicions of that sort cloud the mind and tie the tongue" (614).

Tacitus, through the mouth of Messalla in the *Dialogus,* gives a very plausible reason for the decay of the older oratory under the Empire: "Great oratory is like a flame: it needs fuel to feed it, movement to fan it, and it brightens as it burns. [This figure of the torch comes from the declamation schools. Seneca in *Controversia* x says that Porcius Latro invented it and that Ovid imitated it in the *Amores.*] At Rome, too, the eloquence of our forefathers owed its development to the same conditions. For although the orators of today have also succeeded in obtaining all the influence that it would be proper to allow them under settled, peaceable, and prosperous political conditions, yet their predecessors in those days of unrest and unrestraint thought they could accomplish more when, in the general ferment and without the strong hand of a single ruler, a speaker's political wisdom was measured by his power of carrying conviction to the unstable populace. This was the source of the constant succession of measures put forward by champions of the people's rights, of the harangues of state officials who almost spent the night in the rostrum, of the impeachments of powerful criminals and hereditary feuds between whole families, of schisms among the aristocracy and never-ending struggles between the senate and the commons. All this tore the commonwealth to pieces, but it provided a sphere for the oratory of those days and heaped on it what one saw were vast rewards. . . . It is better, of course, that such horrors should not occur at all, and we must regard that as the most enviable political condition in which we are not liable to anything of the kind. Yet when these things did happen, they furnished the orators of the day with ample material. . . . I do not mean that it was worth the country's while to produce bad citizens, just in order that our orators might have an ample supply of material; but let us bear in mind the point at issue, realizing that our discourse is dealing with an art which comes to the front more readily in times of trouble and unrest. We all know that the blessings of peace bring more profit and greater happiness than the horrors of war; yet war produces a larger number of good fighters than peace. It is the same with eloquence. . . . In consequence of the long period of peace and the unbroken spell of inactivity on the part of the commons and of peaceableness on the part of the senate, by reason also of the working of the great imperial system, a hush has fallen upon eloquence, as indeed it has upon the world at large. . . . In Macedonia and in Persia eloquence was unknown, as indeed it was in all states that were content to live under a settled government. . . . What is the use of one harangue after another on public platforms, when it is not the ignorant multitude that decides a political issue, but the wisest of monarchs" (36–41).

How "the wisest of monarchs" might sidestep a plea and at once silence an oration by demanding a declamation is well illustrated by Philostratus' story of Heliodorus, who appeared before Caracalla to plead for the Celtic tribes. The emperor ordered him, instead, to declaim on the fictitious theme: "Demosthenes, after breaking down before Philip, defends himself against the charge of cowardice." After hearing him declaim, Caracalla made him an advocate of the treasury. "He is now," says Philostratus in *Lives of the Sophists,* "spending his old age at Rome, neither greatly admired, nor altogether neglected" (626).[22]

That the exercise of controversia in the declamation schools did in fact furnish "a practical preparation for judicial eloquence" is well documented by Brother E. Patrick Parks,[23] who points out that the overworked courts under the complex administrative machinery of the Empire offered many careers for the advocates who received their training in the schools of declamation. How success as an advocate might lead to the highest posts in the civil administration is illustrated by the story Gibbon tells of Mallius

[22] F. A. Wright surmises that he was the same Heliodorus who wrote that most exciting of Greek romances, the *Aethiopica.* See *A History of Later Greek Literature,* p. 301.

[23] Parks, *The Roman Rhetorical Schools as a Preparation for the Courts under the Early Empire,* p. 19 ff.

Theodorus: "He was distinguished by his eloquence while he pleaded as an advocate in the court of the Praetorian praefect. He governed one of the provinces of Africa . . . and deserved, by his administration, the honour of a brass statue. He was appointed vicar, or vice-praefect, of Macedonia. Questor. Count of the sacred largesses. Praetorian praefect of the Gauls. He was named Praetorian praefect of Italy in the year 397. While he still exercised that great office, he was created, in the year 399, consul for the West." [24]

Erasmus in *De ratione studii* (1511) revived the tradition in the Renaissance, giving high praise to prosopopoeia—"that sort of exercise, which was used by the ancients, which draws themes from historical material. For instance: Menelaus makes a speech urging the Trojans to return Helen. Or, Phoenix urges Achilles to rejoin the battle. Or Ulysses urges the Trojans to return Helen, rather than go on with the war" (*Opera,* 1703 ed., I, 526).

And in his prefatory epistle, dated 1506, to his translation of Lucian's *Tyrannicide* and his reply thereto, Erasmus likewise praises all the exercises of declamation: "I greatly desire that this sort of exercise—no other is more fruitful—should be restored to our schools. For if we were diligently drilled from boyhood in this exercise of declamation, following the precepts of Cicero and Quintilian and the ancient examples, there would not be, in my opinion, such a dearth of good speaking among those who profess oratory publicly" (*Opera,* 1703 ed., I, 265).

In his *Compendium rhetorices* of 1543 [25] when he uses an example to illustrate a precept, he draws from the themes of school controversiae. Thus he uses the familiar theme of the ravisher of two girls on the same night and the theme dissuading Cicero from begging Antony for his life.

---

[24] Gibbon, *The Decline and Fall of the Roman Empire,* Chapter XVII, Note 122.

[25] *Opus Epist.,* X, Appendix XXII, pp. 396–405 (Oxford, 1941), translated by Hoyt Hudson in *Studies in Speech and Drama in Honor of Alexander M. Drummond* (Cornell University Press, 1944), pp. 326–340.

School exercises in controversiae were again revived in 1581 by Alexander van den Busche, called Le Sylvain, whose *Epitomes de cent histoires tragicques* got into English literature and English rhetoric in a translation by Lazarus Piot under title of *The Orator: Handling a Hundred Several Discourses, in forme of Declamations.* The theme of each fictitious or legendary case is stated, followed by a speech or model theme on each side in accusation and defense. As the epistle "To the Reader" indicates, *The Orator* was intended to be an aid to the teaching of rhetoric. "I have thought good . . . to present thee with certaine Rhetoricall Declamations, the use whereof in every member of our Commonweale, is as necessary, as the abuse of wilfull ignorance is odious. In these thou maiest learne Rhetoricke to inforce a good cause, and art to impugne an ill." Among the themes, drawn from Livy as well as from Seneca, occur the following which I have cited in this chapter: the wife who slew her tyrant husband; the man who repudiated his agreement to allow the foster father of the exposed children to keep one of them; the pirate's daughter; the infant witness; Flaminius; the brave veteran without hands; the poisoner who accused her daughter as an accomplice; the ravisher of two; the maternal grandfather who kidnaped his grandson; the mutilated beggars.

Such were the exercises of suasoria and controversia that afforded the advanced students in the schools of rhetoric an opportunity to put into practice the precepts they had learned from the lectures of their professor and from the study of choice models for imitation. To adapt them, especially the controversiae, to modern educational procedure would, I believe, be more difficult and less profitable than to adapt the elementary exercises. But in the Roman schools, adjusted to the conditions of Roman life in the forum and assembly, they contributed a distinctly useful experience when taught by wise and practiced teachers.

EPILOG: RHETORIC IN SCHOOL AND SOCIETY

GUIDED by the precepts of the past, which I have quoted in my own treatment of peroration, I shall perorate briefly, recapitulating some few of the conclusions which from time to time I have endeavored to draw from Greco-Roman theory and practice in the teaching of rhetoric. I shall, however, spare my readers rhetorical amplification and appeals to their feelings.

First, I wish to consider what lessons ancient philosophies of teaching and learning may have given us for our own classroom teaching. Philosophically educational thinkers can be seen to fall into two familiar categories: the theoretics and the empirics—those who have a strong belief in the efficacy of teaching sound doctrine through rational precepts, and those who have an equally strong belief in free experiment and assiduous practice as leading inevitably to improved learning. Today, as in the past, there is a human tendency to exaggerate one's own educational position because one's opponents make exaggerated claims for the unique validity of their educational positions. In imperial Rome there was a passion for orthodoxy in rhetoric as well as in theology and a tendency to place more confidence in traditional precepts than we do today. Experiment and innovation were frowned upon. What was traditional was right. Indeed as long as there were Roman schools—that is, until the Germanic invasions destroyed Roman civilization—these schools taught rhetoric pretty much as it was

taught when Cicero was a boy. In our schools today there has been
a strong movement in the opposite direction. Progressive education has had a tendency to turn its back on the past in its laudable
effort through experimentation to understand the present and
prepare young people for the future. In fear of the kind of traditionalism which bogged down Roman education modern teaching
neglects a study of the traditions of the past which might well
help illuminate the present and the future.

But why go to extremes? Or if we do go to extremes, why stay
there? I urge in teaching—including the teaching of rhetoric—
the same friendly working together of theory and practice that
Horace urged for nature and nurture. The same issue between
theoretics and empirics which has agitated the teachers of rhetoric
has also agitated the doctors of medicine. I approve as common
sense the statement made in the preface of his *De medicina* by
Cornelius Celsus; he approves a combination of practice and experiment with scientific theory in medical education, because the
via media is likeliest to lead to truth.

Next, I wish to recall and emphasize the habitual association of
rhetoric in the best of ancient schools with all the liberal arts
which went to make up encyclopedic learning (*encyclios paideia*)
or cycle of instruction. The same teacher, whether in grammar
school or school of rhetoric, who taught the arts of speaking and
writing, also read great poems, histories, and public addresses of
earlier ages with the boys. The Roman schools did not suffer
from departmentalization as ours do. Rhetoric was not something
to be taught as a separate and isolated skill, but an organic art, at
work "discovering all possible means to persuasion in any subject."
When so integrated with all the component elements of humane
learning, rhetoric today as in antiquity can vitalize and fructify the
mind and spirit of youth. It can still be taught as the art of discourse, teaching the student to think well and live well while it
teaches him to speak well.

A related lesson which we might learn from the experience of the ancients in teaching rhetoric is the lesson that learning which sets up as its only goal the understanding and appreciation of what is learned is incomplete and sterile. Unless the student is led to organize and synthesize the learning he acquires by exercises in making and doing, speaking and writing, the learning is not truly his own. This art, which teaches the student how to acquire learning, to organize it, and to present it persuasively to an audience, is traditionally called rhetoric. Without rhetoric, designated by whatever name, liberal education cannot successfully humanize and civilize the young. As Isocrates truly declares, "None of the things which are done with intelligence are done without the aid of speech."

We might also learn from Greek and Roman teaching of rhetoric that the teaching of the arts of speaking and writing was in antiquity and can be at all times an agent for the teaching of morality. And we are beginning to realize what floods of barbarism are let loose when morality is not taught. The phrase "original sin" may seem old fashioned, but sin is not. It is a commonplace of universal observation that children by natural impulse are liars, thieves, and vandals. Only if some rudiments of morality are inculcated by parents and teachers will the little savages acquire some semblance of civilized conduct. Now all ancient teachers believed that rhetoric should teach virtue and justice. Plato was indignant because he recognized that rhetoric cannot make men just. But Isocrates, Cicero, and Quintilian pointed out in many passages which I have quoted that training in rhetoric can and does contribute to civilizing young men. "When anyone elects to speak or write discourses which are worthy of praise and honor, it is not conceivable that he will support causes which are unjust and petty," says Isocrates. After his father, in the *De partitione,* had given an account of the rhetorical principles of awarding praise and blame, "which have power not only to teach us to speak well, but also to live honorably," Cicero Junior says: "You have taught me, not only how to praise others, but also how to be worthy of praise myself." Quintilian sums up the theme that the orator must be a good man, doing and speaking no evil. Training in rhetoric cannot alone, or with other educational helps, make a youth prudent, temperate, courageous, and just, but it fails in its traditional educational duty if it does not throw its weight in favor of these cardinal virtues. Teachers may be assured that some measure of success will follow.

The final lesson I wish to draw from ancient experience in the teaching of rhetoric is a warning. Rhetoric, which flourished in democratic Greece and Republican Rome, dried up and in part decayed under the benevolent dictatorship of the best of emperors as well as under the despotism of the bloodiest of tyrants. Teachers of rhetoric should lead the fight for freedom of thought and discussion. When real issues of legal, social, and political importance are debated in public print and public assembly, they may be and should be debated in schools. To be sure the Roman boy learned a great deal from debating the issues of fictitious cases. Our students can learn even more from debating actual issues. But freedom of speech is not to be justified on the ground that speakers and writers on live issues do not like to be muzzled. The traditional and still valid justification is that free discussion by speakers and writers will enable the citizens to discover those probabilities most likely to be near the truth and by "the powers of conjecture to arrive generally at the best course," as Isocrates put it. For we must never forget that rhetoric debates, not what has been demonstrated scientifically, but those issues which are uncertain and contingent. In the absence of certain knowledge, it can only hope to arrive at informed and probable opinion as to what in a given situation is just, honorable, and expedient. The most dangerous enemies of civilization are those fanatics who exalt their opinions, or the opinions of some leader, to an altar of orthodoxy and stifle all discussion or dissent as heretical. But I fear I am making an appeal to the feelings—and that I promised not to do.

It was the declaimer Scaurus, quoted by Seneca in his *Contro-*

versiae, whose reminder touches me now. "It is a greater virtue to know how to stop than how to speak." So however difficult it is, I must strive for that virtue and now conclude with the ancient leavetaking of Roman rhetoric. *Dixi,* I have spoken.

BIBLIOGRAPHICAL REFERENCES

PRIMARY SOURCES

For the convenience of readers here is appended a list of Greek and Roman primary sources in available editions and translations. All translations in the body of this book, save those listed in the Preface, are the author's own.

Aphthonius *Progymnasmata*
    Translated by Ray Nadeau, in *Speech Monographs,* XIX, No. 4 (November, 1952), 264–285.
Apuleius *Metamorphoses*
    With an English translation by W. Adlington revised by S. Gaselee. Loeb Classical Library. London, 1915.
Aristotle *De poetica*
    Translated by Ingram Bywater, in *The Works of Aristotle Translated into English,* Vol. XI. Oxford, Oxford University Press, 1924.
    With an English translation by W. Hamilton Fyfe. In same volume with "Longinus" *De sublimitate* and Demetrius *De elocutione.* Loeb Classical Library. London, 1932.
—— *Rhetorica*
    With an English translation by John Henry Freese. Loeb Classical Library. London, 1926.
    Translated by W. Rhys Roberts, in *The Works of Aristotle Translated into English,* Vol. XI. Oxford, Oxford University Press, 1924.
    Translated by J. E. C. Welldon. London, Macmillan and Co., 1886.
—— *De rhetorica ad Alexandrum* (Anonymous treatise, formerly attributed to Aristotle.)
    Translated by E. S. Forster, in *The Works of Aristotle Translated into English,* Vol. XI. Oxford, Oxford University Press, 1924.

Augustine *De doctrina Christiana*
Translated by Marcus Dods, in *City of God and Christian Doctrine*. New York, Charles Scribner's Sons, 1907.
Dods's translation is also in Schaff, Nicene and Post-Nicene Fathers.
De doctrina Christiana, IV, with a translation by Sister Thérèse Sullivan. Washington, D.C., Catholic University of America, 1930.
Ausonius *Professores*
With an English translation by Hugh G. Evelyn White, in Ausonius, Vol. I, Book v. Loeb Classical Library. London, 1919.
Cassiodorus *De rhetorica*
Translated by Leslie Webber Jones, in *An Introduction to Divine and Human Readings,* pp. 148–158. New York, Columbia University Press, 1946.
Cicero *Brutus*
With an English translation by G. L. Hendrickson. Loeb Classical Library. London, 1942.
Translated by E. Jones. In same volume with John Selby Watson's translation of *De oratore*. New York, Harper & Brothers, 1875.
—— *De inventione*
With an English translation by H. M. Hubbell. In same volume with *Topica* and *De optimo genere oratorum*. Loeb Classical Library. London, 1949.
—— *De optimo genere oratorum*
With an English translation by H. M. Hubbell. In same volume with *Topica* and *De inventione*. Loeb Classical Library. London, 1949.
—— *De oratore*
Books i and ii with an English translation by E. W. Sutton and H. Rackham; Book iii with a translation by H. Rackham. 2 vols. Loeb Classical Library. London, 1942.
Translated by John Selby Watson. In same volume with E. Jones's translation of *Brutus*. New York, Harper & Brothers, 1875.
—— *De partitione oratoria*
With an English translation by H. Rackham. In same volume with *De oratore*, Book iii. Loeb Classical Library. London, 1942.
—— *Epistolae ad Familiares*
With an English translation by W. Glynn Williams. 3 vols. Loeb Classical Library. London, 1927.
—— *Orator*
With an English translation by H. M. Hubbell. Loeb Classical Library. London, 1942.

—— *Rhetorica ad Herennium* (Anonymous treatise, formerly attributed to Cicero.)

Commentary and English translation of Book 1 by Ray Nadeau, in *Speech Monographs,* XVI, No. 1 (August, 1949), 57–68.

Texte revue et traduit par Henri Bornecque. Paris, Garnier, n.d.

With an English translation by H. Caplan. Loeb Classical Library. London, 1954.

—— *Topica*

With an English translation by H. M. Hubbell. In same volume with *De inventione* and *De optimo genere oratorum.* Loeb Classical Library. London, 1949.

Demetrius *De elocutione*

With an English translation by W. Rhys Roberts. In same volume with Aristotle *De poetica* and "Longinus" *De sublimitate.* Loeb Classical Library. London, 1932.

Dio Chrysostom *On Training for Public Speaking*

With an English translation by J. W. Cohoon, Discourse 18 included in Dio Chrysostom, Vol. II. Loeb Classical Library. London, 1939.

Diogenes Laertius *Lives of Eminent Philosophers*

With an English translation by R. D. Hicks. 2 vols. Loeb Classical Library. London, 1925.

Dionysius of Halicarnassus *De compositione verborum*

Greek text, with an English translation and notes by W. Rhys Roberts. London, Macmillan and Co., 1910.

—— *Epistula ad Pompeium*

With an English translation, notes, and an essay by W. Rhys Roberts, in *Three Literary Letters.* Cambridge, Cambridge University Press, 1901.

Donatus *Ars Minor*

With an English translation and an introduction by Wayland Johnson Chase. University of Winconsin Studies in Social Science and History. Madison, 1926.

Erasmus *Compendium rhetorices*

Translated by Hoyt H. Hudson, in *Studies in Speech and Drama in Honor of Alexander M. Drummond,* pp. 326–340. Ithaca, Cornell University Press, 1944.

Gorgias *Encomium of Helen*

Translated by LaRue Van Hook, in Isocrates, Vol. III. Loeb Classical Library. London, 1945.

Hermogenes *Progymnasmata*
Translated by Charles Sears Baldwin, in *Medieval Rhetoric and Poetic,* pp. 23–38. New York, The Macmillan Co., 1928.

Horace *Ars poetica*
With an English translation by H. Rushton Fairclough, in *Satires, Epistles, and Ars Poetica.* Loeb Classical Library. London, 1926.
The Art of Poetry, with an English prose translation, introduction, and notes by Edward H. Blakeney. The volume also has a verse translation by Ben Jonson. London, Scholartis Press, 1928.

Isidorus *Etymologiae*
Edited by W. M. Lindsay. Oxford, Clarendon Press, c1911.

Isocrates *Against the Sophists*
With an English translation by George Norlin, in Isocrates, Vol. II. Loeb Classical Library. London, 1929.

—— *Antidosis*
With an English translation by George Norlin, in Isocrates, Vol. II. Loeb Classical Library. London, 1929.

—— *Panegyricus*
With an English translation by George Norlin, in Isocrates, Vol. I. Loeb Classical Library. London, 1928.

John of Salisbury *Metalogicon*
Edited and translated by Daniel D. McGarry. Berkeley, University of California Press, 1955.

Juvenal and Persius *Saturae*
With an English translation by G. G. Ramsay. Loeb Classical Library. London, 1918.

"Longinus" *De sublimitate*
With an English translation by W. Hamilton Fyfe. In same volume with Demetrius *De elocutione* and Aristotle *De poetica.* Loeb Classical Library. London, 1932.
On the Sublime, Greek text with an English translation and an introduction by W. Rhys Roberts. Cambridge, Cambridge University Press, 1907.

Lucian of Samosata *Works*
Translated by H. W. Fowler and F. G. Fowler. 4 vols. *The Dependent Scholar, The Way to Write History, Tyrannicide, The Disinherited,* and *Phalaris* i and ii, in Vol. II; *The Rhetorician's Vade Mecum,* in Vol. III. Oxford, Clarendon Press, 1905.

Martianus Capella *Rhetorica*
Book v of *De nuptiis Philologiae et Mercurii et de septem artibus*

liberalibus libri novem. Edited by Adolf Dick. Leipzig, Teubner, 1925.

Persius *Saturae* (*See* Juvenal and Persius)

Petronius *Satyricon*
With an English translation by Michael Heseltine. Loeb Classical Library. London, 1913.

Philodemus *Rhetorica*
Translated by H. M. Hubbell, in *Transactions of the Connecticut Academy of Arts and Sciences,* XXIII (September, 1920), 243–382.

Philostratus *The Lives of the Sophists*
With an English translation by Wilmer Cave Wright. Loeb Classical Library. London, 1922.

Plato *Dialogs*
Translated by Benjamin Jowett. Oxford, Oxford University Press, 1920.

—— *Gorgias*
Translated, with an introductory essay, by E. M. Cope. Cambridge, Deighton, Bell, and Co., 1864.
With an English translation by W. R. M. Lamb. In same volume with *Lysis* and *Symposium.* Loeb Classical Library. London, 1946.

—— *Ion*
Translated by Allan H. Gilbert, with selections from *Republic* and *Laws,* in *Literary Criticism: Plato to Dryden.* New York, American Book Co., 1940.

—— *Phaedrus*
With an English translation by H. N. Fowler. In same volume with *Euthyphro, Apology, Crito, Phaedo.* Loeb Classical Library. London, 1919.

Pliny *Epistolae*
With an English translation by William Melmoth revised by W. M. L. Hutchinson. Loeb Classical Library. London, 1915.

Plutarch *De audiendis poetis*
With an English translation by Frank Cole Babbitt, in *Moralia,* Vol. I. Loeb Classical Library. London, 1927.
How a Young Man Should Study Poetry, translated by Frederick Morgan Padelford, in *Essays on the Study and Use of Poetry.* New York, Henry Holt and Co., 1902.

Quintilian *Declamationes*
Major Declamations, formerly attributed to Quintilian. Edited by Georgius Lehnert. Leipzig, Teubner, 1905.

Minor Declamations, possibly by Quintilian. Edited by Constantin Ritter. Leipzig, Teubner, 1884.

—— *Institutio oratoria*

With an English translation by H. E. Butler. 4 vols. Loeb Classical Library. London, 1921, 1922.

Institutes of Oratory, or, Education of an Orator, literally translated with notes by John Selby Watson. 2 vols. London, Bohn, 1856.

Seneca the Elder *Suasoriae*

With an English translation and notes by William A. Edward. Cambridge, Cambridge University Press, 1928.

—— *Suasoriae et Controversiae*

Edited by Adolf Kiessling. Leipzig, Teubner, 1872.

Controverses et Suasoires, nouvelle édition revue et corrigée avec introduction et notes. With a French translation by Henri Bornecque. Paris, Garnier, 1932.

Suetonius *De grammaticis et rhetoribus*

With an English translation by J. C. Rolfe, in Suetonius, Vol. II. Loeb Classical Library. London, 1930.

Tacitus *Dialogus de oratoribus*

With an English translation by William Peterson. In the same volume with *Agricola* and *Germania.* Loeb Classical Library. London, 1914.

Valerius Maximus *Facta et dicta memorabilia*

Edited by Karl Kempf. Leipzig, Teubner, 1888.

Traduction nouvelle avec notes par Pierre Constant. Paris, Garnier, c1935.

SECONDARY WORKS

Amos, Flora Ross. Early Theories of Translation. New York, Columbia University Press, 1920.

Arnim, H. von. Leben und Werke des Dio von Prusa. Berlin, 1898.

Atkins, John W. H. Literary Criticism in Antiquity. 2 vols. Cambridge, Cambridge University Press, 1934.

Baldwin, Charles Sears. Ancient Rhetoric and Poetic. New York, The Macmillan Co., 1924.

—— Medieval Rhetoric and Poetic. New York, The Macmillan Co., 1928.

Bevan, Edwyn R. "Rhetoric in the Ancient World," *Essays in Honour of Gilbert Murray*. London, 1936. Pages 189–213.

Blass, F. Die attische Beredsamkeit. 3 vols. Leipzig, 1887–98.

Boissier, Gaston. "The Schools of Declamation at Rome," *Tacitus and Other Roman Studies*. Translated by W. G. Hutchinson. London, 1906.

Bonner, Stanley Frederick. Roman Declamation in the Late Republic and Early Empire. Liverpool, University Press of Liverpool, 1949.

—— The Literary Treatises of Dionysius of Halicarnassus. Cambridge, Cambridge University Press, 1939.

Bornecque, H. Les Déclamations et les déclamateurs d'après Sénèque le père. Lille, 1902.

Brown, Rollo Walter. How the French Boy Learns to Write. Cambridge, Harvard University Press, 1927.

Bryant, Donald C. "Aspects of the Rhetorical Tradition—1. The Intellectual Foundation," *Quarterly Journal of Speech*, XXXVI (April, 1950), 169.

Caplan, Harry. "The Decay of Eloquence at Rome in the First Century," *Studies in Speech and Drama in Honor of Alexander M. Drummond*. Ithaca, Cornell University Press, 1944. Pages 295–325.

Clark, Albert Curtis. The Cursus in Mediaeval and Vulgar Latin. Oxford, Clarendon Press, 1910.

Clark, Donald Lemen. "Imitation: Theory and Practice in Roman Rhetoric," *Quarterly Journal of Speech*, XXXVII (February, 1951), 11–22.

—— "John Milton and 'the fitted stile of lofty, mean or lowly,'" *Seventeenth-Century News*, Supplement (Winter, 1953).

—— John Milton at St. Paul's School; a Study of Ancient Rhetoric in English Renaissance Education. New York, Columbia University Press, 1948.

—— Rhetoric and Poetry in the Renaissance; a Study of Rhetorical Terms in English Renaissance Literary Criticism. New York, Columbia University Press, 1922.

—— "The Place of Rhetoric in a Liberal Education," *Quarterly Journal of Speech*, XXXVI (October, 1950), 291.

—— "The Requirements of a Poet," *Modern Philology*, Vol. XVI, No. 8 (December, 1918).

—— "The Rise and Fall of Progymnasmata in Sixteenth and Seventeenth Century Grammar Schools," *Speech Monographs*, XIX, No. 4 (November, 1952), 259–63.

Clarke, Martin Lowther. Rhetoric at Rome; a Historical Survey. London, Burns & MacEachern, 1953.

Cole, Percival Richard. Later Roman Education in Ausonius, Capella and the Theodosian Code. New York, Teachers College, Columbia University, Contributions to Education Series, 1909.

Cope, E. M. An Introduction to Aristotle's Rhetoric. London, 1867.

Crane, R. S. Critics and Criticism Ancient and Modern. Chicago, Chicago University Press, 1952. (Reprints McKeon's articles on rhetoric.)

Cucheval, M. Victor. Histoire de l'eloquence latine depuis l'origine de Rome jusqu'a Cicéron. 3d ed. Paris, 1892.

D'Alton, John F. Roman Literary Theory and Criticism. London, Longmans, Green & Co., 1931.

Donnelly, Francis P., S.J. Principles of Jesuit Education in Practice. New York, P. J. Kenedy & Sons, 1934.

Downey, June Etta. Creative Imagination; Studies in the Psychology of Literature. New York, Harcourt, Brace & Co., 1929.

Duff, John Wight. A Literary History of Rome in the Silver Age, from Tiberius to Hadrian. New York, Charles Scribner's Sons, 1930.

Gilbert, Allan H. Literary Criticism: Plato to Dryden. New York, American Book Co., 1940.

Grasberger, Lorenz. Erziehung und Unterricht im klassischen Alterthum. 4 vols. Würzburg, 1864–81.

Gwynn, Aubrey Osborn, S.J. Roman Education from Cicero to Quintilian. Oxford, Oxford University Press, 1926.

Haarhoff, Theodore J. Schools of Gaul; a Study of Pagan and Christian Education in the Last Century of the Western Empire. Oxford, Oxford University Press, 1920.

Halm, C. Rhetores Latini Minores. Leipzig, 1863.

Hendrickson, G. L. "The Origin and Meaning of the Ancient Characters of Style," American Journal of Philology, XXVI (1905), 249.

—— "The Peripatetic Mean of Style and the Three Stylistic Characters," American Journal of Philology, XXV (1904), 125.

Hofrichter, W. Studien zur Entwickelungsgeschichte der Deklamation. Breslau, 1935.

Hollingworth, Harry L. The Psychology of the Audience. New York, American Book Co., 1935.

Hubbell, Harry M. The Influence of Isocrates on Cicero, Dionysius and Aristides. New Haven, Yale University Press, 1914.

Hunt, Everett Lee. "Plato and Aristotle on Rhetoric and Rhetoricians,"

Studies in Rhetoric and Public Speaking in Honor of James Albert Winans. New York, Century Co., 1925.

Jaeger, Werner W. Paideia: the Ideals of Greek Culture. Translated from the German by Gilbert Highet. New York, Oxford University Press, Vol. I (2d ed.), 1945; Vol. II, 1943; Vol. III, 1944.

Jebb, Sir Richard Claverhouse. Selections from Attic Orators. 2d ed. Vol. II. London, The Macmillan Company, 1893.

Johnson, Francis R. "Two Renaissance Textbooks of Rhetoric," *The Huntington Library Quarterly,* VI (August, 1943), 437.

Jullien, Emile. Les Professeurs de littérature dans l'ancienne Rome et leur enseignement depuis l'origine jusqu'a la mort d'Auguste. Paris, 1885.

Kohl, R. De scholasticarum declamationum argumentis ex historia petitis. Paderborn, 1915.

Krause, J. H. Geschichte der Erziehung, des Unterrichts und der Bildung bei den Griechen, Etruskern, und Roemern. Halle, 1951.

Kroll, Wilhelm. Rhetorik. Pauly-Wissowa. Realencyclopädie der classischen Altertumswissenschaft. Supplementband, VII. Stuttgart, 1940.

Lupton, Joseph H. A Life of John Colet. London, 1909.

McKeon, Richard. "Literary Criticism and the Concept of Imitation in Antiquity," *Modern Philology,* XXXIV (August, 1936), 1–35.

—— "Rhetoric in the Middle Ages," *Speculum,* XVII (January, 1942), 1–32.

Marrou, Henri-Irénée. Histoire de l'éducation dans l'antiquité. Paris, 1948.

—— Saint Augustin et la fin de la culture antique. Paris, 1938.

Milton, John. "Of Education," in F. A. Patterson, ed., *The Works of John Milton.* 18 vols. New York, Columbia University Press, 1931–38. Vol. IV, pp. 275–91.

Nicolau, Mathieu G. L'origine du "cursus" rythmique et les débuts de l'accent d'intensité en latin. Paris, 1930.

Norden, Eduard. Die antike Kunstprosa. 2d impression. Leipzig, 1909.

Ong, W. J. "Historical Backgrounds of Elizabethan and Jacobean Punctuation Theory," *PMLA* (1944), 349–53.

Parks, E. Patrick. The Roman Rhetorical Schools as a Preparation for the Courts under the Early Empire. Baltimore, Johns Hopkins Press, 1945.

Prescott, Frederick Clarke. The Poetic Mind. New York, The Macmillan Co., 1922.

Ritter, C. Die Quintilianischen Deklamationen. Tubingen, 1881.

Roberts, William Rhys. Greek Rhetoric and Literary Criticism. New York, Longmans, Green & Co., 1928.

Saintsbury, George A. A History of Criticism and Literary Taste in Europe from the Earliest Texts to the Present Day. 3d ed., 3 vols. London, 1908–17.

Scott, Izora. Controversies over the Imitation of Cicero as a Model for Style. New York, Teachers College, 1910. Contributions to Education, No. 35.

Smiley, Charles Newton. Latinitas and ἑλληνισμός; the Influence of the Stoic Theory of Style as Shown in the Writing of Dionysius, Quintilian, Pliny the Younger, Tacitus, Fronto, Aulus Gellius, and Sextus Empiricus. Vol. III. Madison, University of Wisconsin, 1906.

Stapleton, Thomas. Tres Thomae. Douai, 1588.

Summers, Walter Coventry. "Declamations under the Empire," *Proceedings of the Classical Association,* X (January, 1913), 87–102.

—— The Silver Age of Latin Literature. London, 1920.

Thompson, Craig Ringwalt. The Translations of Lucian by Erasmus and St. Thomas More. Ithaca, Privately Printed, 1940.

Van Hook, LaRue. "Alcidamas versus Isocrates," *Classical Weekly,* XII (January 20, 1919), 89.

Wagner, Russell H. "The Meaning of *Dispositio,*" *Studies in Speech and Drama in Honor of Alexander M. Drummond.* Ithaca, 1944. Pages 285–94.

White, Harold Ogden. Plagiarism and Imitation during the English Renaissance. Cambridge, Harvard University Press, 1935.

Wilson, Thomas. The Arte of Rhetorique, ed. by G. H. Mair. Oxford, Oxford University Press, 1909.

Wolf, Peter. Vom Schulwesen der Spätantike. Studien zu Libanius. Baden, 1952.

Wright, Frederick Adam. A History of Later Greek Literature, from the Death of Alexander, 323 B.C. to the Death of Justinian, 565 A.D. New York, The Macmillan Co., 1932.

INDEX